Doing Documentary Work

Each year The New York Public Library and Oxford University Press invite a prominent figure in the arts and letters to give a series of lectures on a topic of his or her choice. The lectures become the basis of a book jointly published by the Library and the Press. The previous books in the series are *The Old World's New World* by C. Vann Woodward, *Culture of Complaint: The Fraying of America* by Robert Hughes, *Witches and Jesuits: Shakespeare's Macbeth* by Garry Wills, and *Visions of the Future: The Distant Past, Yesterday, Today, Tomorrow* by Robert Heilbroner.

Doing Documentary Work

Robert Coles

The New York Public Library
OXFORD UNIVERSITY PRESS
New York   Oxford

Oxford University Press

Oxford   New York
Athens   Auckland   Bangkok   Bogotá   Buenos Aires   Calcutta
Cape Town   Chennai   Dar es Salaam   Delhi   Florence   Hong Kong   Istanbul
Karachi   Kuala Lumpur   Madrid   Melbourne   Mexico City   Mumbai
Nairobi   Paris   São Paulo   Singapore   Taipei   Tokyo   Toronto   Warsaw

and associated companies in
Berlin   Ibadan

Copyright © 1997 by Robert Coles

First published by Oxford University Press, Inc., 1997

First issued as an Oxford University Press paperback, 1998

Oxford is a registered trademark of Oxford University Press

The Publisher gratefully acknowledges permission to include here
portions of chapter four that were originally published in the *New Yorker*,
the *New Repubilc*, *Commenweal*, and *Karitan*.

Library of Congress Cataloging-in-Publication Data
Coles, Robert.
    Doing documentary work / Robert Coles.
        p. cm.
    Based on a series of lectures.
    Includes index.
    ISBN-13 978-0-19-511629-8

    ISBN-13 978-0-19-512495-8 (Pbk.)

    1. Documentary mass media.   I. Title.
    P96.D62C65   1997
    070.1—dc21   97-292

23 22 21 20 19 18 17 16 15

Printed in the United States of America

To my colleagues and friends at Duke University's
Center for Documentary Studies and at
DoubleTake Magazine

Contents

Doing Documentary Work

Introduction

A t one point early in *Let Us Now Praise Famous Men*, James Agee stops to contemplate the awesome task before him, that of doing justice to the lives of the tenant-farmer families he and Walker Evans had met in July of 1936. They had been sent south by the editors of *Fortune* magazine to do a story on the agricultural economy of that region. They had chosen central Alabama as their locale, the heart of the so-called black belt, a phrase meant to describe not a racial population but a kind of earth, rich and productive for growing crops. They had made their way, with the help of others, to three families, all of them white—and now faced the task of figuring out what to try to learn, and then what to offer the readers who would challenge their words and images. That documentary task troubled Agee enormously—some, reading him, might say needlessly. He reveals to us in the first pages of his book the aesthetic, intellectual, and moral struggle he waged as he spent time with those fellow citizens, fellow human beings, then considered what to report of what he had witnessed. He refers to "the cruel radiance of what is," and seems to despair of ever being able to render it. Soon enough, he turns to anger and scorn, which he directs at those who sent him and Evans south, at himself, even at his eventual readers. "It seems to me curious, not to say obscene and thoroughly terrifying," he writes, "that it could occur to an association of human beings drawn together through need and chance and for profit into a company, an organ of journalism, to pry intimately into the lives of an undefended and appallingly damaged group of human beings...." That is the mere beginning of a very long sentence which, in its sum, charges the editors of *Fortune* and their two employees, James Agee and Walker Evans, with (at a minimum) insensitivity, thoughtlessness, arrogance. As for us who may happen to pick up the book that came of this journalistic assignment, we are all too likely to be as culpable in our own way as the writer surely is, as he has reminded us many times. Late in a section titled "Education," Agee refers to his "self-disgust," which he attributes less to his "ignorance" than to his "inability" to declare adequately what might be done to remedy the distress he has seen; and he also chastises himself for an obvious "inability to blow out the brains with it [his description of what needs to be done on behalf of the people about whom he is writing] of you who take what it is talking of lightly, or not seriously enough."

I suppose such intense, dramatic, scattershot anger can be dismissed as mere rhetoric—an ingenuous or coy effort to engage the reader, through the writer's confessional remarks, in a necessary moral introspection: how earnestly and thoroughly might one take such a book to heart? Still, Agee's anger is ultimately less personal than his heated language sometimes suggests. He is constantly railing, really, against our very humanity as writers and readers, even as he tries so passionately and brilliantly (and prolixly, some would aver) to uphold the humanity of those others who share his nationality and race, even his own not-so-distant background (his father was of Tennessee-yeoman ancestry), though of course not his educational level, his class. A central source of tension in the book is Agee's sense of inadequacy to the task at hand—his sense that any manuscript he will complete and send to a publisher won't convey so very much that matters about the lives of the people he has met, and yes, his worry that his readers won't realize that to be the case, because he as a writer might persuade and charm them, his caveats notwithstanding, into the dangerous notion that when they have finished reading *Let Us Now Praise Famous Men* they will have learned just about all they need to know on a subject not exactly central to most of their lives.

In desperation, at the very start of his writhing documentary writing (doomed to futility and inadequacy, we are repeatedly warned) Agee issues a mock challenge: "If I could do it, I'd do no writing at all here. It would be photographs; the rest would be fragments of cloth, bits of cotton, lumps of earth, records of speech, pieces of wood and iron, phials of odors, plates of food and of excrement." He most certainly *might* have done "it," abstained from the considerable labor and public agony, the performance, a skeptic might say, of his book, now readily and justifiably called an idiosyncratic work of genius by so many of us—but quite apparently he couldn't stop himself from giving us this extended spell of writing, warts, multiple self-condemnations, and all. We who follow him, as readers of his torrent of words, have every right, every responsibility to figure out the psychological and ethical conundrum he almost nonchalantly (the book is full of such provocative asides) tosses our way. Was he frivolously, self-indulgently carried away, hence this book with all its rage as well as its penetrating, large-minded lyricism? Was he right in his suggested alternatives to a book, even in his mention of photography as somehow more truthful and adequate to the job at hand—never mind the other suggested (and provocative) offerings? Was he reminding us, ironically, in a remark that on its surface seems so dismissive, even denigrating to writers, how important words can be—the means, after all, by which the idea of the "fragments" and "bits" and "pieces" and "phials" and "records" and "plates" are conveyed to you and me? Of course, the rock-bottom issue is *which* words, meaning what kind of language, written by what person, possessed of what acquaintance and knowledge, acquired in what manner, justifies both the exploratory effort made (that time spent in central Alabama during the summer of 1936) and the several years' worth of additional exploration (their tangible form called "drafts") that culminated in the publication of what Agee with scarcely concealed and distancing derision refers to as a book?

I will be coming back to Agee and his book in this book, but here I want to indicate with his help some of the occupational hazards, as it were, of so-called documentary work. The intense self-scrutiny Agee attempts is, one hopes, an aspect of all writing, all research. In my work, that of psychoanalytic psychiatry, we properly put great emphasis on the capacity for self-deception, under the sway of early and now unconscious influences, not only of our patients but of ourselves—so-called "transference" in them, "counter-transference" in us. Unfortunately, our journals and books stress the former far more than the latter, perhaps out of the all-too-human inclination toward self-protection; and unfortunately, the words "transference" and "counter-transference" don't quite encompass or explain the possible range of mental responsiveness, conscious and unconscious,—or, put differently, knowing and unwitting—that characterizes our unspoken, never mind quite explicitly avowed, way of getting along with one another. Not all of our irrationality, even, stems from childhood experiences within a family. Moreover, as we get older a host of social attitudes grow within us, a consequence of the kind of life we have lived, and they bear down on us constantly, making us sensitive here, relatively indifferent or even callous there. Each of us brings, finally, a particular life to the others who are being observed in documentary work, and so to some degree, each of us will engage with those others differently, carrying back from such engagement our own version of them.

The word *documentary* certainly suggests an interest in what is actual, what exists, rather than what one brings personally, if not irrationally, to the table of present-day actuality. Documentary evidence substantiates what is otherwise an assertion or a hypothesis or a claim. A documentary film attempts to portray a particular kind of life realistically; a documentary report offers authentication of what is otherwise speculation. Through documents themselves, through informants, witnesses, participants, through the use of the camera and the tape recorder, through letters or journals or diaries, through school records, court records, hospital records, or newspaper records, a growing accuracy with respect to a situation, a place, a person or a group of people begins to be assembled. Agee is getting at that mode of inquiry when he provocatively makes mention of cotton and the earth and cloth as well as the more obvious "variable" of speech that is heard and remembered in notes taken—his way of urging us to pay the closest attention to anything and everything that is a part of the life we are attempting to get to know. But his repeatedly acknowledged, fiercely declared impatience with himself and his readers, his outbursts of scorn, self-directed but also hurled indiscriminately at those who happen to open his book, remind us that a search for the factual, the palpable, the real, a determined effort to observe and authenticate, and, afterwards, to report, has to contend, often enough, with a range of seemingly irrelevant or distracting emotions—the search for objectivity waylaid by a stubborn subjectivity. These days (far more than in Agee's time) that subjectivity is amplified for writer and reader alike by a cultural interest in all things psychological, so that Agee's outbursts, or those of Orwell in his documentary writing (*Down And Out In London And Paris, The Road To Wigan Pier*) get quickly characterized by my students, by me, as manifestations of "guilt" or "shame"—an angry nervousness that belies a sense of complicity in some wrongdoing, or an embarrassment connected to one's good luck as it is rubbed into one's awareness by the sight of others utterly down on their luck.

At other moments in history, the strong expressions of personal feeling in an Agee might have been differently regarded—an expression of proper social outrage, or a righteousness quite in keeping with the task at hand: the moral underpinnings of social inquiry. Today some of us want no part of that—want, rather, a "value-free" social science, for instance. To connect again with my own profession's introspective struggles, I remember well the desire for "neutrality" that some of us young psychiatrists kept expressing, our wish, even, to cover our personal tracks, in order that our patients would tell us a "truth" uninfluenced (as much as possible) by our attitudes and values, as expressed in the books and pictures we might be tempted to put in our offices, for instance, or what we might absent-mindedly say about ourselves or others, not to mention the events of the day—hence those dimly lit rooms, bereft of "stimuli," of hints and more of ourselves. The point was to encourage our patients to use us in a certain way: we weren't *ourselves*, we were "objects of transference," or "instruments" (note the depersonalized language) by means of which our patients would discover *themselves*. They would do so, we hoped, one after the other, no matter the variations in them, because we had striven mightily for a kind of resolute impassivity, a disappearance, almost. Some of us in our theoretical talk referred to ourselves as a "screen," an interesting image—a blankness upon which others "projected" themselves, their attributions with respect to us amounting to a collective revelation about their past experience with parents and siblings.

But how much self-effacement is really possible, either in a clinical setting or out in that "field" where fellow human beings are "studied"? We psychiatrists may keep our mouths shut most of the time, and when we speak, we may be very careful to do so in an even-handed way that eschews emotionality or judgmental passion. We may be properly wary of showing our feelings, and we may furnish our offices in such a way that little of ourselves is visually there for our visitors. But those offices are located in certain neighborhoods; they are hardly "value-free"! Moreover, it is impossible for us to attend everything we hear or see with a fine impartiality. We notice what we notice in accordance with who we are—and, like Agee and Orwell, we are paid money for our efforts to understand others, who as patients are presumably "poorer" than we are (that is, in trouble, hurt, bewildered). Even as Agee and Evans poked and peered at the downtrodden, we watch every move, listen to every word of the downcast. No question, we have had medical training, hospital and clinic experience—we clothe ourselves in the intimidating garb of science, and with some justification. We are "trained," a word that is meant to certify ourselves and reassure those who come to our offices. Writers or photographers don't go through such a spell of study, but they have their own apprenticeships, and presumably the editors of *Fortune* had confidence in the ability of Agee and Evans to do a thorough job, come back, and render accurately what they had seen and heard. Still, many patients have accused their doctors of failing to understand them in a full and just way, and not a few doctors have joined Agee in a public lament of what is or is not possible in a clinical setting—have even been willing to resort to a strenuous criticism of the work they nevertheless keep doing, even as Agee, for all his complaints or asides kept doing his self-directed work as an observer, a writer, and ultimately delivered a manuscript to a publisher.

To take stock of others is to call upon oneself—as a journalist, a writer, a photographer, or as a doctor or a teacher. This mix of the objective and the subjective is a constant presence and, for many of us, a constant challenge—what blend of the two is proper, and at what point shall we begin to cry "foul"? Here the moral side of our nature can trouble us, if not haunt us—Agee's exclamations, Orwell's diatribes (I shall come to them later), and the "indignation" Erik H. Erikson dared summon for his psychoanalytic colleagues as a most important and desirable quality (this at a time when detachment and "cool" were decidedly the postures those colleagues found desirable, or rather, mandatory, even as Agee and Orwell were and are regarded by many readers—many of my students, certainly—as impossibly hotheaded, and thereby untrustworthy as the dispassionate social observers they ought to have been). One person's *ought* is another person's *naught*, of course; and we go through cycles and eras, times when documentary writers or photographers are inclined (and expected) to be relatively aloof from their chosen "field of study," their "subjects" (again, the evocative and suggestive power of language!), or times when the hope is for a virtual entanglement of those under scrutiny and those giving them the once-over—to the point where some social science research has been called, with firm approval, "participant observation," wherein those much discussed "roles" that sociologists and anthropologists struggle to define end up merging.

I bring up these matters because they keep coming up, I notice, in seminars I teach, attended by writers and photographers and filmmakers and journalists and social scientists who have tried to put into words or represent through pictures (or on film) what they have witnessed as observers, as reporters, as (a catchall word) documentarians. Again and again, our discussions center on the attitudes these men and women have toward their work (its nature, its possibilities, its limitations) and toward themselves as the individuals (outsiders, people of relative privilege) who are doing that work. Sometimes the issue is methodological—how one does a specific project, how one writes it up or puts together the visual documents obtained. Sometimes the issue is psychological or personal—how one comes to terms with a host of emotions that keep arising as one leaves a campus, a privileged suburb, even an only modestly comfortable or conventional life, to take the measure of others who are different in this or that way. Nor is the issue always a matter of class—specifically, a reasonably well-off investigator spending time with poor families. No question, much of the documentary tradition has featured that kind of encounter: a journalist or essayist or photographer or university-connected researcher or filmmaker who wants to learn how it goes across a particular set of railroad tracks and then returns with the makings of an article, a book, a film, a series of pictures to be put on display or published. But documentary writers and photographers have also crossed other barriers—of race, obviously, of region or nationality, of culture. Sometimes, as a matter of fact, such fieldwork involves moving "up" rather than "down," to the point where one thinks of a parodic version of Orwell's first book—"up and about" in, say, two "gold coast" communities. I well remember the personal responses and difficulties of three students of mine who did such work, tape recorders and cameras in hand, minds on the line, with as much to consider as their colleagues in the seminar who had taken themselves to ghettoes or to migrant-labor camps.

Ultimately such students, such fieldworkers, sort out the questions that keep coming to mind as partly psychological, partly moral—though there is (and ought be) a blur when one looks for a boundary between the two. Nor are those who do documentary work only a problem, as it were, to themselves. To be sure, there is plenty of soul-searching, as we shall see; but there is also the obvious reality of the observed, who have their own notions about what these visitors, these outsiders, these men and women on a mission of sorts, intend to do, are doing—and will do, later, when they have departed. I am afraid that not enough is made of the terms of entry, the terms of departure in so-called "fieldwork"—what has been arranged, for instance, for the observer, at the start, by various scouts, informants, or intermediaries, and what has happened toward the end of a particular stay, in the way of pledges, avowals, or worries expressed and even threats made. Agee's "Late Sunday Morning" in *Let Us Now Praise Famous Men* more than hints at what can happen as two Yankees, laden with gear, show up: "When they saw the amount of equipment stowed in the back of our car, they showed that they felt they had been taken advantage of, but said nothing of it." In that one sentence, necessity confronts an only apparent, fearful courtesy, and wins the day—though at a price.

To do his work, Evans needed his cameras. The white landowners who were taking him and Agee to meet some of their tenants would not be anything but polite and welcoming. Still, their eyes had widened at the invitation, and reservations (if not outright apprehensions) had crossed their minds. Agee's mind, too, had been stirred—he had seen below the surface of his hosts, even as they had perhaps seen below his ostensibly cordial and (by implication) beseeching manner. Soon enough, as he accepts the favors of these men, he is beginning to take note of their authority, their fearful power over those who work for them, and he is, right away, turning on the hands that feed him. He also wastes no time in turning on himself. There he is, showing up at the homes of these tenant farmers with their bossmen. He has begun to realize, of course, that such a start to his work is not without significance, without consequences for the nature of that work. No question, someone had to help him meet these shy, easily intimidated, impoverished people who lived in out-of-the-way places and were hardly prepared to be available in the comfortable "coffee shoppe" where Agee and Evans had met the landowners. Moreover, these two visitors from up north were on a specific assignment. They didn't have all the time in the world to spare, nor were they free simply to hang around, letting time and conversations and the accidents of particular acquaintance give shape to the direction of their work. They knew whom they had to see before they left New York City, and whom they had to see upon arrival in Alabama—the "contacts" who would presumably pass them along to those whose lives would become the subject matter of a proposed text to be illustrated by Evans's camera work.

A powerfully suggestive writer, Agee could offer so very much to consider through a remembered moment's exchange, relayed in the very first paragraph of that introductory section: "Walker said it would be all right to make pictures, wouldn't it, and he said, Sure, of course, take all the snaps you're a mind to; that is, if you can keep the niggers from running off when they see a camera." In a rather candidly devastating statement, four sentences further along, he lets us know, with respect to one of the two (white, of course) landlords chauffeuring them around, that "nearly all his tenants were Negroes and no use to me."

Agee is frank to tell us that no matter his avowed, painfully uttered sympathy for, and empathy with, the people whose lives get presented in his book—the lyricism constantly extended them by a gifted poet and essayist who happened to be on a magazine's errand—he and his friend were quite capable of being cannily practical. The use of the vernacular in those passages is especially devastating—and revealing: of how much we can take for granted, if we are certain people and if certain other people are our sponsors. As for those who, anyway, don't count—they are not going to be any problem. They're of "no use" to these temporary visitors, whose high-mindedness, whose generosity of soul, whose fineness of sensibility don't stand in the way of their lives as, right now, negotiators: take us where we'll get the job done, to people who will cooperate (that last word a signpost in documentary work—the degree to which "respondents" are willing to be forthcoming). I say the above not with animus or out of sarcasm. Agee himself was simmering while with those two bossmen, and his later recall and use of the vernacular, though it implicates him and Evans (they said not a word in disagreement or protest), lets us know what he thinks of them, shows all too clearly their smug sense of themselves, their smug indifference to the others (whose toil enabled them to be who they were, relatively well-to-do people). Soon enough Agee's bitterness and rage would be on the lookout for fuller expression. He was thwarted by his "research" needs, the exploratory requirements of a journalistic project, from telling off these two, who were (the ironies keep mounting) doing him a big and important and utterly necessary favor, but his mind was resourceful, and others (the liberal intelligentsia, for instance, back home) would get quite a slamming, to the point where they seem far more malevolent, at times, than those two fellows who owned the land tilled by Agee's "three tenant families," as they get called on his book's title page.

As for Agee's departure from Alabama, one can only speculate on what happened to him as he took leave; but he never did write that article for *Fortune*. In a sense, his mission failed; and it surely did, to some considerable extent, because of his passionate desire to make some kind of amends to people whom he would eventually present to the world as hurt, yes, but as almost enviably noble—as, indeed, worthy of the Biblical "praise" due "famous men." I doubt that Agee and Evans knew they were going nowhere with their article when they actually departed Alabama, but I suspect they had set the stage for their future blocks and impasses and temporizations, their inability to come up with a "product" or deliver the goods, by the way they (most especially Agee, one suspects) said good-bye to the people with whom they had stayed, and, more generally, to the situation in which they had immersed themselves so thoroughly. The self-recriminations that keep making their way into *Let Us Now Praise Famous Men* bespeak a moral agony somehow unsettled in the South, and hence a force to be reckoned with down the line, in the Northern world of typewriters and editorial offices.

So it would go with Orwell, when he left Wigan, where he did his observational stint with miners the very same year that saw Agee and Evans in Alabama with tenant farmers. *The Road To Wigan Pier* offers almost unlimited admiration for miners, to the point of veneration—while others near and far do less well, for sure: the shopkeepers of Wigan, for example, or the intellectuals of London, including the very folks, the editors of the New Left Book Club, who gave Orwell his documentary commission. Orwell never does tell us how he gained access to a given world, what he shared with those he met as to his intentions, and how he said his farewell; but as with Agee, the vehemence of his assault on the world to which he belonged before he left for Wigan—the world, after all, whose inhabitants would be his readers—makes one wonder not only about his particular documentary effort, but about those initiated by all of us. If we don't somehow settle a certain score with ourselves, never mind those we go to "study" (to be crude, calling upon Agee's chosen crudity, those we "use") while we are out there, in that elusive, ever-changing entity abstractly called "the field," we are apt to show that amoiguity of feeling to others in our writing, maybe even in the editing we do of our film footage, or the titles we give to our photographs, the selections we make, the way we arrange them. I will be coming back to such matters in the pages ahead with the help of my students, not to mention through an examination of my own documentary journey, with its attendant missteps, its blind spots, its dead-end detours. Here I have wanted to set my sightings, and thereby give a clue to one of this book's purposes, one of its destinations: a look at what happens to those of us who venture into streets not our own in pursuit of the awareness those streets (one hopes) can offer—what happens morally and psychologically within us, and what subsequently happens to us as writers, photographers, filmmakers, or academic researchers.

Of course, as several students in one of my early seminars on this subject pointed out to me, the "field" can be one's own backyard—the critical matter being an attitude toward the daily life that surrounds one: how consciously and deliberately (with a documentary goal in mind) does one go about the routines of a life? More on that, too, during a later discussion. Here I acknowledge a great debt to those students I've already begun mentioning, from those seminars I have taught for nearly twenty years now, at Harvard and at the Center for Documentary Studies at Duke. The so-called "literary-documentary tradition" served as the mainstay of that teaching for a long spell: the writing of Agee and Orwell, already mentioned; books such as *An American Exodus*, by Dorothea Lange and Paul Taylor; various collections of photography, from those of Lewis Hine and Doris Ullman to the range of work sponsored by the Farm Security Administration (FSA); as well as Walker Evans and the images of Russell Lee, Marion Post Walcott, Ben Shahn, Edward Rothstein. I have also called upon Frederick Wiseman's documentary films, which in their sum amount to a major examination of American institutional life as it concretely affects those who are a daily part of it: students and teachers in our schools, workers and customers in our stores, patients and doctors and nurses in our hospitals.

All of that reading and visual matter, supplemented by guest appearances, such as J. Anthony Lukas's *Common Ground*, Oscar Lewis's *Children of Sanchez*, Studs Terkel's *Working* and *Division Street*, has prompted in us many thoughts about the work we ourselves have been doing: each member of the seminar has been engaged in doing documentary work, be it the taking of pictures, the making of a film, or the writing of a report, an essay, an extended description of others, of oneself with others. In time we have begun to realize, together, three major domains of concern and discussion, hence the first three sections of this book. As befits those who are attending a seminar under the auspices of a university, we have constantly struggled with matters of the intellect (perhaps too much so, and with no small risk of pride and self-importance). What kind of work are we doing, and to what purpose? How are we to proceed— through which intermediaries in pursuit of which men, women, children, living in what neighborhoods? How does our work compare with that of others who work for newspapers, who do more traditional social science (survey research, for instance), or who do a kind of social history that does not entail interviews with ordinary folk? When does enough turn out to be enough—when, that is, do we leave reasonably satisfied, and if so, with what messages given to the people with whom we have worked? What *is* our responsibility to such people, and how ought it be acknowledged? What about ourselves—when does honorable inquiry turn into an exercise in manipulative self-interest, even (that word of words!) "exploitation"? Who is to make such judgments, calling upon what criteria? As for ourselves, in the lonely corners of whose minds a certain vague yet ever so pressing moral awareness can restively lurk, ready in the most unexpected moments to pounce on us, bear down on our sense of who we are and what we've become—what ought we to consider appropriate or inappropriate in this kind of relatively idiosyncratic endeavor, of a kind not usually regulated by the rules of departmental disciplines, by textbooks that spell out steps and routines and procedures and the theories that justify them?

Speaking of theory—how to think of "documentary studies" in the abstract, as well as in the implementation of the concrete? Speaking, too, of the personal and ethical, as so many of the above questions do—how to talk directly, candidly (using what kind of language), about the psychological hazards of such work, and, too, the ethical challenges that appear, it sometimes seems, from out of nowhere? Moreover, what to make of one's interventions, as a writer, as an editor of tapes or notes, as the person who picks and chooses words, crops and cuts photographs, splices constantly the tapes of a documentary film? When do selection and arrangement and a response to narrative need, in the form of one's comments and asides, become so decisive that one story ("raw interview material" or "unedited footage" or photographic film that hasn't been sorted or sequenced) has turned into quite another? What of pictures cropped (with a possible attendant shift in emphasis, focus, not to mention the substance of a scene)? What of films that move back and forth across time and space while presenting an apparent narrative and chronological continuity? When does fact veer toward fiction—and how are those two words to be understood with respect to one another: as polarities, as contraries, or as kin, working a parallel, often contiguous territory, and borrowing from another now and then? It is such questions that I hope to discuss in the chapters ahead.

In a sense, I have been preparing to write this book, and especially the introductory words to it, for over thirty-five years—it was in 1960, actually, when I began to do so, began to scribble notes about the nature of the work that my wife, Jane, and I were doing as we tried to make sense of what we saw on the streets of New Orleans amidst the struggle of school desegregation, and as, too, we tried to make sense of ourselves, as witnesses, as onlookers and listeners, as individuals doing "research," as people trying to figure out what mattered and why (and, therefore, who we were, never mind what others were saying, or trying to accomplish, and why). Since that New Orleans encounter on our part (an accident of fate) with the four black children who endured the resistance of months of mobs, assembled daily to heckle and threaten them, I have spent my working life trying to understand how children (and their parents, and indeed their grandparents) manage to live under a variety of circumstances. The result has been a series of books about children (the five volumes of the *Children of Crisis* series, the three volumes of the *Inner Lives of Children* series), and, too, books in which I've worked with photographers, responded to photographers who have also done documentary work: *The Old Ones of New Mexico* and *The Last and First Eskimos* (with Alex Harris); essays connected to the work of Dorothea Lange, Doris Ullman, and Thomas Roma. In much of that work I've tried to discuss (in chapters titled "Method") the nature of documentary work as I've experienced it. I've also been teaching courses for many years which draw upon the documentary tradition. I've described that teaching, to some extent, in *The Call of Stories: Teaching and the Moral Imagination* and *The Call of Service: A Witness to Idealism*—the ways in which certain novelists or photographers help us understand the world, help us figure out, too, the obstacles to such an understanding. This book belongs with those two—a continuing exploration of how we might, through the reading of narrative, through the effort of service, through projects in the "field," do justice to the complexity of observable life, to the moral responsibilities and hazards that confront us as we try to change aspects of that life, and, finally, to the nature of the documentary work that brings us closer to the world around us, but that also poses many questions and challenges for us to consider.

A good portion of this book was originally presented as three lectures, delivered in May of 1996 at the New York Public Library, as a contribution to a series there sponsored in collaboration with the Oxford University Press. I thank the editors of the Press and the officials of the Library for their courtesy and kindness toward me. A substantial part of the last chapter was first published elsewhere in a different form. I thank the magazine editors who let me thereby again explore themes examined more fully here. I also want to mention right off the gratitude I feel day by day for the written and spoken words of Dr. William Carlos Williams. I'd have had a different life if I'd not known him, and as the reader will see, his lyrical statements run through the pages ahead, a leitmotif for me as I try to make sense of my own work and that of others. I thank, finally, my colleagues at the Center for Documentary Studies at Duke University and those who are part of the community at *DoubleTake* magazine, which is published there, for the great privilege of being connected to them—and I dedicate this book to all of those individuals, with much affection.

one

The Work

Locations In Theory

The noun *document* goes back centuries in time. It is derived from the Latin *docere*, to teach, and was originally, of course, used to describe something that offered clues, or, better, proof, a piece of paper with words that attested evidence. In our time, a photograph or a recording or a film have also qualified as documents. In the early eighteenth century (1711), the word *document* became more active—a verb, whose meaning conveyed the act of furnishing such evidence; and eventually, as with the noun, the range of such activity expanded: first one documented with words on paper; later, one documented with photographs and a film crew. Interestingly, the verb would get used this way, too: "to construct or produce (as a movie or a novel) with authentic situations or events," and "to portray realistically." Here the creative or imaginative life is tempered by words such as "authentic" or "realistically," which, are nonetheless potentially subjective or elusive: a distance has been traveled from the documenting that has to do with words on paper (court records, school reports, letters, journals, and diaries) offered as proof that something happened in, say, a judge's chamber or a classroom. In the early nineteenth century (1802) the adjective *documentary* emerged—a description of evidence, naturally, but also as "relating to, or employing documentation in literature or art," again an encounter of the factual or objective with the imaginative. In this century (1935) the noun *documentary* arrived, telling of a product, the "documentary presentation of a film or novel." The one who did such work got a name in the 1940s—well, two names: *documentarian* (1943), and *documentarist* (1949). Just before those two words entered the language, and as if in anticipation of them, *documentarist* came into use (1939), "a specialist in documentation"—a person who furthered the tradition of old-fashioned documenting, as indicated by that word *documentation*, itself a bequest of the late nineteenth century (1884), and meant to refer to historical verification and substantiation.

This search through words for contemporary meaning helps bring into focus a twofold struggle: that of writers and photographers and filmmakers who attempt to ascertain what *is*, what can be noted, recorded, pictured; and that of presentation—how to elicit the interest of others, and how to provide a context, so that an incident, for instance, is connected to the conditions that informed and prompted its occurrence. Again and again, as I listen to my students compare their efforts with those undertaken by sociologists or anthropologists, by newspaper reporters and staff photographers responding to a day's event within the confines of a dispatch to be filed, by historians writing about a certain place and time or about those who commanded armies (or whole countries), I hear the connections those students make to the work of such individuals—yet, too, the distinctions made, the possible differences explored. Nor do we in those discussions always arrive at clear-cut contrasts and mutually exclusive definitions. Often we settle for descriptive characterizations or demarcations of professional territory, unashamedly heavy with qualifications—a documentary effort in itself: an attempt that summons the narrative side of the verb *document*, as opposed to its more specific reference to the accumulation or designation of various items as firm proof of something.

Historians are, perhaps, our oldest professional observers of human affairs—or, perhaps, it is best to say that writers or essayists are such, since Thucydides certainly did not have any graduate professional training, was not certified by any academic institution as knowledgeable about the past or the unfolding present. Long before there were universities with departments of history, there obviously were writers who tried to discover for themselves and their potential readers what actually happened at particular times, in particular locations, and how (and why) what occurred did end up taking place. In so doing, those writers varied with respect to their passion for factual certainty and specificity, and with respect to their interest in discursive comment, in personal or moral (or even spiritual) reflection. Even when a historian doesn't intend to ruminate or ramble along byways, even when he or she means to stick to dates and numbers and descriptions based on "data," on firsthand observations put down in ledgers, in letters, in communiqués, or in news reports or dispatches published in daily or weekly or monthly publications— there still remains the task of assembling information, choosing what matters, what might be (is to be) left out, what is to be discussed briefly or summarily, what is to be highlighted, considered in great detail. The issue, finally, becomes one of judgment, and thereby a subjective matter: an opinion of someone whose mind has taken in all that information, that documentation, and then given it the shape of sentences, of words used, with all their suggestive possibilities. Needless to say, even a history that insists on the primacy of statistics, of such numbers as given us by computers, will have to confront the same challenge of emphasis, of interpretation, of choice, of presentation through words, whereby the person who fed "data" into a computer is now the one using a computer in a different way, pressing letters that turn into something that is said, asserted.

By the late sixteenth century (1593), some students of their fellow human beings began to make reference to a science of "anthropology." They were not interested in a chronology or an interpretation of events, but rather in sorting people out, by virtue of their appearance, their residence, or their habits and customs. There is, of course, a historical side to all this (inevitably quite speculative): the emergence over time of various human races out of the obscurity and outright mystery of the most ancient history, which precedes all recorded data and rests upon archeological artifacts as they, like today's computer printouts, get fitted into someone's narrative, a story of the development of those races over an indefinitely long span of time. The nineteenth-century physical anthropologists (and their kinfolk, archeologists) had the company of social or cultural anthropologists, who concentrated their energies on how various groups of people behaved. Charts were developed that conveyed "relationships," "interactions," authority held and wielded, submission accepted without question. Such patterns of activity, such hierarchies of influence, such diagrams that told of consanguinity, of belief or conviction, became a body of knowledge, a field of learning, given the ultimate institutional (social, political, cultural, economic) sanction of departmental status in today's colleges and universities.

So it has gone with sociology, a term that came upon us in the middle of the nineteenth century (1843). There is an obvious overlap between the work of cultural anthropologists and sociologists— though the former, by convention rather than theoretical necessity (the anthropology of anthropologists!) have usually chosen the pre-literate, pre-industrial world as the beneficiary of their close, usually residential attention. In contrast, sociologists have given themselves over to a systematic (that word counts!) study of the way so-called groups of people come together and behave—a process of consolidation and, often, deterioration that might be called the rise and fall of classes and castes and regions and even nations. The connection of such inquiry to history as well as cultural anthropology is clear; and again, the role of the scholar's personal life is evident—his or her attitudes with respect to the attitudes of others under scrutiny, and his or her imaginative life as it gets expressed in the embrace of concepts, of generalizations, of hypotheses, which are collections of words meant to offer or convey an idea, a suggestive or organizing principle, a manner of looking at things, a gesture of interpretation, of coherence.

This move from concrete particulars to abstract pronouncement is crucial to science as we now commonly know it. It can be said, without animus, that careers are usually made in the social sciences as a consequence of one's willingness and capacity to move from the specific instance to the more general, the conceptual. Such a posture of formulation is not, however, always regarded as speculative (and thereby a close cousin—more anthropology!—to the imaginative). Instead, we hear of *science*: a systematic ordering of knowledge presumably based on the sifting and sorting of information, on the testing of hypotheses through experiments, through direct observation, though it is not unfair to say that, by and large, natural science and social science differ decidedly in the ability of their respective practitioners to perform tests that will definitively corroborate or dismiss various hypotheses. Still, social scientists aim for the general, hope to promulgate "laws" or postulates that give a sense of order and structure to what obtains in this world.

In contrast, journalists (who also document aspects of human behavior) respond to the particular, tell us the news—recent events that have occurred. Some journalists do so briefly, tersely, paying attention only to factuality and chronology; others give themselves (or are given) more leeway—are both chroniclers and interpreters of the news. Even the most factual kind of journalism, of course, can be suggestive, poignant, arresting—art giving shape to the presentation of reality. On the other hand, an interpretive essay in a newspaper or magazine is usually presented to the reader as the response of the publication's editors, through a writer, to something that has happened or is now going on: events with all their ramifications. In certain magazines, however, journalists may become something else—essayists who regularly contemplate those events and fit them into the larger frames of reference that historians or social scientists pursue.

The essayist is himself or herself confined by the nature of a chosen medium, even as the journalist has to contend with the confines of a newspaper story—but an essay allows for more space, for a mix of literary and analytic sensibility, for that other mix of factuality and opinion, and for the particular writer's idiosyncratic approach to a given topic. The essay gives journalists or others writers discursive freedom, and gives novelists a chance to mull over factuality directly, rather than at the remove of their created fictional characters. The essay also allows social scientists a chance to abandon *their* created "characters" (the theories they construct) for the possibilities and challenges of an ordinary language meant to inform and persuade the "common reader," as opposed to one's professional colleagues. Such essayists offer what used to be called "social knowledge"—Henry James commenting on Italy's gifts or on his native America revisited, Dickens observing that same America as a visiting lecturer, and, closer to our time, the poet James Agee and the novelist George Orwell trying to understand what they had witnessed and felt in Alabama, Yorkshire, and Lancashire in 1936.

A close examination of what came of the last two of those writers once they'd finished their observations, and a close reading of what they ultimately wrote about their experiences, helps clarify our thinking about the various ways observers can respond to what they have seen and heard and come to believe. It is no accident that both Agee and Orwell "failed" with respect to their respective missions, from the point of view of their assigning editors. *Fortune* magazine wanted Agee to do a strong piece of investigative magazine journalism. He was to spend a limited amount of time with a specific kind of people, in the company of a photographer, who was to capture pictures that would convey the (grim) reality of their lives. Instead, Agee turned his time in Alabama into a major moral and personal crisis. He lost sight of his magazine's interests and became excited and challenged by the commands and demands of both his aesthetic sensibility and his conscience. He stopped being interested in a limited, reasonably balanced, or even-handed discussion of a particular social and economic question facing the nation at the height of the Great Depression—the struggle for survival of a Southern agriculture heavily dependent on the relationship between the landowner and his tenant farmers. He turned, instead, to a different kind of language, a different way of seeing the world of central Alabama. He never even wrote the article for which he was commissioned. He quit the magazine that had sent him South, an assignment that enabled him to meet and get to know the world that had gotten him so aroused, so engaged. For several years he labored in both elation and despair with an enormously unwieldy manuscript, the result of a thorough reinterpretation of his position as an observer and a writer with regard to those he had encountered and tried to understand. The result, as we all know, was a book whose very title, Biblically connected (from the book of Ecclesiasticus), is exhortative and morally impassioned—a far cry from the tone of *Fortune* articles, not to mention those of so many other magazines. That book is deliberately rambling, lyrical, fiercely provocative, utterly idiosyncratic; it is also very long, at once detailed in its descriptive evocations of a kind of daily life and long-winded in its attempt to assault the supposedly conventional mind of its reader—as if the central issue is not only the suffering and marginality of Dixie tenant farmers but the assumptions (moral and intellectual) of the presumably well-off and well educated people who had the spare change in 1941, the Depression still not licked, to go buy such a book.

Orwell's Wigan Pier book also conveys a strain of moral anxiety; of all ironies, the reader is offered a measured disavowal of the author from Victor Gollancz, the one who had sent him north from London in the first place, so that the New Left Book Club might publish yet another piece of extended muckraking journalism, this one about the life of coal miners. Instead, Orwell wrote with a novelist's capacity for (interest in) the complexities and ironies of a given observed life; and he gave a much broader context for his discussion than that expected (and wanted) by his sponsors, hence their need to disclaim, at least partially, what they did publish (out of their essential fair-mindedness—others might not have been so obliging). Orwell found his own relatively entitled world in many ways lacking compared to the one he had glimpsed up north. He turned on those whose company he ordinarily kept, the London intelligentsia, just as Agee could not resist taking one swipe after another at his (Harvard, Manhattan, literary) background. The "road" Orwell took as a consequence of his visit to Wigan turned out to be toward a land of personal, moral reflection, of storytelling narration, of social and political polemic, of combative and sometimes erratic digression, of vivid presentation of moments experienced, remembered, and considered to be of significance without recourse to the justifications of social theory, political practicality, even journalistic custom or convenience. He threw his writing, as it were, in the face of those who ended up perplexed, but actually a good deal more forgiving of him than he attempts to be of them.

Later on I will try to guess what it was that got these two writers so intemperate, so angry, while on these particular missions; but here it is important to note their departure from ordinary journalism, from the conventional social essay, long or short. Both Agee and Orwell seem to know that they are in uncertain territory as they try to address their audience. They move back and forth from a posture of calm, even dry recitation of facts and figures to one of heated advocacy or derision. They also move from the third-person voice to that of the first person—a shift that tells a lot about their connection to the people being described, and about their intentions as writers. When they want to convey a kind of factuality (how cotton grows and is harvested, how miners do their work and the economic consequences of that work, coal production for a capitalist society), they can be impersonal, specific, exact, even statistical. When they want to get something off their chest, want to let others know how they reacted, on the spot, to something they had seen or heard, or how they ended up feeling later, when back on their own turf, about what they recalled, then the words "I" and "me" come to the fore, not to mention unconcealed sarcasm, even open contempt or rage toward certain others—though never, of course, are the targets of such emotions the tenant farmers or coal miners whom they have gotten to know, and that refusal of any criticism whatsoever obviously deserves our attention.

To be more abstract about both Agee and Orwell as social observers and writers (and about a kind of writing that combines reportage and reflection, delivered in a prose that is affecting, summoning, suggestively descriptive), certain polarities or tensions ought to be mentioned: the demands of reality as against those of art; the demands of objectivity as against those of subjectivity; a quantitative emphasis as against a qualitative one; the tone a first-person narrative offers as against one executed in the third person; a voice seeking to be contemplative, considered, as against one aiming for passionate persuasion, or advocacy, or denunciation; a distanced, analytic posture as against a morally engaged or partisan one; an inclination for the theoretical, as against the concrete, the practical; a narrative, rendered in personal or vernacular or even confessional language as against one replete with a technical or academic language.

Needless to say, a writer, a researcher, even, can move back and forth, draw upon one or another side of these various equations, or, again, polarities. As I well remember, when I submitted articles (they were not called "essays") to pediatric, psychiatric, and psychoanalytic journals, a word used, a single adjective, can raise the eyebrows of an editor or a "peer review" committee. When I wrote up my observations of migrant farm children for a journal read by physicians, and, especially, by my fellow psychiatrists, I tried to describe the various states of mind I observed in the children I met. In so doing, I called upon psychiatric and psychoanalytic terminology and wrote in the passive, third-person voice: "The defense mechanisms most frequently seen were..." and so it went! At one point, however, I inadvertently got myself and my editors into some trouble by using the word *poignant* to indicate the condition of some of the children: "In many of their drawings the children doing self-portraits refrained from putting land under themselves, a poignant denial of their very condition as young farm workers." I was discussing the use of one of the so-called defense mechanisms—now, when psychology fuels the American vernacular, a far better known maneuver of the mind than was the case back then (1966). I was dealing, really, with an irony, though I consciously restrained myself from using that word or its adjectival or adverbial versions, lest I introduce myself as an implicit commentator in a paper meant to be an account of "field research" done in the tradition of psychoanalytic child psychiatry— hence pages given over to accounts of "intra-psychic" conflict, and accounts, too, of the various "defense mechanisms" as they "were observed" (not as, actually, I stumbled into them!).

All went well, it seemed, until an editor's red pencil chanced upon that word, *poignant*: why was "it used," he wondered (not "Why did you use it")? I explained that I found it ironic, poignantly so, that children who put in long hours beside their parents harvesting crops (that is, working the land on their hands and knees, often, or stooped over) won't put that same land in their drawings or paintings of themselves. My editor friend (I knew him well, respected him) understood clearly what I was indicating, but noted that in this particular journal the word *poignant* would "stand out." I did not find that possibility especially worrisome, but he did. He pointed out that the word "in question" is a "subjective one"—my personal sense of something as opposed to a reaction of the child that I had "documented" through my "research." I remember being intrigued by the use of "documented"—a different use, surely, than the one Dorothea Lange, say, had in mind when she did her "documentary fieldwork" or "research" with migrant families during the 1930s. I also remember telling my editor friend that all of the "research" I had written up for this "paper" was "subjective"—an estimate or interpretation on my part of what I thought I had seen and heard happening in the lives of children, in their minds, rather than a chronicle of what happened independently of my mind (an account of the unfolding of an objective series of events).

True, "our discipline" is inescapably "subjective," I was told—yet "there are degrees." After all, I was tape-recording interviews and analyzing them for topics mentioned—"thematic analysis"; and I was collecting hundreds of children's drawings and paintings and putting all of them under a microscopic lens (my imagery!), that of, again, psychiatric and psychoanalytic perusal: "self-image," as reflected, for example, in the presence or absence of intact limbs, the manner in which facial features are presented (*if* they are), the character of clothing summoned, and again, the location the child chose for a self-portrait, or a picture of a parent, or too, a building: a landscape under a full sky, with sun, with trees and flowers, or a landscape which shows dark clouds, few if any plants or trees, no flowers. I knew not to speak, in that regard, of a pastoral, let alone a bucolic, scene, or a bleak or grim one—florid language! But it seemed to me *poignant* that children who lived so intimately with the land seemed to want no part of it when they sketched themselves, or, perhaps, *poignant* that they showed themselves with literally no ground under them, and thus, by no big leap of the mind (so I felt), symbolically groundless, meaning adrift and vulnerable and without the ties to a specific location (a city, a town, a community) that most of us simply take for granted.

In the end I cut the word *poignant*, because an editor felt that the word had to do with *me*, my personal or subjective evaluation of what he called the "objective data" I had obtained, those drawings. He was, interestingly, not at all averse to any interpretations of those drawings I wanted to offer, so long as I made clear that such was my interest in a separate section devoted to that kind of activity. But to describe a proposed "mechanism of defense" casually as poignant, without discussing my reasons for so insisting, was more than this editor wanted to allow. Anyway, he kept repeating, the issue is the children, not me—*poignant* being a word that tells of my mind as it came to be moved, affected by what I'd seen. I missed seeing that word in print, but I wanted to have my article published, and at that point in my career it was such articles in such journals that would—well, would *make* that career. Of course, I could have chosen, then and there, to write up my experiences with (as opposed to my research among) migrant farm families in a magazine (rather than a journal) and in a first-person narrator's voice, with emphasis on events, on anecdotes, on stories, and, yes, on ironies noted, on the poignancy of certain moments, certain situations, as I remembered them, making no mention of tape-recorded interviews with their "standard questions" posed and the answers to them "carefully analyzed" (that adverb, so often used, can be all too self-serving!). In so doing, I would have "taken risks," as I've heard folks say, by "writing for the public" rather than for "the profession"—and then I would be turning into a bit of a migrant myself: on the move. Location matters for those migrant families, as I gradually learned; they had to be at the right place (the crops just ready to be picked) at the right time (the grower has started recruiting willing farm laborers, field hands). And so with a writer's career—a person tries to figure out when to write what for which publication, and how to do so, meaning with one kind of language or with quite another kind.

No doubt for some readers and scholars, no matter what I would write, no matter how abstract or technical or impersonal the language, I was still on very dubious ground throughout my stay with the migrant families I met in Florida, Texas, and elsewhere. They were a mere handful of souls, rather than a "sample of respondents." I often asked them whatever came to my mind, so the questions varied from day to day, family to family. In contrast, I might have spent a lot of time trying to figure out which questions I'd be (uniformly!) asking, and why, and then arrived with them, and only them, in mind; or, better, with a questionnaire in hand, to be filled out either by them or by me, putting checks in boxes in accordance with what I had been told. Later a computer would be summoned and results tabulated, with scores or findings the eventual outcome: a "project" rather than a series of personal encounters or interviews. Each of these phrases places the individual doing the work in a location as surely as does a migration of a family from, say, Belle Glade, Florida, to the eastern shore of Maryland: a choice, in both instances, as to what will be harvested! Additionally, there is the matter of one's purpose as a writer. If one submits a paper to a journal, one is furthering the cause of "science," and (less eagerly or openly stated) one's career. If I write an article for a newspaper or a magazine on the same subject, but in a different voice and manner, with different shades of meaning put forth, then I am certainly furthering my writing career, and I may well be called a "participant observer" or an "advocate" by readers or colleagues, or by myself in what I say or imply about myself: someone who has become "involved" with those he has met, or (pejoratively) "over-involved"; one who worked alongside those he was getting to know (as a researcher and a writer) but (moving across the spectrum) one who began arguing on their behalf or doing things on their behalf (collecting money, going into court as a lawyer, setting up a clinic as a doctor, doing some teaching). Such a step need not be mentioned, of course, in the writing one does, nor need it *necessarily* become a force that gives shape to the nature of that writing. Nevertheless, I can imagine the driest writer of social science giving of himself or herself passionately to those once "studied," and I can, conversely, imagine a passionately eloquent essayist or journalist having little interest in working actively on behalf of those whose cause he or she has advocated.

Once more, the issue is that of location—how a particular writer or researcher decides to commit himself or herself with respect to those others being studied, watched, heard, made the subject of a writing initiative. It is possible to argue, surely, that the abstract polarity of observation-participation, like all the foregoing polarities, doesn't do justice to the nuances and subtleties of human involvements—that even the most austerely detached social scientist (or insistently impartial journalist or essayist) will be touched or affected by the act of going somewhere, being with those who are later described, handed over to others through words (or pictures). In this century of the unconscious, that is, the very notion of detachment contends with our commonly held conviction that all the time the mind unwittingly responds to the world in ways that can make a difference in what we think and feel, and how we give expression to our ideas. An observer of migrant workers may, for instance, quite readily refrain from using a word such as *poignant* in the articles he or she writes for scientific journals, yet keep amassing statistics that tell their own dramatic, even startling story of vulnerability and deprivation. By the same token, someone deeply and openly involved in the social and political struggle being waged by migrants may, once with pen in hand, or at a computer, veer a bit toward detachment, not out of a shift of opinion or commitment but in simple response to the imperatives of language as an instrument of communication. If I shout and scream (in response to the strong feelings churning inside me), if I write words that convey such an attitude, I may well be undoing my mission as an advocate or polemicist, one who wants to persuade or convince others. Besides, to write particular words or to take specific pictures is to stand at some remove from the entire range of what can be said or photographed, and to take such a step moves one at least a measure away from that full participatory zeal that some activists hold up for themselves and for others as ideal.

How well I remember, in that regard, some of those "soul sessions" of SNCC (the Student Non-Violent Coordinating Committee) during the early and most dangerous and demanding years of the civil-rights struggle in the South. Again and again those young men and women warned one another (warned themselves) about the dangers of "doing a lot of thinking"——not the kind of remark a psychiatrist who had worked in an academic setting was used to hearing. I wanted to hear more, of course, even as I had already concluded, without hearing any explanation, that such an attitude was, in some way, "defensive." (We bring theory, inevitably, to our exploratory field work, however open-minded we try to be—not necessarily out of intention, but as a consequence of our mind's natural capacity to remember what it has learned or has considered to be true.) When one of SNCC's leaders decided to address the matter, to take on reflection as against action, he did so this way: "You have to go stand up to those sheriffs, with guns in their holsters, and their hands on the guns, and you start doing a lot of thinking, 'sifting and sorting,' my mom used to say, and you're through, you're washed up, you're scared stiff. You think better of it—and that means you pull back. Let me tell you, I'm not accusing anyone [with those words, that description of what takes place]; I'm just remembering—from my life, from last month, when I was going to picket a courthouse, and I started thinking and thinking, and that was *it*: I never got there."

As those nearby listened and nodded I found myself not especially surprised: *of course* a person confronted with fear and danger doesn't spend a lot of time weighing matters, lest indecisiveness, at the very least, become the winner. Still, why did it matter so much for these youths to spell all that out—especially when, in a way, doing so only made for the very consciousness (self-consciousness) that they kept abjuring? But I was not respectful enough, I fear, of their capacity to consider in their own way what had come to my mind:

I suppose we're getting ourselves into trouble right now by talking about all this—saying we shouldn't do this kind of thing! Someone came by [the SNCC Atlanta office] the other day [April, 1964], and he said we should keep records, because we're making history, and afterwards, people will want to know what happened. I said, hey mister, you folks will be able to 'know'—you'll know by what we *did*. You start poking around, interviewing, you'll hear a lot of talk, a lot of agreement and disagreement—that's not history, that's people saying something. History is when you come together, when we're here, and we go there—to do what we believe is right, even if you can be shot dead, and it's noon and the sun is out and you're an American, killed for wanting to be able to vote.

There was so much more, a long and fiery oration of sorts, whose purport (again, irony!) was the futility and vanity of mere words, not to mention documentary evidence meant to chronicle and explain, to account for a particular historical moment. At that same meeting, however, another SNCC leader cautiously raised, yet again, the matter of such documentation, not on behalf of the particular historian who had visited the SNCC office (who was black) but on behalf of SNCC itself: "I think we shouldn't forget that one day we'll win this struggle, and then we'll want to look back and remember. We'll want to tell our kids and our grandchildren what happened—and you do forget. Hey, I'm twenty-eight, and I forget things already! So, if we kept some records, and they're *ours*, not someone else's, then that's not bad."

But what "records" did she have in mind? An intense discussion followed, one that (more irony!) I was tape-recording (as a long-standing member of the planning group then preparing for the Mississippi Summer Project, the effort to initiate voting registration in the Delta of that state with the help of hundreds of college students from across the land). At a certain moment the matter of "oral history" was broached—again, a professor's desire to do interviews. Now a discussion of that matter ensued. These young men and women were aware that a machine can both record what is going on and shape it. They knew the inhibitions that arise when one knows that one's words are going to last, so to speak, rather than disappear into the privacy, the complexity, the ambiguity of each person's memory. Suddenly, Bob Moses, our leader, looked at me, with my machine at my side. He smiled and asked: "Is this oral history?" I didn't know how to answer. I finally came up with "No." I was asked to explain myself. I spoke of the systematic stories, the life histories of individuals (in the tradition of, say, Oscar Lewis, the anthropologist) which at the time constituted oral history in my mind. Well, what about my tape-recorded "material"—how to classify it? I said that I used such tapes to help me understand what I was hearing and seeing in connection with my work as a "participant observer," work mainly done with SNCC. Well, how *did* I use the tapes, and what would I do with them down the line: whose were they? (This was back a ways, chronologically, in the history of oral history, and, too, in the recent chronicle of self-consciousness that inevitably developed and led to the phrase "participant observation." Surely, though, for generations individuals have both taken part in a particular social or political struggle and stood far enough away to take some measure of what was happening, then share what they had concluded with others through writing, or, in this century, through photographs).

I found myself "defensive," perplexed, ingratiating. Whatever "they" wanted, I'd do; but I did feel I could "learn more" by being able to "listen a second time." But why not "just take notes"? one SNCC member asked. Why "hang on our every word"? another person wondered. Anyway, do I tape-record my patients' comments and go over *them* that closely? Is research any different in its requirements than therapy? What kind of research was I doing, anyway? Psychiatric? Sociological? Historical? All (or none) of the above? We weren't very systematic in our conversation. There were urgent practical matters to take up. I offered to stop tape-recording our talks (I only did so sometimes, never when major decisions of an especially sensitive kind were being made). No, I was told, I should continue— but the tapes ought be the property of SNCC. I gladly assented. Meanwhile, before we put the matter to rest, I had to contend with some other tough questions about the nature of my work. Was I looking for certain "traits" in my SNCC colleagues, some "personality type" that fitted them all? Was I trying to be a "shrink" when I talked with them—despite my day-to-day work alongside them as a volunteer, like all the others who were offering their time and energy in the hope of helping to make a difference? How *did* I think when I was talking with people? Was I interested in getting to know individuals, as fully as possible, or was I on the lookout for general statements or descriptions, for "data," as one youth put it with barely concealed derision?

To this day I think back to that long time with friends, with "brothers and sisters" in a struggle, but also with tough skeptics who were themselves rather knowing about so-called "methodological issues" in research, many of those young men and women having majored in one or the other of the social sciences, and not a few having taken philosophy courses—hence a discussion of the analytic as against the phenomenological mode of vision, and of how such distinctions apply to fieldwork. "A heavy time, our talk," Bob Moses described it—he who had been enrolled as a doctoral candidate in philosophy before coming south to work with SNCC, and, ultimately, to lead us all into that Mississippi Summer Project. It was Bob who pursued that "talk" most strenuously. He pointed out to me the tendency of many of us Americans of this century (and not only social scientists, but also essayists and journalists) to look for this or that "common denominator," to try to find conceptualizations that serve as umbrellas, or as probing and explanatory instruments. He commented, at one point, "In Europe there are 'phenomenologists'—they take each person as an individual, and try to do the best they can to get to know the person. Here, so many of you folks are trying to explain everything, everybody with these 'general laws'—you impose ideas on people. That's what a professor of mine said is wrong about a lot of social science—and the newspaper and magazine editors who take it so seriously: the 'rage,' he said, 'to reduce,' to simplify, to explain with a definition or conclusion that is supposed to include, to take care of, to account for everything."

Bob stopped talking just as (we thought) he seemed ready to

launch upon one of his carefully delivered lectures: the young philosopher back in the classroom. We waited a few seconds, then I
responded with my agreement—though I added that a tentative
(rather than reductive) analytic or categorical approach to the world's
various human events offered its own suggestive possibilities: theories
as speculations, rather than reifications, as ways of merely trying to
sort things out rather than to banish the complexities of life through
resort to distinctions that are fixed or dogmatic. But Bob, it turned
out, had not stopped for good; he was thinking in his own inimitable
way, and now we heard more:

I know, I know—but this is not a temperate, or, as you put it, 'tentative'
age! We love explanations and we forget that they are—*that*; instead, we
turn them into discoveries, conclusions that aren't really subject to disagreement, because so-and-so has handed down a *law*, a *rule*, a division of
people, a formulation about society. We don't say: that's his opinion, his
idea, and I have my own. We buy his words and *believe*; or we don't, and
we turn to someone else, who suits our appetite better. It's the *appetite* I'm
worried about! I guess I'm saying that these days that way of thinking—
of exploring the world—is the only dish [of food] around. In Europe,
phenomenology is on the menu, too! In America, a guy like you makes
your reputation when you're here, studying us, if you come up with a
bunch of psychological and sociological *ideas* about us: who we are, in
our heads, and what our background is, and what 'ideology' we're pushing—and then you write your stuff up, and pretty soon it's news, and
you write a book, and it's used in classrooms, and those poor students,
they don't end up knowing *me*, and *Jim* [Foreman, another SNCC leader]
and maybe *Bob Zellner* and *Dottie* [two other SNCC leaders, then husband
and wife]; instead, they know about 'types' and 'problems' and 'beliefs'—
anything to bunch folks together in any way the one doing the 'research'

(or the newspaper article or the magazine piece) can figure out, and the catchier the way it's done, the bigger the payoff.

I sit silent, troubled. I more than got his point, and I followed the line of argument readily, because I had heard him speak it before. I worry about a certain cynicism that comes across, and, ironically, I do in my mind exactly what Bob has alleged that people like me are wont to do: I conclude that he is exhausted and frightened by what will be going on, soon enough, in the summer ahead, and so he is lashing out a bit, targeting privileged outsiders as calculating or simple-minded, or both—unable or unwilling to try to fathom the variousness of the world they are approaching, the idiosyncratic and the peculiar, the ambiguous and the paradoxical and the inconsistent, the fatefully accidental nature of so much that occurs, the mere luck, good and bad, that gets so much going. Yet (I counter in that unspoken conversation with myself), it most certainly is hard to do justice to human particularity when one is trying to understand a social or political event. True, hundreds of individuals make up the SNCC cadres, but no matter the individuality of those men and women, they are united in certain ways that deserve mention (and analysis): the deeds they do together, the shared ideas and ideals they continually express. Anyway, I conclude, these modes of thinking and of expression are not mutually contradictory; they are alternative visions, or ways of looking and then sharing what has been observed with others.

We were interrupted by an important phone call, and soon enough these SNCC leaders would be on the road once more, driving through the long night from Atlanta to Jackson, Mississippi. Just before Bob left, though, he joked with me, through resort to travel imagery—and why not finish an argument by drawing upon the deed that was around the corner, an automobile journey, with the choice of roads always a serious question, given the hostility of the South's state and local police? "You're trying to see the big picture, I guess," he said. "But we're the ones, each of us, who make up the picture." With that conjunction, "but," Bob drew more than a distinction—he drew a contrast, one he quickly underlined as genetic in nature:

Don't you see, that's been our story—the black story: everyone calls us something! It's so hard for any single one of us to be seen by you folks [white people], even the kindest of you, even our friends [among you] as a person, nothing more. That's where we are; that's where we're coming from; that's our 'place' in all this! You folks—can be yourselves! You can wander all over the map. You can be here and you can be there. You can go set up your tent wherever you think it'll do you good! That's great—for you! That's what it means to be white, and have a good education. You can look at things with a microscope or a tele-scope, and from way up in the mountains and down near the seashore, and when it's sunny and when it's raining cats and dogs, and then, later, when you write or you publish your photographs—you're not a *white* writer, or a *white* photographer. You're free of the biggest label of them all, the one that defines us every single minute of our lives! So, you can take all roads, and you can stop at any gas station or restaurant while on the way. Us—we're trying to get people to give us just a *little* break, to call us Mister or Missus, to let me go where I please without thinking I might get arrested, and even killed. So, it's location, man, location, for us: where we're at, and where you're at, and where we can go, and where you can go—that's why I favor stopping to look at one person, then the next, and not running all which ways to corral folks into someone's pen, some circle, with a fence around it.

What one thinks, he was reminding me, can depend upon who one is—the possibilities in life open and available, the limitations of life very much present (and threatening). I was struck by his desire to locate me, locate himself, and then ironically, go further: make a general statement, a conceptualization of sorts, tied to the obvious reality, the constant shadow of racial experience. In a sense, Bob's plea for a new notion of individuality had foundered on the obvious imperative of racial awareness. No single black person can be altogether free of a tie that somewhat defines all who make up a people—even as the obverse holds, too, for whites insofar as they try to comprehend blacks: each of us, in so doing, is the "other," inescapably. Still, if Bob was trying to plead for particularity, even as he insisted upon an important general (racial) truth, I was asked to think twice about the basis of my support for an interpretive, a modestly theoretical and analytic stance for those of us who look at others in the hope of learning about how they live, what they uphold, and why they do various things, then make a "document" of what we have learned: the writing, the photography that mobilize language and visual intelligence (and talent) to the task of informing others. We take our stand, as it were, locate ourselves with respect to how we think, how we work, how we present our observations, by dint of our "orientation." But maybe we ought to go back further, realize (again, the irony) that even as a plea for individuality can stem from the awareness of being part of a general (a group) experience, so a plea on behalf of the value, the worth of generalities (theories) can depend upon specific privileges, unavailable to others as a conse-quence of race or, one can speculate, class, gender, nationality. (The ideological indoctrination of students and scholars in totalitarian states cuts off for many even the contemplation of various ideas).

Documentary work, then, can itself be documented—can be fitted into a grand scale of classifications or categories, or can be more cautiously regarded as a series of individual stories: so-and-so, and how it came that he or she did such-and-such work. (I am speaking here not only of motivational analysis, but of a person's complex life as it got connected with, say, politics, economics, or history itself: Dorothea Lange, for example, the San Francisco portrait photographer of the well-to-do, chanced upon the desolate early-1930s world of the Great Depression, and with it a career that might otherwise never have materialized.) Put differently, where we locate ourselves with respect to our vantage point as documentarians will tell us not only about what (whom) we'll see, but who we, the viewers, are—the lives that enabled or encouraged us in one direction prevented us surely or sorely from pursuing another direction, as Bob Moses, in his challenging way, at once philosophical (abstract) and earthy (concrete), was at pains for me to know many years ago, in a conversational aside whose lack of pretentiousness in no way interfered with its telling import.

I remember discussing with Erik Erikson two years later, in 1966 (I taught in his Harvard College course at the time, and was a member of a seminar he was offering), the details of that relatively brief moment with my SNCC friends. Erikson was himself working on the subject of nonviolent social and political action, though not in connection with students taking on the segregationist South, but rather with Gandhi's challenge to imperial British rule. We sat in his Widener-library study and shared experiences, each of us trying to apply psychoanalytic thinking to historical events as they had unfolded in the early years of this century across the Pacific Ocean or here at home in the very decade that was then, for us, the present. I can still hear us, comparing notes and telling of our confusions, our apprehensions, the obstacles we'd encountered as we tried to talk with individuals who turned out to be, themselves, confused or apprehensive, or fearfully reluctant, or all too anxious that we hear from them so very much, to the point where we wondered what, in fact, we were hearing that meant all that much. At a certain point in the discussion, Erikson interrupted himself, changed tack, became ruminative rather than complaining, and, finally, turned confessional:

"Sometimes I have to distinguish between what I am hearing, and what I wanted to hear from the person, before I even met him!"

A knowing look came my way—and as I recall, I looked down at the floor, a tell-tale response on my part. Erikson didn't mean to incriminate himself or me; he was being "methodological"—pursuing psychoanalytic self-scrutiny in the tradition of the Freud who dared to examine frankly his own dreams, not to mention those of his patients, and also in the tradition of St. Augustine, who let little in the way of self-observation pass him by. Erikson was ready to amplify, to connect us not to sin but a modest kind of twentieth-century (psychiatric, psychoanalytic) virtue: "That's our job, to make sure where we stop and our patients start: their concerns as opposed to our sense of what their concerns 'really' are—or should be!"

Silence for both of us, as we each had our memories to share with ourselves, those in connection with our clinical work and those in connection with our "fieldwork," our documentary efforts to learn from others about what they were doing (or had seen others do), and our efforts to fit what we had learned (or surmised) into a presentation for others (or, more skeptically, a performance for others) that would obtain their interest (a matter of consent), and then (we hope, surely) their agreement (a matter of assent). Finally, I speak, tersely and a little anxiously. I say that we can at least offer *that* to this kind of research, this doing of documentary work: our willingness to put ourselves on the line in this way, our willingness to indicate that the documentarian, the listener and the one who sees, the witness, can be both a vehicle and an obstacle on a journey. More silence, and then I recite a clinical truism: that the analyst must constantly look within, hence the parallel need in "fieldwork" to take into account the person (ourselves) who is offering an account of others—it being so easy, in contrast, to read those oral histories, those personal essays, those theories, or even those statistically laden reports, or to look at those photographs, with their titles and the terse or extended descriptions under them, or the film footage with its voices and visions, and forget (a negation of the whole point of documentary work) the person's life that preceded and now informs this time when he or she has become that listener, that witness.

I was, of course, repeating what I had heard my important and imposing teacher say. I was affirming what takes place all the time in human affairs: our connectedness (in this case as teacher and student), our membership (even if it be temporary) in whatever "community" we are trying to "study," and thus our ability, our inclination, our need to accommodate ourselves to one another, and our participation in what we aim to observe—our participation, obviously, as well, in what we thereafter document or give to others as a stimulus for *their* participation. In that last regard, needless to say, this chain of information sought, information offered, information sorted, and information presented goes a step further: the book reader, the museum visitor, the moviegoer is himself or herself receptive or resistant, willing to say yes, determined to say no, or interested in doing both (as a matter of firm, energized principle sometimes, rather than open-mindedness). The complexity of this amplification of the matter mounts, of course, as we take into consideration not only the individual documentarian and the individual respondent, but the larger world that bears down on both: the historical moment, with its cultural preoccupations, political shifts, and social fads and concerns—all of no small significance in determining (let us be frank) whether there will be any audience for a completed documentary project, or even whether such a project will ever be done.

Even as George Eliot, in *Middlemarch*, wondered about the countless lives that go unnoticed, undocumented, so that their outcomes are unknown, we might wonder about the many documentary ideas that never even get formulated, much less brought to the attention of editors, museum curators, owners of film houses—the times preclude this idea for the tape recorder, the camera, the film crew, or the person with writing goals (and ambitions) sitting with pen and paper, or at a computer. To be sure, some documentarians have taken on many "principalities and powers," even as Gandhi and those SNCC workers did—and, again, as Bob Moses once observed, "When you're weak, you're strong that way." He expanded with the obvious: that there are people ready to align themselves with the poor, with the marginal rather than the powerful; and so, to be a bit cynical, those living and working "at the bottom" have their potential audience, too—as SNCC's leaders quickly learned when they went to the fanciest colleges in America, talked with some of the luckiest and most favored and best-connected students in the country, and found in them a welcoming audience and, soon thereafter, a substantial pool of eager followers (though not leaders).

Speaking of theory, and of individuals who have challenged it (thereby establishing their own relationship to it, and even turning an oppositional stance into a theoretical position, that of the antitheorist), I recall my college study of the poetry of William Carlos Williams, and my eventual good fortune in getting to know him, in accompanying him on his medical rounds and home visits. I recall his refrain, his cry of the heart, all through the long, lyrical examination of a city's, a country's social history that is his great poem, *Paterson*: "No ideas but in things." Williams was constantly on the observational prowl, through those back alleys and supposedly dead-end streets, up those tenement-house stairs, where his often immigrant, almost invariably impoverished, even destitute patients lived in an America deeply troubled at the time (the 1930s) when he began work on that poem, and on his stories (published, first, as *Life Along the Passaic River*, his effort to tell of his doctoring life at the remove of fiction). I remember him taking notes after we left an apartment—words heard, phrases used, incidents relayed, beliefs or convictions expressed, gestures and mannerisms noted. All the while, as we walked or drove, he would scorn those who tried to do too much with such information, or indeed with no such information, those who proceeded with their minds made up, or their minds conjuring something up, their minds at work on speculation, on distanced opinion, on surveys, polls, summary descriptions, or, as he once characterized a kind of research that might be journalistic or social-scientific, "Fly-by-night invasions or raids."

Williams's sarcasm could be intimidating, sometimes wrong-headed, but it was also brusquely confronting and provocative. "The thing itself," he kept reminding himself, was his "subject": how to describe people, places, customs, gesticulations, signs, waves of the hand, a smile or a frown, a withdrawal or an approach, the trembling of one person, the wide-eyed interest of another, and how to do so in a language that is itself worthy of those attended, a language that salutes them by drawing unashamedly from them, drawing upon the vernacular of a certain neighborhood oft visited over the decades of a doctor's or a writer's working life. But Williams wrote in Rutherford, in that delightfully comfortable, unpretentious Victorian clapboard home on Ridge Road; and he could be candidly forthcoming about the significance of even those few miles that separated him from—well, "them." "I tell you," he once tried hard to tell me, "there are days that I wonder what I'm doing in my study, of all places!" When my face seemed to indicate my answer—that he was writing there (and why not!), he continued as if I'd become a potential antagonist: "Don't you see—that's it: I'm not seeing *here*, I'm remembering. When I'm *there*, sitting with those folks, listening and talking—the flow of it!—I'm part of that life, and I'm near it in my head, too. The words are coming to me, and I have to push them away, because I've got to ask those medical questions and use my stethoscope. Back here, sitting near this typewriter—it's different.

I'm a 'writer.' I'm a doctor living in Rutherford who is describing 'a world elsewhere,' as I said it [in Paterson], and it wasn't a compliment to myself, and it wasn't only the exhortation people think, something for all of us to do. 'A world subject to my incursions'— get it? *Subject, incursions!* The lord and master to whom a world is 'subject,' and who makes his quickie 'incursions.' That's a bigshot word [incursions] for a bigshot guy!"

Scorn turned to self-reproach. The writer's effort to respond faithfully but also imaginatively to a scene he himself regularly joins as a visiting participant (house calls all day, often nonstop) prompts him to wonder (speaking of the imagination) how it might go were he writing in the very midst of things, with his eyes and ears, as he once put it, "bombarded," his brain jogged by what *is*: the immediately audible and visible, rather than intermediation, modulation, intrusions, and too, the lapses and distortions of a mind now distanced yet struggling to encompass (find a direction toward, find the direction of the life in) that "world elsewhere."

In his own fashion, Williams could become a kind of theorist, a feisty, no-nonsense, street-savvy one who knew in his bones that location made a huge difference, not only the location of a particular documentary project with respect to someone's analytic scheme of things (it is *this*, it is *that*, it should go under some other name, be described as something different) but the very location of the person doing the project, and of course the reasons behind that location (racial or occupational or psychological, as Bob Moses and Erik Erikson reminded themselves and reminded us). "I stand here ironing," Tillie Olsen has her worn and worried mother say at the start of her fine and well-known story by that title—a poor woman's remembrance of a family's hurt, precarious past; and so with Dr. Williams as he wondered about where to stand, as he tried to iron out his take on a life only down the road, it seemed, only as far away as yesterday's doctoring. He faced the understandable worry over what to say later, under different circumstances, about what happened then, there, with them: the matter of the specific location of oneself as documentarian amidst one's struggle to locate oneself as an observer and writer, as someone who saw and now wants to represent, in the sense of conveying or picturing, so that others will say or feel (Williams liked the expression) "I got it," or, better, "I'm really getting it."

two

The Person As Documentarian

Moral and Psychological Tensions

S ome of the upbraiding Dr. Williams directed at himself, including his confessional moments in *Paterson* and in his somewhat autobiographical short fiction, was not only meant to serve an intellectual purpose—that of an anti-intellectualism, a broader adversarial position to stake out than one of skepticism with respect to theory. When this writing doctor tells us that he could be self-absorbed, all too indifferent to others even while treating them as a doctor and, later, writing about them in poems and stories, he is asking us to consider the vocational hazards of a certain kind of work—the moral and psychological questions that confront us explicitly or by implication as we who take stock of others also try to live our own lives with some self-respect.

Dr. Williams's persistent notion that he ought somehow to do some of his writing *in medias res* (as near as possible to the world he kept saying he was trying to render as carefully, directly, intimately, and knowingly as possible) might not have been only a subject of the intellect, of the search for a methodology that ensured better, more accurate writing by moving closer to "things," with "no ideas" to distract our view, our sense of them. To urge "no ideas," of course, is to have an idea, to push it on the reader, one more paradox an author does well to let stand rather than try to "resolve," that rather cool, slippery word some of us use today, without letup, as we consider patients' problems or those posed by scientific inquiry to be matters ultimately in need of "resolution." But a moral issue was also at stake. There he was, after all, living quite comfortably in Rutherford, for all his occasional bellyaching that certain patients didn't (couldn't) pay him except through resort to a barter economy: "They pay me with a cake or bread they've made, and I thank them, but to be honest, I'd much rather have the dough than the cooked dough! Then, I feel bad for complaining about not getting my damn fee!"

That half-irritable, half-bemused, blunt, offhand comment shocked me, a twenty-one-year-old college student whose professed idealism and gentility had yet to be looked at closely by himself, let alone by someone else called a psychoanalyst. Later, I thought of that comment and others like it often—when I worked in the South, studying school desegregation, or participating in the activities sponsored by SNCC, or still later, while trying to learn how migrants live, or the people of Appalachia, or of northern New Mexico, or of Alaska. I list those commitments, those places, with obvious pride, and I remember much of the time spent visiting families in their homes with an increasing nostalgia, which, I suspect (I have to admit), glosses over plenty of troublesome moments, as I saw in those individuals what they (the families themselves, or their neighbors or advocates) most certainly saw in me—my fortunate life, made even more fortunate by this documentary work, and their far less fortunate, indeed quite vulnerable lives.

Even, for example, as Dr. Williams could wonder what it would be like to write about others right where they were (maybe, in wondering, he was prodding himself, moving himself nearer imaginatively to the world he meant to evoke), I can recall the questions of the black children I was trying to get to know in New Orleans in the early 1960s, as they struggled past heckling, threatening mobs in order to desegregate schools abandoned (for a while) by the enraged white population. Where do you live? Where's that? Do you like it there? Let's see, how would I get to your place? Those questions were put to my wife, Jane, and me over and over, though more to me than to her, because she was able to be more relaxed and less explicitly inquisitive than I was (she could quietly and casually watch and hear, and overhear, while I was forever making everyone self-conscious with my inquiries). Such questions were asked not only out of curiosity but out of annoyance: When will you be leaving us alone, when will you return to your home? Those questions were reminders, too: you not only live someplace else, someplace that is off limits to us, you *are* someplace else, in the sense that you are someone else: different in enough ways, no matter our momentary time together, for us to take notice, to consider, and, in so doing, maybe, to feel ourselves wanting, lacking.

Those questions do not, of course, go unnoticed by those of us to whom they are posed. Questions of fact are easy: we reply with the knowledge we have acquired. Questions that have moral implications are harder to hear, are not so easy to answer, and, for many of us, persist long after they have been asked—indeed, become *our* questions, posed to ourselves. When I first read James Agee's *Let Us Now Praise Famous Men*, I was put off: page after page of anger directed at nameless others, including the reader. Agee is constantly proclaiming his inadequacy as a writer. He is constantly taking swipes at his own kind, writers and intellectuals from the Northeast. He gets sardonic in many ways, even with the use of a statement made by President Franklin D. Roosevelt on one of his campaign trips: "You are farmers; I am a farmer myself." Now it is easy, in that instance, to ride along, to salute Agee for his clever humor—the *nerve* of that FDR, to connect himself, the millionaire product of the aristocratic gentry, so unqualifiedly with the millions of American men of the soil who were barely scraping by at best. We are reminded simply by the sight of that sentence, placed at the start of a chapter titled "Money," that politicians can be glib and even absurd in their pietistic wish to bring us all together as a citizenry when in fact huge differences separate us.

Still, if any rich American gentleman "farmer" was worrying about other farmers far less well off, surely FDR would qualify as the one. The Southern rural people, the white yeomen, whom Agee glimpsed in the summer of 1936 were about to vote overwhelmingly for this President, whose agricultural programs, no matter their inadequacy, surely attested to a desire on his part to make things better for those whom he embraced with the remark Agee offers in sheer, angry irony. Moreover, in his chapter "Education," Agee laments the inadequate facilities of the schools available to the children he has met, describes "overcrowded" classrooms, worries about "ill-paid" teachers who also have "anxiety over their jobs"—concern that they will lose them, so desperate was that time for many parts of the United States. Yet, as with FDR, he turns on those same teachers (and anyone else available, it sometimes seems) with outspoken derision: "Nearly all teachers and clergymen suffocate their victims, through this sterility [of their thinking and manner] alone." In one breath, he wishes better for such teachers but in the next breath, he would deny them what he himself, in company with FDR, managed to get: "I could not wish any of them that they should have had the 'advantages' I have had: a Harvard education is by no means an unqualified advantage."

That remark, of course, does not escape the notice of my Harvard students, and in fact manages to serve what we begin to realize in class may have been Agee's purpose—that we stop and think about who we are, the ones who come to size up others and, later, let the world know what is there to be noticed and what is very much not there (adequate housing, say, or solidly constructed schools in which teachers are appropriately salaried and enabled to do their work with the assurance that they are respected). Agee has been waging a battle in the section titled "Education" similar to the one he carries on throughout his book: a struggle against smugness and complacency. He has a keen eye and ear for the conceits and deceits of his own kind, and he clearly regards his own kind with skepticism, if not outright disdain. He is moved to a radical critique of a society, is worried about the costs of accommodating the status quo—something that takes place, he keeps insisting, in the schools, among other places. Prophetically, he worries (half a century ago) about psychology and psychiatry as potential instruments of complacency and self-congratulation—the normative aspect of what gets called "mental health," an attitude of conformity that receives a medical or therapeutic nod: "As a whole part of 'psychological education' it needs to be remembered that a neurosis can be valuable; also that 'adjustment' to a sick and insane environment is of itself not 'health' but sickness and insanity."

For my students, for all of Agee's readers, here is an author who intends to be unnerving, indeed; who refers to his "self-disgust"; who even threatens to "blow out the brains" of those who don't take his preoccupations, his train of thought, his "convictions" and passions "seriously enough." This is all rhetoric, we are tempted to say, or, more favorably, here is some good, clean anger that is meant to jolt us from the kind of acquiescence, moral and psychological, that tempts us constantly, and that commonly takes the form of this question: What can I possibly do to change all this, either in Alabama or nearer to my own home? Not that Agee provides an answer, a specific agenda. He is all the more frustrating and enraging to many of us who love his lyrical writing, admire enormously his defiantly, brilliantly idiosyncratic voice, and cherish his moral energy and his shrewd and sometimes hilarious capacity for social satire, yet can't help feeling—well, beaten up as we turn the many pages of what he provocatively disdained as a book. Agee keeps telling us that he is confused and at a loss for advice on what ought be done on behalf of the tenant families he has met; and he keeps venting his splenetic wrath in a determined assault on a range of targets, and of course any of us qualifies as one or another of them. We exult in his fury at hypocrites and phonies, even (some of us) in his disparagement of all fancy entitlements and prerogatives by his singling out the oldest and fanciest of institutions, his own alma mater, Harvard, for a good kick in the pants. Yet after a while this rancor, this moral alarm and outrage, this exasperation that is poured on objects and institutions large and small, on individuals prominent and obscure, begins to wear thin, because it seems almost reflexive— and this from someone who is determined to use language in such an original, compelling, unsettling manner that it will, he must have hoped, break the hold of various clichés and stereotypes and banalities upon our thinking.

When we in class contemplate the above, try to fashion for ourselves an attitude toward this utterly unique stretch of words, so confrontational and goading one moment and so exquisitely expressive, original, and suggestive the next, we begin to realize, in time, that our rationality, our capacity to analyze carefully a "text" may help us to discard this book as hopelessly flawed by inconsistencies, by near hysteria, by a rambling self-indulgence—but also to realize that those very aspects of failure (and others, too) are exactly what make Agee's sustained exhortation so powerfully instructive. For his bile, his seemingly hopeless inconsistencies, his self-accusations, his search for targets at which to aim his bitter, tart asides, are (at a lower frequency, perhaps) not unfamiliar to many of us. Like him, we have left one world for another—have worked, for instance, as tutors with ghetto children in summer programs, near home or far away. Like him, we have felt overwhelmed, quite at a loss to figure out what ought to be done that will really make a difference—what we, in fact, or anyone might hope to accomplish. Like him, we have often found ourselves better at realizing what isn't working than at finding out what might work. Like him, too, we have found people and institutions well worth our criticism: loafers and even con artists who work in the various programs set up to serve the so very needy people whose obvious plight touches us, worries us, and leaves us occasionally at wit's end. Like him, we get caught—inevitably, it seems—in various contradictions. We come to admire some of the people we meet, admire their ability simply to survive against such great odds. Indeed, as we get to know how overwhelmingly adverse those odds sometimes are, we imagine ourselves trying to face up to them, and conclude that we would fail to do so. All the more reason, then, to admire these souls, with their luck so poor, their chances so grim. All the more reason to strike out at those who are on top, wherever they are—to remark on their heartlessness or duplicity or pretentiousness, their insincerity. Surely if they were more honorable, things would be better here or there, wherever it is in the "lower depths" that we happen to be.

However, we know in our heart of hearts (as Agee knew) that we ourselves won't be where we now are (as volunteers, as members of Vista or the Peace Corps) for the rest or our lives; far from it. How inviting, then, to search for people to condemn—and how much easier to notice blemishes in others than in those vulnerable people with whom we are working. To spare such people, we can turn on ourselves if necessary, bask in a certain kind of self-directed censure. So it was that Agee extolled those three tenant-farm families, asked us to "praise" them with unreserved conviction, even as he no doubt couldn't bear to think about some of their warts, their blind spots, their mean and narrow sides. I remember hearing reference made to Agee's book during the march from Selma to Montgomery that Dr. Martin Luther King, Jr., led in 1965—and the person so referring was as surprised at what came to his mind as the rest of us were to hear it: "We're near the place Agee and Evans stayed thirty years ago. Some of those same people could be right there on the road, calling us every swear word they could think of!"

The point was not to condemn either Agee or the people of Hale County, Alabama, whom he came to know and so very much admire; rather, it was to remind us, then and there, how eagerly we want to think well of people, under certain circumstances, and how reluctant we can therefore be to notice their limitations and worse. The man who spoke was black, an admirer of *Let Us Now Praise Famous Men*, and he was quite willing to move from the racism of Hale County, in 1936 and 1965, to the black world of the Mississippi Delta during the summer of 1964: "I remember all those white college students telling me how much they loved their black host families in Canton [Mississippi], where they were staying. Lord, they sang their praises. They were saying what Agee said—and a lot of them brought his book with them: let us now praise these famous folks, these humble people who are putting us up and feeding us and taking us to their churches and showering us with all their attention, [and] who'd give us the shirts off their backs if we'd take them. I knew some of those folks real well, and hey, I'm not the one to bad-mouth them! They *were* fine folks. But they weren't angels sent down here from heaven—and some of them knew how to be scoundrels every now and then, like you and me. Once, during one of those long middle-of-the-night talks, I'd been listening to all the praise being heaped on all the host families, and finally, I had to stop those kids, and say: 'Come on, you're here to fight the worst segregation in America, and now you're telling me that *these* people are the best people you've ever met in the world, you're saying that! Now, if that's the case, why should we end segregation? Why should we worry whether those families can go stay in a Howard Johnson's Motor Lodge? Why should they even bother going to those all-white schools or restaurants? Why not salute the state of Mississippi—it's produced the finest, the most thoughtful and sensitive families we'll ever see, until [God's] kingdom come!"

The man stopped to let me savor that ironical moment, to recall it himself, to scratch his head and to sip some iced tea on that warm, humid, early spring Alabama day. I was shaking my head. I was thinking about Agee and his great admiration for *his* hosts; and yes, I was thinking about some of my own responses to the various black and white families I'd met in Louisiana and Georgia, to my talks with the children of both races who had initiated school desegregation. In the black homes, I went out of my way to give everyone the benefit of the doubt, to notice hospitality, generosity, warmth, liveliness, humility, spirituality—and there was plenty of all that to notice in certain homes. But in other black homes there was a cold distrust and irritability, and even a frank unfriendliness that I also went out of my way to understand, to explain to myself, but not to stress for others, for I was, meanwhile, expressing again and again my unstinting admiration for the obvious bravery of every one of the black children I had met—who encountered threatening street mobs (New Orleans) or an everyday icy rejection inside classrooms (Atlanta)—in order to make a start of school desegregation in the deep South of Georgia and Louisiana.

I am not saying that I refused any mention of certain unattractive traits in certain black families. Rather, I emphasized the attractive and appealing qualities in the families I liked best—to the extent that my descriptive writing, both in professional journals and for the so-called lay public, drew heavily from my notes taken while working with the children of those families. True, I protected myself with necessary qualifications, reminded my readers (and myself) that I was not doing interviews in the Promised Land but in the still deeply segregationist South. Yet more and more I downplayed the troubles I encountered in favor of the resiliency I also encountered. Since none of the children, thank God, got into any psychiatric trouble, I had no ethical problem of a professional nature; I was not trying to paint a rosy picture where none existed. Instead, I was ignoring family tensions or moments of rudeness and callousness in certain families (toward the children, or toward my wife and me) in favor of a general awe—legitimate, I felt then and feel now—toward people who did indeed successfully face down a spell of hell.

On the white side of the tracks, however, I had considerably less trouble acknowledging the less attractive side of human nature as I spotted it in the families whose children were the first to attend school with black classmates. With those families, I could be relentlessly observant, especially when I heard nasty comments directed at black people. When I heard such comments directed *by* black people at black people, sometimes within a family, and sometimes with devastating meanness and seriousness, I could only turn my head away, or shake that head with a kind of sad resignation and understanding that I did not feel among my white informants—*their* "racism," obvious and vocal, was, after all, a "subject matter" I was present to document, both among the children and among their parents and teachers. In a sense, I had from the very start protected myself from certain troublesome moments that arrived in the course of the research—I had defined the nature of that research: to learn how black children managed the serious social and educational stress of school desegregation as it took place in the racially embattled south; and to learn how white children, only reluctantly sent to those desegregated schools against a history of fierce and unrelenting opposition, managed their new school life in classrooms with black boys and girls.

I proceeded, therefore, to follow closely the entry of the black children, follow closely their psychological ups and downs, follow closely the gradual success of their initiative; and follow closely, too, the open and all too pitiless resentment and resistance of white children and their parents (and many teachers) in those early days and weeks and months—and follow closely, as well, a gradual if reluctant accommodation. With such a self-imposed mandate, one that seemed in obvious accordance with that vaunted virtue "common sense," I was spared the need to pursue a Tolstoyan rationale that would acknowledge malice and sin as fairly universal and moments of decency or charity as not any one kind of person's property, in favor of a "research methodology" that concentrated on certain kinds of "evidence": the anxieties of black children, as expressed in their drawings and conversation, and the psychological strengths that they nevertheless displayed; the fears of white children, as expressed in their drawings and remarks, and their day-by-day willingness, over time, to live with the inevitable, the necessary, and their slow but steady capacity to see their new classmates as individuals rather than as members of another race, to the point where there were finally moments of real (psychological) integration in these at first fearfully desegregated classrooms.

I have memories of queasiness, of biting my lips as I heard unattractive comments and worse in certain black homes, and of scratching my head in disbelief as I heard wonderfully kind and sensitive remarks spoken by white parents (to their children, to other children, to my wife and me) who at the same time were unalterably opposed, so they said, to "this integration thing," a phrase I heard in house after house, not all of them occupied by followers of the devil. No wonder, then, I was as quick as my black minister friend, who spoke to me in 1965, to observe, the earnest enthusiasm of those white students for all black folks in the Delta of Mississippi. No wonder I was jolted by his remarks on Agee's writing in his most celebrated book—I'd never thought to connect his hymns of affectionate, appreciative, near reverential enthusiasm for those tenant farmers, and especially their children, with some of my own less compelling, less sonorous, less affecting, less memorable tunes; nor had I been able to connect his near worshipful ballads of amazement at the dignity of his hosts with the responses of those college students during the summer of 1964, and with my own responses for four years prior to that summer. (Agee unashamedly uses musical imagery in *Let Us Now Praise Famous Men*, imagery that is meant to take on the shape of an oratorio of sorts, or an opera, with Agee himself as a singer, desperately trying to perform a most demanding role.)

Nor do I now withdraw what I once felt or said—try to rewrite it all at a much later time for a much different era. In the long retrospect of a life, I simply understand a bit more adequately the moral and psychological tensions that this documentarian encountered as he did his work, and realize how those tensions influenced the way he thought, the way he went about doing his interviews, the way he wrote them up, the way he presented them to the world. In that regard, I well remember Kenneth Clark's observation to me when we talked (in 1960) about the plan I had to get to know those New Orleans black children who pioneered desegregation in that old cosmopolitan port city. "If you were Negro and poor, you'd be hearing different words from those [Negro] children, writing up a different research project; and you sure wouldn't even be thinking of (not in your wildest dreams!) doing interviews with white children and their parents—or with the schoolteachers."

He had stated the obvious, and though I was embarrassed by what he said and felt more than vaguely ashamed (for all of us in

America, not just for myself), I didn't (I couldn't, I guess, and still can't) realize the full import of his comment. There I was, in pursuit of some objective truth, so I thought, of a kind I could apprehend with those so-called "tools" of a particular "trade": Anna Freud's "direct observation"; the use of crayons and paints to enable a child's psychological expression and an observer's documentary expression; the interviews I would do with parents, with teachers, with relatives and neighbors, all tape-recorded, all to be heard and heard again, the themes noted and analyzed—a mid-twentieth-century psychiatric and psychoanalytic investigation. There Dr. Kenneth Clark was, however, first telling me that a darkening of my skin's pigment would make all that scientific know-how and planning irrelevant, and then going further, saying these unforgettable words to me: "I couldn't do that project, either—even in the Negro homes." I wanted to know why! "I'm a Northerner, and I've lived a protected, comfortable life; it would be hard to leave it for that world of danger and violence." Meanwhile, race and class presented no apparent problem for me—indeed, served to protect me not only literally but figuratively: I was a white knight who needed have no fear, and who thought (had to think) he could go anywhere, talk to anyone. I cringe, today, at my naïveté and my self-assurance, and maybe my unknowing (as it often is!) arrogance—even as I frankly doubt that without such a psychological, never mind racial and social, background I could have gotten even to first base on either side of those railroad tracks I visited in those beleaguered Southern cities of the early 1960s.

But the considerable obstacles in the way of such an inquiry, to which Dr. Clark was alluding, would soon yield to another kind, not sociological or historical or even necessarily racial: What are one's obligations not to oneself, one's career, the academic world, or the world of readers, but to the people who are, after all, slowly becoming not only one's "sources" or "contacts" or "informants,"

but one's graciously tolerant and open-handed teachers and friends—
there, week after week, with answers to questions, with hands ready
to pick up crayons, with the courtesy and hospitality of food and
drink, with advice, with revealing second thoughts to discussions one
had long ago put aside, but most important, *there* in their available
yet so vulnerable and hard-pressed and precarious lives? Toward the
end of my stay in New Orleans in 1964, Ruby Bridges' mother and
I were sitting over coffee and cake (she was a wonderful cook and
hostess), and she was talking about the future, that of her child and
her family. At a certain point, however, I began to realize that she
was also talking about a particular human involvement, which she
and her daughter (and her husband and her other children) had been
enjoying, coming to an end: "We'll be missing you. We've got so
used to your coming here, that we forgot you're only going to be
with us so long, and then you'll be on your way! Ruby told me she
was sure you'd stay here [in New Orleans] and that we'd see you
the way we have, because you're our friend, so that's when I told
her 'he is' [their friend], but he's got his work to do, and it's all
over, so he won't be visiting us like in the past—maybe now and
then."

I was surprised, embarrassed at her directness. I'd always had
trouble ending my "relationships" with my patients; all that talk of
"termination" (the very word!) used to bother me, the recitation by
my supervisors of the forthcoming anxieties and moodiness—yet it
was always true. An intense human connection was about to be
concluded, an affair of the heart, often enough, put to rest, hence
the sadness and the apprehension. But in clinical work there is an
entire tradition that helps one sort out such feelings and move on—
the two of you are doctor and patient, or the group of you are a
doctor and a family with whom you've tried to work, and you've
done so in a clinic or an office, with the clock setting its own limits
and helping to define what is happening: a professional life, with its

"hours." There, in Mrs. Bridges' humble yet tidy kitchen, with the aroma of her French market coffee and her mouth-watering coffee cake cut into enormous slices (a clear and present temptation), it seemed quite different: "termination" felt like a kind of finality, a death, for which I hadn't prepared myself. There were no colleagues with whom I might have discussed this, no clinical seminar at which I could have made a presentation; rather, I was learning about the documentarian as loner, out there in that "field," stumbling along, and now brought up short by the thoughtful remarks of one of the people he was "observing," "studying"—as if Mrs. Bridges had decided that this fellow needed a bit of the "help" his kind is known for offering others.

What started as a casual comment on the part of Mrs. Bridges turned into a long conversation. I knew that she was a careful observer herself: she worked in the home of a well-to-do white family, and she watched them and listened to them attentively. She asked me about my future plans, asked me where I'd eventually settle down. She and my wife, Jane, had become good friends, and Jane and I had ourselves been discussing some of the questions Mrs. Bridges was putting to me—including the one that both Jane's parents and mine had very much in mind then: When would we start a family? I realize today that in a sense Mrs. Bridges was with me *in loco parentis* that morning. Jane, a teacher, had gone to visit with Ruby's schoolteacher, and Mr. Bridges was at work. In the quiet of a modest apartment a sensible, tactful, wise wife and mother and worker and fellow citizen, a fellow human being, a friend of four years by then, was helping me to think of my own life, not hers or her daughter's. She was also, by gentle indirection, bringing up moral as well as psychological matters. "I hope you won't forget our people," she said, after we'd discussed my future plans. I was surprised, speechless. What did she mean—or what was she implying? I answered, finally, with rote reassurance: of course not. Still, later that day, driving along the Gulf Coast on my way to a SNCC meeting in Biloxi, where I'd previously lived for two years while in the air force as a psychiatrist (under the old doctors' draft law that made us all serve in the military at some early point in our careers), I kept going back to that remark with a rising curiosity, and, I admit, with no small amount of discomfort—as if I'd been quite subtly and politely accused of something. My thoughts went like this: I've been deeply involved in this school desegregation struggle for four years, and also in the larger civil-rights effort being waged by SNCC, soon to culminate in the Mississippi Summer Project of 1964. Why would I *ever* want to forget Mrs. Bridges, her daughter, their family, all the other families Jane and I had been so fortunate to know? Why would I ever want to forget the "people" Mrs. Bridges had mentioned, the people who had, in fact, not only tutored me daily as I went about my work, but also had given that (psychiatric) work a kind of focus and direction and meaning it had hitherto and otherwise sorely lacked?*

Other *whys* also came to my mind, I'd better admit. Why was Mrs. Bridges saying that, *then*? Surely she wasn't merely giving voice to an offhand "hope"; she had more for me to contemplate. Why had she referred to "our people," rather than to her specific family, or perhaps to others I'd come to know in that endlessly intriguing, inviting, exhausting "city that care forgot"? Anyway, why was I now so preoccupied with that one brief assertion, that polite wish, it could be considered, that sensitively spoken acknowledgment of a parting soon to come? For me, it seemed, a handful of words, offered in passing, not portentously or reprovingly, had become quite some-

---

* I had made this lack quite clear, actually, in an article that I wrote before I started my Southern fieldwork; it was published just as that work began: "A Young Psychiatrist Looks at His Profession," *Atlantic Monthly*, July, 1961.

thing else—a worry, rather than a hope of Mrs. Bridges', a worry that addressed me, my purposes and values, my life. A worry, finally, that had become an accusation, I gradually realized as I looked at the quiet, blue expanse of the Gulf of Mexico while standing under a noonday sun and a clear sky beside my car as it was being filled with gas at a familiar Esso station in Gulfport, Mississippi. Suddenly clouds of worry, of self-criticism, of egoistic alarm came over me. Mrs. Bridges had become a stand-in for the "people" she had mentioned, and, beyond them, for the people of the world who get observed and studied by those of us who start our projects, conclude them, and go on to new projects, which will also be finished, "world without end"—all to our personal credit, if not our glory: we build a documentary life, with its bibliography, with the critical response of fellow writers, with a reputation.

Right now, the reader (and the writer) of these words can wonder skeptically about the usefulness of such a line of reasoning, surely one that Mrs. Bridges, to be fair to her, didn't have in mind as desirable when she offered me more cake, more coffee, and more milk and sugar. She had by then become quite identified with the fate of her city's black people, as combatants do when they get caught up in a cause that needs fighting. She was getting ready to say a good-bye on behalf of lots of folks in the Crescent City, and she was proud of her "people," letting me know that they were worth everyone's continuing attention in those 1960s, the very start of which had marked a birth of sorts for those "people." She had that much more reason to be a bit concerned, if not apprehensive, as we all are when a new baby arrives: Will it get the necessary attention it deserves, or will folks somehow overlook it or forget it, to its great detriment? For me, though, what was a general concern on the part of Mrs. Bridges became a quite pointed personal accusation: I was proving to be, finally, a self-absorbed traveling salesman, peddling my documentary (my careerist) wares, which she and others were asked to purchase, through the time and energy they gave to me, week by week.

There was a Dostoyevskyan uproar in my mind, I began to realize, though I'd taken no ax to anyone's head—or had I? So much had been given to me by all those children and by their parents and their kinfolk, and now I was taking a final leave! Suddenly, standing there near my new sports car, I thought of those kin, and in particular of Ruby's family, and the hard, hard praying they did in those church services (no air conditioning, despite the humid heat, *so* oppressive at times), praying that went on and on, hours of it, hours of witnessing and testifying, hours of the blues, hours of lyrical exclamations, hours in which people who had virtually no "literacy," no command over the written word, recited passage after passage from the Old Testament (the warnings and appeals of Jeremiah and Isaiah and Amos and Micah) and from the New Testament (the living example, the parables and dire warnings and spirited series of summonses Jesus gave to His disciples, and, through them, to all of us of a mind to take notice). Suddenly, there by the shore of the Gulf, I felt engulfed—voices, through the memories of experiences, came over me, at me. This is a needless melodrama, a narcissistic indulgence, I told myself, but ironically, those descriptions, intended as interpretive reassurance, joined with the others in a collective complaint, allegation, indictment, denunciation: you and your kind!

My car's thirst replenished, I moved on toward Mobile's Government Street, where I was to meet Jane at one of our favorite haunts, Morrison's, a *Southern* cafeteria, meaning a place where very good food could be quite pleasantly eaten. All during that time my father kept coming to mind—certainly not because he, like Mrs. Bridges, had now become an accuser of mine. (He was not even a "liberal," never mind a purveyor of "liberal guilt"!) I kept remembering his admiration of George Orwell, not only the Orwell of

Animal Farm and *1984* but the early documentary Orwell of *Down and Out in London and Paris*, *The Road to Wigan Pier*, and *Homage to Catalonia*. I had read those books at his behest while in high school, and eventually, a decade after the scene I am now describing, I would be teaching those books, along with Agee's giant documentary companion to them, in a seminar fancily titled "The Literary-Documentary Tradition." But now, an hour or two out of New Orleans, on the old Route 90, I was going back and forth between Mrs. Bridges and my English-born, politically conservative, engineer dad and his intellectual buddy Mr. Orwell. Especially, I was remembering *Wigan Pier*, and the tremendous anger its author vented toward the English left, toward, really, his confreres, toward himself. My mom, politically liberal and psychologically alert and astute, had often asked, much to Dad's annoyance: "Why is he being so nasty—to the very people who wanted to be of help to the miners?" Suddenly, her words arrived, along with my dad's. I remembered their various discussions in which Dad celebrated a wonderfully clear and sensible and honest writer's interest in sharing with others his experiences, the sights he'd seen, the knowledge he'd picked up, and, as a consequence, the views he'd developed; while Mom took note of a certain querulousness, a rancor, even a sense of disgust that could come over him, out of nowhere, it might seem, though for her the cause, again and again, was not hard to figure, as she would let us know by wry, pointed resort to specific pages, specific passages.

In *Wigan Pier*, which she knew best, Mom often cited the very first, brief paragraph, a mere two sentences: "The first sound in the mornings was the clumping of the mill-girls' clogs down the cobbled street. Earlier than that, I suppose, there were factory whistles I was never awake to hear." Right off, she reminded Dad, Orwell admits to his privileged status: he refers to others, those whose fate he will be documenting, who have to rise early to get to work in time for the blowing whistles. He could sleep until the muse (or his stomach or his bladder) told him to get up. Soon we find out where he was sleeping (at least for a while): in a lodging house run by a couple, the Brookers, who become, in this skilled writer's hands, a Dickensian pair: "Mrs. Brooker, our landlady, lay permanently ill, festooned in grimy blankets. She had a big, pale yellow, anxious face. No one knew for certain what was the matter with her; I suspect her only real trouble was over-eating." As for her husband: "Mr. Brooker was a dark, small, bored, sour, Irish-looking man, and astonishingly dirty. I don't think I ever saw his hands clean."

That is a mere beginning for those two hapless members of the petit bourgeoisie who provide a powerful satirist a juicy target, which he obviously relishes. Yet, we learn, Mr. Brooker was himself a former miner—and one wonders whether Orwell would have lanced him so mercilessly had he still been a miner, and had he offered to put this visiting observer up for a few days. In any case, the emphasis Orwell puts on the Brookers' dirt, on their shabby home, on the "disgusting" food they serve, described in great detail, is selective indeed. Neither the miners' dirt nor their food seems to bother this compassionate, even smitten observer. It is impossible to watch them "at work," we are told, "without feeling a pang of envy for their toughness." At another point we learn that "nearly all of them have the most noble bodies," and in the same chapter that offers such descriptions we are told in expansive (intimidating) detail not only how very hard such men work, but the extremely important, productive significance of their labor. ("Practically everything we do, from eating anise to crossing the Atlantic, and from baking a loaf to writing a novel, involves the use of coal, directly or indirectly.")

The matter then gets pushed further—to the utmost details, to an autobiographical specificity. Orwell and others need their "comfortable coal fire," and, of course, the electricity that the coal enabled. But Orwell doesn't stop with that vivid insistence upon connecting himself and his daily working life to that of the miners—a fair enough gesture, a decent gesture from a man who in many ways embodied decency (nowhere more tellingly than in his third documentary book, *Homage to Catalonia*, with its story of political cunning and betrayal from both the right and the left in the Spanish Civil War). He suddenly makes other connections—ones my mother noticed, ones she mentioned to us—on behalf of those hardworking, underpaid "men of the earth" (a phrase I used to hear in West Virginia to describe our own coal miners): "The cricket crowds may assemble" and "the Nancy poets may scratch one another's backs," all because the miners toil mightily. In a conclusion to what has obviously been a paean of thanksgiving to the miners and a sardonic assault on everyone else, Orwell thunders: "You and I and the editors of the *Times Literary Supplement*, and the Nancy poets and the Archbishop of Canterbury, and Comrade X, author of *Marxism for Infants*—all of us *really* owe the comparative decency of our lives to poor drudges underground, blackened to the eyes, with their throats full of coal dust, driving their shovels forward with arms and belly muscles of steel."

A few pages earlier, our documentary observer had envied these "poor drudges." He had called them "splendid men," referred to their "most noble bodies," and admired, too, their camaraderie, their bravery, their patience, their commitment to their work. Their habits had seemed beyond reproach. The observer-writer who could loath the Brookers for the omnipresent dirt in their house could now give us this mixture of fact and personal response to fact: "From what I have seen I should say that a majority of miners prefer to eat their meal first and wash afterwards, as I should do in their circumstances." The miners' workday lunch turns out to be "a hunk of bread and dripping and a bottle of cold tea." Orwell doesn't dare criticize that repast, which was gobbled up fast, he learned, virtually on the run—but had the Brookers served *him* such an offering at teatime (or at any time) we can only imagine (and my mom did once ask my dad, my brother, and me to imagine) the withering scorn their paying guest would reserve for them, later on, when he had returned to the London literary world (which, in turn, he punched with the same vehemence directed at those most marginal boarding house operators who made the mistake of letting him have one of their rooms).

I bring up this contrariness of Orwell's now because although I had learned about it as a youth, courtesy of my folks, I had a new view of it that day in 1964, after I'd talked with Mrs. Bridges and then took off in my fast car. Suddenly both Orwell's contrariness and Agee's, too, so evident from the very first pages of *The Road to Wigan Pier* and *Let Us Now Praise Famous Men*, made a kind of sense to me that hitherto had escaped me. Now, I was no longer interested in enjoying the marvelous vitriol and the striking inconsistency of attitudes of these two masters of caustic observation; now, I realized how readily a documentary writer or photographer or filmmaker can feel, irrationally but all too understandably, *accused*—by himself or herself, never mind by someone else. Guilt, I kept hearing during psychiatric and psychoanalytic training, has to do with a feeling of remorse that follows the commission of a misdeed, a wrong, a crime—though that kind of self-blame, that feeling of having done bad, as it were, can also come in response to the imaginary, or from a sense of moral inadequacy. Shame is a subjective aspect of such haunting guilt, an admonishing consciousness of one's shortcomings or improprieties, one's failures of omission and commission. Orwell's seemingly self-indulgent outbursts against upper-crust London's literary and religious life and Agee's similar tendency to fire away contemptuously at people not unlike himself in occupation or political attitude, now seemed not just evidence of mulish crankiness, a refusal to accept with a calm common sense the ordinary or expectable from certain people, but a covert expression (who knows with what degree of a writer's awareness!) of their own agitated apprehensiveness as writers—an awareness that they, too, are worthy of the cutting comments they level at those others who, again, are more like them with respect to social and cultural background than like tenant farmers or miners.

No wonder, then, my mind returned to Orwell that afternoon, as I kept hearing Mrs. Bridges' musing remark with respect to both the literal and the moral nature of my future life. No wonder, also, a moment in the Harvard Faculty Club months later in 1964, well after the Mississippi Summer Project was over. I had been invited to the Club for lunch by Erik Erikson, an exciting moment for me: I admired Erikson's work enormously, and to be in touch with him, to be at lunch with him, to be asked to help teach in his course—all of that was very heady for me. But I had just finished my stay in Canton, Mississippi, and before that had spent time in McComb, deep in the Delta, where all of us staying in one of those "freedom houses" found ourselves being arrested one morning, put in jail, after our home had been dynamited—presumably on the assumption that we were collectively suicidal. To be away from that constant struggle with potentially murderous sheriffs (three people who belonged to the project had been killed by a sheriff in Philadelphia, Mississippi, of all ironically named places, before we'd even begun our work) was a great relief—yet, some of us had noted, days after coming North, that we weren't in the mood to be all that celebratory. I had attributed our seeming despondency, our irritability, our quickness to turn on certain people who said anything that for any reason rubbed us the wrong way, to a "weariness," the tense exhaustion that followed a tense spell of social struggle. But I fear that "weariness" didn't quite fill the explanatory bill. Suddenly, in the illustrious Harvard Faculty Club, where I'd never been before, some professors sat down near the table where Erikson and I were sitting, and their not especially soft chitchat resounded in my ears, and hit me in some part of my head that connected with feeling rather than thinking.

Suddenly, I was full of annoyance, if not disgust: who *are* these big shots, I thought, sitting here in all their immodesty, their unconcealed egoism, their quite evident privilege? My restlessness become quickly evident to Erikson, whose artist's wide-eyed openness to human experience was matched only by his remarkable capacity to sit still, listen, and fathom, with lightening speed, a speaker's intent. "You'd rather be back in Mississippi?" he asked. I immediately shook my head and wondered, naively, What gave him that idea? I was getting ready to be more specific in my denial; I was glad, frankly, to be alive and uninjured. I was about to say how happy I was to be back North, how pleased I was by the prospect of teaching in his course, when he looked around the dining hall, looked back at me, and said, "Some of them are sitting ducks for us, aren't they!"

Erikson's resort to a folksy saying explained both an obvious tension in the air and an incongruity in my mind (from those Delta Freedom Houses to this, in one week). The issue, he had gently indicated (in response not to what I'd said, but to what I'd shown in a glowering face) was not these people nearby, eating their lunch and conversing spiritedly about matters of the intellect, but my own readiness to use them, to keep looking long and hard at them rather than inward at the turmoil of memories, aspirations, worries that inhabited my own head. Moreover, as is so often the case with the one who scapegoats, the issue was finally what bothered me about myself: the wish to follow suit, to join those professors, to be one of them down the line—and to do so by writing up the documentary research done in the very place I'd just left. The more I let myself get worked up about people sitting in the Harvard Faculty Club whom I really didn't know, the more time I spent bashing folks in the tradition of Agee and Orwell, the less time I'd have to do what Mrs. Bridges was quietly hoping I'd do—hold her "people" in memory, remain in touch with them in whatever way seemed suitable. We forget about others in many ways—sometimes by becoming newly preoccupied with a righteousness that turns into self-righteousness, and feeds on any and all victims, many of them made up on the spot.

Now, years later, as I talk with students, or as I conduct and write up yet another research project, I realize how nearly inevitable certain moral and psychological tensions are for those of us who do the interviewing, the picture-taking, the filming in places like the Mississippi Delta or, for that matter, a mile or so down the road from this or that university, where a "community service" project has brought some students to tutor or to work with the sick, the elderly, the severely troubled. Presumably, for those students the idealism is there, at work, even as those who involved themselves in the Mississippi Summer Project were doing so out of a strong conviction that segregation had to go, once and for all, and that they were willing to take personal risks in the struggle to get rid of it. Still, those young people, both black and white, had not forgotten their own lives, the futures that awaited them, even as my students, hard at work in ghetto schools, neighborhood health centers, homes for the elderly, prisons, or Habitat projects, do not forget deadlines for tests and papers, fellowship applications, or graduate-school examinations. Nor do those students overlook the requirements of our seminar: that they document in some manner the world they have chosen to enter, by keeping a journal, by writing essays, by using a camera or a tape recorder, by collecting the words and the drawings of children, the related memories of the elderly, and the stories told by young and old alike as they go through their lives—as a means of getting a good grade, furthering their ambitions. All of the above takes place, of course, alongside the different aspects of our ongoing lives. But sometimes collisions take place—as when a Mrs. Bridges, ever so graciously, wonders aloud about the nature and duration of a particular commitment. And so it is with others who receive students into their homes or schools or are interviewed by reporters, featured in photographic essays, or seen in documentary films, and who ask silently or quite openly: Who are these visitors, these avowed doers of good, these earnest documentarians, and what are they up to, and what will they end up doing, or where will they end up going, and what will come of all this, for us and for them?

Moreover, from "our" point of view—that of the volunteer who does "community service," or a documentary project in connection with such service, as a means of understanding it, conveying its significance to others, reflecting upon its aims, its worth, its successes and failures, or who is making a career out of documentary photography or film, or a kind of oral history, or socially engaged journalism that requires "fieldwork" as its mainstay—what are our responsibilities to those with whom we come to spend our time, to whom we pose questions, or whom we ask to pose while we go click, click, click, or our videocameras roll on and on? How ought we regard ourselves, with what degree of scrutiny of our motives and our manner, of why we go where we do, and how we behave while there? Afterwards, what, if anything, ought we keep in mind? Should we keep in touch with those whom we have enlisted as informants, as participants in our project? Put differently, what kind of moral and psychological accountability should we demand of ourselves, we who lay claim to social idealism, or to a documentary tradition that will somehow (we hope) work toward a social good— expose injustice, shed light on human suffering, or contribute to a growing body of knowledge stored in libraries, in museums, in film studios?

Such questions are all too appealingly general, and founder on the shoals of particular lives and the ethical and personal quandries they present. We are not ordinarily living in a realm of multiple-choice questions, of either/or answers—nor does a finger-wagging absolutism (rules promulgated for any and all occasions) satisfactorily address what for many continues to be an intensely felt self-scrutiny that unavoidably seems to go with the territory, the work chosen.

As I consider this matter of responsibility and accountability on the part of documentary writers, photographers, and filmmakers, I think of the courses I have taught, with titles such as "Community Service and the Documentary Tradition," "The Literary-Documentary Tradition," "The Literature of Social Reflection," and "Moral and Social Inquiry." For each course, I have selected reading matter that illustrates a variety of approaches to documentary writing, photography, and film; and I have selected students (for the seminars) or teaching assistants (for the large courses) who have had reason to mull over these vocational matters, which have a way of becoming quite personal matters: men and women who have worked in service projects, for instance, and tried to document what they have observed and learned; or journalists or historians or filmmakers or photographers or social scientists who have visited communities suffering from a so-called social problem or crisis or racial struggle—those matters that get "studied," that make for "good" documentary projects. All the time in our discussions the students, the young teachers who are also documentarians of one kind or another, bring up matters close to their lives and hearts, matters that Mrs. Bridges put before me long ago. How long does one stay with a project, and with what kind of commitment of time and energy? That general question seems easy enough to answer; yet, as Mrs. Bridges was implying, one can get some "news," make some "observations," obtain some "data" "conduct" some interviews, take some pictures, film a scene, wrap up one's project, and leave forthwith; or one can linger and try to learn something other than the "answer" to one's original inquiry: learn, that is, whether and how one might be of some use to the people who have given of themselves by answering questions or allowing someone to "shoot" them with a camera.

More bluntly, what, if anything, do we owe those we have "studied," whose lives we have gone to document? Should we, for instance, send back the writing, the photography, the film once it is completed? If so, at what stage of that work's development: as it is being assembled, as it is being edited, before it is published or exhibited or shown on television or in a movie house, or well afterwards, or indeed never? Should we pay our informants for all the time and effort put into making a film or working with a photographer or an interviewer? Should we share our royalties, our artistic fees, our monetary rewards or prizes with the subjects of our documentary project, or share them with a group or fund whose purpose it is to address the particular "problem" we have presented? Then there is the problem of exploitation, frequently mentioned by my more skeptical students, young men and women who are anxious to work with the communities or individuals they choose to observe. Is it "exploitative" to do documentary work, to arrive on a given scene, ask for people's cooperation, time, energy, and knowledge, do one's "study" or "project," and soon enough, leave, *thank yous* presumably extended? How can we do such work honorably, so that those observed get more closely, explicitly connected with it? Should "informants" be publicly acknowledged if they so desire? Should we invite them to those exhibitions or film presentations that commemorate the completion of documentary work? How do we communicate to others, called "potential subjects," our artistic or social or political purposes, let them know what we have in mind, what we hope to do, and why it might be necessary to go to such lengths?

Such questions are concrete and specific, yet they can be all too abstract in a documentarian's mind as he or she sets out to work on a particular project. Sometimes, for some people being observed, the real "issue" is that of "attitude": the observer's manner of approach rather than the substance of a specific agreement or commitment spelled out earlier. "I didn't like those people," I once heard a ghetto mother say, referring to two students, one a photographer and one a journalist, who had come to interview her. I questioned her closely about her reasons. She wasn't able to be specific, but in the end she offered this sense of what was bothering her: "They say good things. They say they're here to help us. I'm sure they're telling the truth; I'm sure they want to make people realize what's going on here, our troubles. I don't know why I get nervous with them; I just don't 'connect' with them the way I'd like to. They say these good things, but they're always rushing, from one thing to another; so they don't have the time of day for you, unless they want something from you, and then they come and smooth-talk you (boy, do they!), and they think we don't see through them! We're not as dumb as they think we are!

"I sure know this: when they're through with their work, they'll be out of here lightning fast, and that'll be the end of them. They come here, people like that, they have their job to do, they do it; that's when they'll sweet-talk you, and when they leave, out they go, and if you get a 'so long,' you're lucky."

Such sentiments are by no means rare among individuals who have had experience with outsiders bent on doing a story about them. When I worked in Appalachia, I was stunned by the familiarity between many mountain people (supposedly so isolated) and various journalists, camera crews, and social scientists (like myself), not to mention Vista workers, college students on leave to do volunteer work or a field project. "There's always someone coming here to ask us if we need something," said the mother of a ten-year-old boy whom I was getting to know, and she described such folks this way:

I don't know where they come from, or why they've decided to come hereabouts—actually, they all say the same thing. They tell you they're wanting to visit, so they can learn more about us folks up here, and they say they know we've got our problems, bad ones, and they're here to make everything better, if we'll just be nice and friendly to them. Well, Lord, I *always* am nice and friendly, and why shouldn't I be! You'd think we weren't going to be [nice and friendly]—that's what they're expecting, I know. [It] beats me, the opinion these folks have of us—[they] think we're ready to shoot to kill when they drive up here, their cars loaded down with [film] equipment. My son Jamie [whose drawings of his hollow life were stark and haunting] started saying he wanted to go run off with some of that stuff. I told him two things: one, it's dead wrong— you don't steal, period! Two, I said, 'Jamie, you'd not know what to do with it all, and no one would want to buy it from you!' He wanted to know how come I'm so smart on the subject! I said, 'Hey, son, they've been here before, and I watched them real close, and you know what?— they have trouble themselves with all those camera machines (*do* they!), so why would anyone up here [in the hollow] want to go looking for one big heap of trouble, and pay for it to boot!'

"Besides, those folks are real watchful: no one's going to snatch something from under their noses! They check on everything all the time, and they're in a hurry all the time. They want to get in and get out, *fast*. When they arrive, they're all smiles, and they give you this speech, and you can tell they're just repeating what they've said a hundred times before, but you smile and you pretend that you're the first who's ever been told you should 'cooperate,' so everything will get better for us up here. Then you say yes, and they barely give you time to turn around and go inside—they're way ahead of you, arranging this and rearranging that, and it isn't as though they remember what they've moved, so they can be kind enough to put it back where it belongs! They want you to talk with them, the camera going—they have a list of questions a mile long, at least, and you better answer them, or they'll look disappointed, and come back at you with the same question, again, or it'll be another one, but it's that last one worked over again, like we do with a second crop in midsummer, if we're lucky with the weather.

"It's not that I'm against them [I had asked]; I know they're trying to tell folks yonder what it's like for us up here. But if you ask me, they've made up their minds about us long before they hit this hollow with those station wagons. How do I know? [I'd asked]. I just do—these people, they'll start sizing everything up, and they grab at what's not so nice, and they're disappointed if you don't have a lot of hurt to show them, and they're plain happy and smiling if you have a sick one, and there's been no lights, because a wire is down. They take all the pictures, and . pepper you with this they want to know, then there's the next thing on their list, and fast as can be, they're packing, and nine times out of ten, I'll bet, they don't even think to say their *thank yous*, and their good-byes. It's not very nice, I say."

The above lessons were learned after three separate film crews did stories on the hollow where this woman lived—and I hadn't yet exhausted *my* list of questions! "Serves us right for being so convenient to you folks, and telling the school people we'd accept visitors," she said, and I recall thinking hard about that word *accept*. To be sure, it was an aspect of a particular vernacular; but it had a message for all of us: we are asking for a kind of forbearance from people who are often considerably more burdened than we are, hence our obligation to think carefully about how we approach such people and how we *are* with them, not to mention how we take leave of them.

Not that some who pursue documentary work don't reflect long and hard on these issues with an introspective energy that a person such as the one I've just quoted can pick up right away. "There was one woman [a reporter]," she told me, "who was so nice I wanted to ask her to stay here and be with us forever!" How had that "niceness" been manifested? "She smiled, and she didn't come rushing at us, and her eyes weren't running all over the place, toting things up and figuring out what to snap and what to ask, before we'd not so much as said hello! I can tell by their faces—it's not what they say, it's what they don't say. The bad ones, once you've said your first yes, it's as if you've given them permission to do anything they want. They'll walk right by you, and start moving things around in your own house, and *telling* you, not asking you, telling you it's *here* you should be, or *there*; and they'll want you ready, pronto, when they're done looking around, to come sit and talk with them, and if you dare look as though you have something else to do, why then you've turned traitor on them, and they'll just pout, and go off and whisper—as if I can't figure out what they're saying. They'd snap a whip at us if they thought they could get away with it. As it is, they keep their tongues in check—but when they drive off, they say all they meant to say earlier."

I ask her what she means by that last remark. She looks surprised at me: poor fellow, you're not thinking so good today! She lets me know just how observant she is of observers: "If you can imagine people in a hurry! They've been here, having to be patient with us. If they could really have their way, they'd want everyone to stop and only pay attention to them, and no one else, and stop living, all of it, but for them. (Can you imagine!) But since we have our chores to do, and the kids to look after, they know to watch their step a little—as much as they have to! So you see, when they're all through, they just hurry up (do they!), and they pack like the Devil is after them, and like my kid brother [who is sixteen and a fast driver] would say, vroom! My husband says if he was blindfolded from the time those folks came to the time they left for good, he'd sure know the difference between [the time of] their coming and they have work to do, and the very last time, when they're leaving for good, just by listening to the way they step on that gas. At the end, it's good riddance!"

She pulls back a bit and retracts some of her critique, acknowledging that "everyone has a job to do" and trying to see things from the point of view of busy camera crews with deadlines, busy journalists with a story to be written fast. Still, I find her statements unnerving, not because she may have overstated something about others, but because there I am, eager to learn, anxious to keep adding information to my growing store of it, and consciously impatient with respect to a line of questioning I'm waiting to pursue. I have refrained from doing so because I don't judge the moment opportune (someone is busy, or we're not yet "there," psychologically). I hope I am under control at that moment, indeed at all times; I hope I keep under wraps my pressing curiosity, my ambition to get to the psychological, the sociological, the cultural heart of the matter, to have a great, breakthrough interview, an almost wondrously revealing and surprising exchange with a child after he or she has made for me (*given* to me) a drawing that is truly amazing in its communicative subtlety, a drawing that hands me an extraordinary opportunity to reveal—well, just how clever someone like me can be under the right set of circumstances. In my thinking, I reassure myself; I defend myself; I console myself; I try to conceal a certain avarice or greed, though when a child, every once in a while, tells me he or she doesn't want to part with his or her drawings, my suddenly pale face, my silence, interrupted by grunts, by pleas, by looks thrown at the parents, reveal the truth: I'm roaring the way the cars do when the film crews are finally through—give me that stuff, so I can press down hard on *my* gas pedal, your artwork safely stashed in one of those manila folders of mine!

Some of my students are less confident of their ability to fake it, to keep their cool no matter how ornery the child or adult who comes their way (*uncooperative*, one can call them, or, to escalate the self-protective jargon, *resistant*, as clinicians call anyone who stays uncooperative too long!). Those young, would-be social investigators, those writers and photographers and filmmakers who want to address, simultaneously, an aroused social conscience, a curiosity about society, and an intellectual ambition already grounded in some experience, some training, some demonstrated competence—a good number of such students can be, I fear, quick to become their own critics, and like that Appalachian mother, though for different reasons, can cover themselves with doubt and hesitation and second thoughts and scruples and qualms, even as they know they've got to plow ahead, ring those doorbells, make those requests, become persistent, even at times importunate, lest the doubts and hesitations of others prevail, and no documentary work get done.

"Some of the time—I guess I could say, a lot of the time— things go all right," a photographer tells me, a college senior. But there are moments, he adds, when he is truly at a loss, and feels that he should apologize when someone whom he has asked for permission to photograph refuses him. The person in question has struck him as interesting, as appealing, as an individual whose daily life he wants to explore both visually and through the interviews he does side-by-side with the camera work. Yet, he can't seem to get the Yes he very much desires. He wonders: maybe he should try a "softer approach"; maybe he should simply be more persuasive; maybe he should pull back, let the matter drop, ask if he might come and discuss things at a later time, "keep the door open"; maybe he should try to figure out some magic remark that will reliably make a dif-ference to the person in question. All of that and more crosses his fevered mind—and then, a reversal of sorts:

I'll be sitting there in someone's home—I've interrupted their life, the nerve of me!—and I think to myself, this is wrong. Why don't I take a polite No politely, and leave? Why am I being so conniving? That's the word I should use! [I had asked] Why *should* that family let me hang around? I use that phrase as if it means I'll be a fly on the wall, and their already difficult life won't be made any worse, but it's not true, and I know it's not true, and they do, too. I suppose I could try to bribe them, pay them, but that's not right—or is it? Why *shouldn't* they be paid? They're poor, and they need the money, and I'll get something out of all this, that's certain. We don't get into it [that subject] when we sit here [in the classroom] talking about someone's photographs or someone's book: we do our 'documentary work,' and we get recognition, and we build our lives up, our careers—and they, there's nothing in it for them. They put up with us! Sure, we're trying to 'help' them in the broad sense, tell the world about their problems. But I'm not convinced that political change takes place because of the photographic work people do. Even the FSA didn't do much for Roosevelt and his New Deal. Once he lost effective control of the Congress in 1938, that was *it*, even though the FSA pictures were pouring out from those [developing] studios. I'm a history major, and I just wrote a paper on the New Deal— and I wish the FSA *did* accomplish more; that way, I'd feel better about what 'photojournalism' can do for all those people we run around trying to catch for some story or other!

It's the old truth my grandfather used to tell us when we were little: if you've *got*, you *get*, and if you don't have a thing, then you're not likely to go too far. He set up these trusts for all of us [grandchildren]; they're not huge, but they help me get by. This isn't work that makes you rich; it's not a profession like medicine or law. You're on your own—you've got to learn on your own, and figure out some angle for yourself, so you can build your reputation and get to do the work you do. Besides, it's hard for a photographer—few places to get your pictures published. Writers have all those magazines and quarterlies, [but] not us! Newspaper work—you're a slave to what some editor thinks will hype the circulation of the paper. So with that trust fund money I can get by, and try to be a 'documentary photographer'; that means finding people willing to put up with me! When I leave, I wonder: why have they been so patient with me? Would I be that patient with other people? Is it their need, their hope that things will get better if my pictures are run in some newspaper, or displayed somewhere? Is it the attention I'm giving them—

that they don't get from others in this tough world? Is it the beginning of a friendship, or is it vanity—they get themselves photographed, and they can look at themselves, like we all enjoy doing! Is it that they don't feel they have the *right*, the right to say *no*, to refuse to let someone poke into their lives? You know—well, they have to 'submit' to the welfare worker, so why not me! Yes, there *are* 'studies' done of people who aren't on welfare—I know. [I had pointed this out.] But the higher up you go [on the socioeconomic scale] the less studies there are—and look at the photographs that cater to the rich: celebrity photography, flattery photography. In your course, all those books . . . they were about poor folks, 'down and out' folks, in London and Paris [Orwell], in Alabama [Agee], in Chicago [Alex Kotlowitz's *There Are No Children Here*], in Georgia [Melissa Fay Green's *Praying for Sheetrock*], in New Mexico [*River of Traps*, by William DeBuys and Alex Harris], in Boston, those poor victims of AIDS [*People With AIDS*, by Nicholas Nixon and Bebe Nixon], and that classic *American Exodus* that you like so much, all those 'Okies' of the 1930's! The novels and the stories you assign—Ellison's *Invisible Man*, [William Carlos] Williams's "Doctor Stories," Zora Neale Hurston [*Their Eyes Were Watching God*], Dorothy Day [*The Long Loneliness*]—it's all about working with people who are down on their luck, and writing about what you've experienced, and taking pictures: *us*, the documentary people, and *them*, the ones [whose lives] we document. I feel the same way about this work, sometimes, as I do about the community-service work I do: I sure get a lot out of doing it, but I'm not sure what it all means for those folks out there I go visit. I know, I know—I tutor, and the kids learn. But it's hard to believe those kids are going very far, lots of them, and meanwhile I feel pretty good about what I'm doing, and I list it on all my applications, and I know it helps my rating go up with the people reading them."

So much happening in this student's mind, his conscience, his soul—the documentarian documenting his own struggles to make sense not only of his work, but that work and his life as they fit into American society. As I sit with such young people I realize that all the worries and misgivings that trouble those involved in community-service work also give serious pause to documentarians: they worry that they will take advantage of others for their own careerist reasons; that they will not really be of much long-term assistance to the people with whom they are spending time; that in some way they are being exploitative or manipulative, and should therefore stand accused in their own eyes; that they are guilty of being fly-by-night observers, given to turning a quick, personal, occupational profit out of a spell "across town," as it were. Why *wouldn't* these young observers, so lucky in so many ways, feel apprehensive, get a case, now and then, of the moral jitters, look at themselves askance in their mirrors as they start and finish their assignments, leaving one person, one family, one community after another?

Small wonder that Agee's passionate, exquisite, and powerfully declared (confessed) anguish, his small-minded digs, and his brilliantly savage and insulting asides take hold with those students who read him, or who encounter Orwell's similarly snide and rude and disparaging remarks. Again and again, students see documentarians trying hard to justify what they have done and how they have done it; or students note the ones who say nothing, thereby stirring up plenty of questions and qualms. I suspect that such men and women, the FSA photographers and our contemporaries ones, the 1930s documentary writers and those writing now, might be pleased to hear students take to heart a whole tradition of documentary work, put themselves in the shoes of those who accomplished various kinds of exploration, try to see and hear as they did, try to sort out various personal and ethical loyalties and obligations as they did. "I suppose," the young photographer quoted above once speculated, "my work with a camera is itself a kind of 'service,' and I should try to hold on to that idea when I get 'down,' and I do. Isn't that what the FSA project was all about—cameras carried all over the country, so that the pain in the ailing country would be brought to light (literally!)? And that *is* a 'service,' I realize, and what comes out of it, all those photographs, *are* useful, not only politically, but for anyone who wants to stop and think about what he's doing, what he hopes to accomplish, when he's 'out there' in a world of hurt and broken families, trying to lend a hand in some way. A friend of mine, tutoring kids, looked at some of the photographs of children I've taken, children like the ones he tries to teach, and he called me to say that just stopping and looking [at the pictures] with a couple of his buddies [who also tutor] gave them a chance to see things a little clearer, because they were by themselves, and they could think and talk, but there those kids were, staring at them. I had put some words I'd recorded under the photographs—and I know they helped, too."

It would take that pragmatic documentary photographer only a week or so to forget that moment of grateful acknowledgment of the value of his work—to resume his all-too-common mood of gloomy skepticism, no small amount of it self-directed. Still, as he would tell us in class one day, documentary work is bound somewhat to pull down those who do it, those who probe and scrutinize the undertow of the world. It sure can help, though, every once in a while, to hear others who read the words and look at the pictures or the films that come from such projects speak of what has happened to them, what has been done for them, what has inspired them—to see words and pictures illuminate the attitude, the actions, the manner of being of readers and viewers.

three

The Tradition

Fact and Fiction

The heart of the matter for someone doing documentary work is the pursuit of what James Agee called "human actuality"—rendering and representing for others what has been witnessed, heard, overheard, or sensed. Fact is "the quality of being actual," hence Agee's concern with actuality. All documentation, however, is put together by a particular mind whose capacities, interests, values, conjectures, suppositions and presuppositions, whose memories, and, not least, whose talents will come to bear directly or indirectly on what is, finally a presented to the world in the form of words, pictures, or even music or artifacts of one kind or another. In shaping an article or a book, the writer can add factors and variables in two directions: social and cultural and historical on the one hand, individual or idiosyncratic on the other. As Agee reminds us in his long "country letter," his aria: "All that each person is, and experiences, and shall ever experience, in body and in mind, all these things are differing expressions of himself and of one root, and are identical: and not one of these things nor one of these persons is ever quite to be duplicated, nor replaced, nor has it ever quite had precedent: but each is a new and incommunicably tender life, wounded in every breath, and almost as hardly killed as easily wounded: sustaining, for a while, without defense, the enormous assaults of the universe."

Such an emphasis on human particularity would include the ups and downs of a life, even events (both internal and external) in that life that would seem to have nothing to do with the objectivity of, say, the world of central Alabama, but everything to do with the world of the writer or the photographer who will notice, ignore, take seriously, or find irrelevant Alabama's various moments, happenings, acts and deeds and comments, scenes. Events are filtered through a person's awareness, itself not uninfluenced by a history of private experience, by all sorts of aspirations, frustrations, and yearnings, by those elusive, significant "moods" as they can affect and even sway what we deem of interest or importance, not to mention how we assemble what we have learned into something to present to others—to editors, museum curators first of all, whose personal attitudes, not to mention the nature of their jobs or the values and desires of *their* bosses, all help shape their editorial or curatorial judgment. The web of one kind of human complexity (that of life in Hale County, Alabama) connects with, is influenced by, the web of another kind of human complexity (Agee and Evans and all that informs not only their lives but those of their magazine and book editors).

So often in our discussion of documentary work my students echo Agee, emphasize the "actuality" of the work—its responsibility to fact. They commonly pose for themselves the familiar alternative of fiction, as though we were dealing in clear-cut opposites: if not the true as against the false, at least the real as against the imaginary. But such opposites or alternatives don't quite do justice either conceptually or pragmatically to the aspect of "human actuality" that has to do with the vocational life of writers, photographers, folklorists, musicologists, and filmmakers, those who are trying to engage with people's words, their music, gestures, movements, and overall appearance and then let others know what they have learned. No one going anywhere, on a journalistic trip, on a documentary assignment, for social-science research, or to soak up the atmosphere of a place to aid in the writing of a story or a novel, will claim to be able to see and hear everything, or even claim to be able to notice all that truly matters. Who we are, to some variable extent, determines what we notice and, at another level of intellectual activity, what we regard as worthy of notice, what we find significant. Nor will technology help us all that decisively. I can arrive in America's Alabama or England's Yorkshire, I can find my way to a South Seas island or to central Africa, I can go visit a nearby suburban mall with the best tape recorder in the world, with cameras that take superb pictures, and even with a clear idea of what I am to do, and still I face the matter of looking *and* overlooking, paying instant heed *and* letting something slip by; and I face the matter of sorting out what I *have* noticed, of arranging it for emphasis—the matter, really, of *composition*, be it verbal or visual, the matter of re-presenting; and here that all-important word *narrative* enters. Stories heard or seen now have to turn into stories put together with some guiding intelligence and discrimination: I must select *what* ought to be present; decide on the *tone* of that presentation, its *atmosphere* or *mood*. These words can be as elusive as they are compelling to an essay, an exhibition of pictures, or a film.

Even if the strict limits of oral history are never suspended (*only* the taped interviews with informants are used in a given article or book, or any comments from the practitioner of oral history are confined to an introduction or to explanatory footnotes) there still remains that challenge of selection, with its implications for the narrative: which portions of which tapes are to be used, and with what assertive or clarifying or instructional agenda in mind (in the hope, for instance, of what popular or academic nod of comprehension or applause). How does one organize one's "material," with what topics in mind, what broader themes? How does one deal with the mix of factuality and emotionality that any taped interview presents, never mind a stock of them, and how does one arrange and unfold the events, the incidents: a story's pace, its plot, its coherence, its character development and portrayal, its suggestiveness, its degree of inwardness, its degree of connection to external action, and, all in all, its dramatic power, not to mention its moral authority?

The above words and phrases are summoned all the time by writers and teachers of fiction. Fictional devices, that is, inform the construction of nonfiction, and of course, fiction, conversely, draws upon the actual, the "real-life." A novelist uses his or her lived experience and the observations he or she has made and is making in the course of living a life as elements of a writing life. I remember William Carlos Williams pausing, after a home visit, to write down not only medical notes but a writer's notes: words heard; a revealing moment remembered; the appearance of a room on a particular day, or of a face brimming with surprise or happiness, a head lowered in dismay, a look of anticipation or alarm or dread, fear on a child's face, those details of life, of language, of appearance, of occurrence for which novelists are known, but which the rest of us also crave or require, as readers, of course, but also in our working lives: we all survive and prevail through a mastery of certain details, or fail by letting them slip through our fingers.

A novelist has to have those details at constant hand. He or she has had occasion in so-called real life to become aware of them but now has to fit this personal learning into a story, a narrative that requires both imagination and an idea of what will reach and touch readers persuasively. Nonfiction involves the same process, though we have to be careful of how we use words such as *experience, observation,* and, certainly, *imagination* when discussing nonfiction. A documentarian's report will be strengthened by what has been witnessed, but will be fueled, surely, by what those observations come to mean in his or her head: we absorb sights and sounds, and they become *our* experience, unique to us, in that we, their recipients, are unique. What we offer others in the way of our documentary reports, then, is *our* mix of what we have observed and experienced, as we have assembled it, that assembly having to do, again, with our imaginative capability, our gifts as writers, as editors, as storytellers, as artists. Oscar Lewis and Studs Terkel, working with taped interviews, pages and pages of transcripts, put all of that together in such a way that makes us readers marvel, not only at what we're told but at how it gets told,—and, before that, at how it was elicited from the various individuals these two met and from anyone who worked with them (Lewis trained a team of colleagues to help him out). Others of us might have met the same people but obtained from them different stories, maybe fewer in number or less interesting, less revealing.

I remember well what one of my psychoanalytic supervisors, Elizabeth Zetzel, who was a rather solidly conventional physician with a mind George Eliot would have called "theoretic," told me as she contemplated my protocols (my daily notes of what I had heard from a particular patient). Psychoanalysis, she said, is not only the uncovering of psychological material; it is two people doing so. Therefore, anyone's analysis, undertaken with a particular analyst, is only one of a possible series of hypothetical analyses, depending on who *else* might be the analyst, and what might be looked at and concluded on the basis of that other person's presence as the analyst, rather than the one now being consulted. I had been zealously on the prowl for certain memories that would, frankly, confirm my clinical notion of what had happened earlier in a certain patient's life, and to what effect. Dr. Zetzel had realized (I would later realize) that this was not only *an* inquiry, or the "correct" inquiry, but *my* inquiry—that someone else might have had other clinical interests, other kinds of memories to pursue, other clinical destinations in mind and, very important, would no doubt have engaged with this patient in a different way. (Nietzsche's aphorism holds here: "It takes two to make a truth.")

Moreover, what I make of what I hear from any patient has to do with what I've learned, and with what I have brought from my life to what has been taught me. Psychoanalysis, then, is a person's continuing narrative, however "meandering" rather than formally structured, as it is prompted by and shaped by his or her life, of course, but also as it responds to a particular listener or observer who has his or her own narrative interests and capacities and intentions (his or her observations, experiences, and, as with artists, talent and imagination—ways of sensing and of phrasing what is sensed, skill at putting him- or herself in another's shoes). A profession also has its narrative as well as its intellectual and emotional demands, and it, too, affects a particular practitioner, here a psychoanalyst, in influential ways: an agreed-upon language; an agreed-upon story called a diagnosis or a clinical interpretation or summary, namely, how we (are trained to) tell ourselves what we're hearing before we get around to letting our patients know what we think. Put differently, we develop, as psychiatric or psychoanalytic listeners, a professional narrative, which is offered in response to the narratives we hear in that unusual room where matters of utter intimacy and privacy become a shared documentary experience limited to two people. Others may be brought into the "act," however, since patients talk to people they know, and so do we, in our professional lives (at meetings) and in our writing lives: we share case histories with our colleagues and stories with readers, and surely we tailor our stories to elicit readers' interest—a tradition that goes back to Freud's first books and accounts for those of the many who have followed throughout this profession's now hundred-year history.

All of the above is as intricate and knotty, but also as evident and ordinary, as what happens every day when any two people talk to each other. The words and the pictorial sense vary on both sides, depending upon who the people are; and if one or both of the two talks to a third or a fourth person, that "report" will also vary depending on the person then doing the listening. We have words for the gross distortions of this process: rumor, gossip. We are less likely to account for the almost infinite possible variations on an encounter that constitute a human exchange, or a human response to the non-human world of the landscape or the multi-human world of a social scene. Naturally, a novelist does go one significant step further—reserves the right to use his or her imagination more freely than a documentarian, and to call upon the imaginary as a matter of course,: personal fantasies, made-up voices given to made-up characters with made-up names, and scenes described out of the mind's visual reveries, even as its verbal ones supply words. All of the above has to be done with judgment as well as provocative ingenuity and boldness. The imaginary life, like the real one, requires a teller's thoughtfulness, canniness, sensitivity, and talent for dealing with language, or with the visual. What emerges, if it is done successfully, is a kind of truth, sometimes (as in Tolstoy, George Eliot, Dickens; we each make our choices from among these storytellers) an enveloping and unforgettable wisdom that strikes the reader as realer than real, a truth that penetrates deep within one, that leaps beyond verisimilitude or incisive portrayal, appealing and recognizable characterization, and lands on a terrain where the cognitive, the emotional, the reflective, and the moral live side-by-side. "I make up stories all day," I hear a wonderfully able novelist say at a seminar on "documentary studies." "Some people would say I tell lies—my 'business' is to write them down and sell them, with the help of a publisher." We all demur, but he rejects what he hears as an evasive politeness on our part. "All right," he provokes us further, "I do a good job, so I get published, and you like what you read. But there are talented storytellers out there, let's call them that, who spend their lives telling stories, persuading people to get wrapped up in them, just like they talk of getting wrapped up in a good novel...and they are telling what you and I would call lies, a string of them, or falsehoods, or *un*truths. Some of them do enough of it that they become known chiefly, essentially, for what they tell *as*—they are 'con artists.' Am I a version of such a person, a successful, socially sanctioned, 'sublimated' version? Is that a useful way of thinking about stories and novels—cleverly or entertainingly put together lies?"

This writer, this novelist who was also a teacher and an effective conversationalist, was forcefully putting a big subject before us. He had, after a fashion, constructed a small story about the matter of storytelling in which he highlighted the matter of fiction as something made up—though often quite full of facts, observations, accurately recalled happenings, and also made up, potentially, of truth, even the highest kind of truth, as many of us would insist. Others in the seminar, of course, spoke of journalism and social science, their claims to another kind of truth, one that pertains to an observed world unconnected to an imagined one; though, again, the journalist's, the photographer's, the social scientist's imagination can all the time influence how a news story or a research project is done, what is obtained in the way of information, remarks, photographs, and how all of that is relayed to others.

I tried, in that seminar, to make sense of my own work, to figure out its nature, and so did we all: this was the purpose of the seminar. During the early 1960s, as I mentioned earlier, I was trying hard to learn how Southern schoolchildren, both black and white, were managing under the stresses of court-ordered desegregation in the South, and how civil-rights activists were dealing with their special, often dangerous, even fatally dangerous lives of constant protest. I was doing psychiatric research and beginning to write up my findings for presentation to professional audiences and journals. By then, I'd also been interviewed by newspaper reporters, because I was immersed in a serious educational, social, and racial crisis. I was privileged (I only gradually realized) to be watching a moment of history. Soon I was not only taking what I heard from children, teachers, parents, and young activists and fitting it all into a language, a way of thinking, a theoretical or conceptual apparatus of sorts (lists of defense mechanisms, signs of various symptoms, evidence of successful adaptation); I was developing a general thesis on what makes for collapse in children under duress and what makes for "resiliency." I had developed a list of "variables," aspects of a life that tended to make a child worthy of being described as such by me: a resilient child. Eventually, with enough knowledge of enough children, I had in mind a broader claim, a more ambitious one, a statement on "*the* resilient child."

I was also seeing, in some newspapers, quotations correctly attributed to me that weren't always my words, and that seemed a bit foreign to me because they had been hurriedly scribbled as I talked. Even my exactly transcribed words, *taped* words, sometimes seemed strange to me, because they appeared out of context; they were deprived of the explanatory remarks, the narrative sequence, that had preceded and followed them. My wife would say, "You said *that?*" I would say yes, and then the refrain: "but the reporter used what I said for his purposes"—and I wasn't necessarily being critical. I had tried to explain something, had tried to speak with some qualifications or even with skepticism, second thoughts, or outright misgivings about my own thoughts, themselves being constantly modified by interviews, by conversations with colleagues, by *consideration* of this or that matter, the reflective aspect of what gets called experience.

The reporters, needless to say, had their own purposes to consider, their own experiences; they had gradually accumulated manners of hearing and remembering, of listening to tapes, based on notions of what they were meant to do professionally. I was meant to move from hearing children talk about what was on their minds to thinking about the *projections* these children summoned, the *denials* or *reaction-formations* to which they resorted; a journalist is used to hearing me, and soon enough, asking me pointed questions that aim for an opinion, an explanation, stated as plainly and unequivocally as possible. *Why* is this child doing so well, given the pressures she has to endure? Why is *that* child not doing so well? What is your explanation for the difference? If my explanation was too long-winded, evasive, abstract, or, finally, unconvincing, the reporter pressed, rephrased, got me to reconsider, to say things differently—until what I said helped him or her understand the subject at hand (and would presumably help his or her editor and readers, who inhabit his or her mind, understand.) Sometimes I was not only surprised, by the printed result, as my wife was, but grateful. Those reporters pushed me to think (and to put things) in ways not familiar to me, and when I remembered what I said, seeing it presented in the context of a story, a part of the reporter's own take on the subject, I found myself learning something, regarding matters with a different emphasis or point of view, responding, it can be said, to the "truth" of that particular interview. All interviews, one hopes, become jointly conducted!

The harder I struggled to make sense of my work, never mind make sense of what others might make of it, the more confused I became: what was I doing, what was I learning, what was I trying to say? I was a child psychiatrist and was learning to be a psychoanalyst, but I wasn't working with patients in an office or a clinic; I was visiting children and their parents in their homes, talking with teachers in schools, and, through SNCC, doing things regarded by cities and states of the South as illegal, a challenge both to laws and to long-standing customs. On the one hand, I had to answer to a certain kind of psychiatric voice in me: why *are* you doing all this? On the other hand, I had to answer to the collective voices of civil rights workers: why are you concentrating your energies on *us*, when there's a "sick" society out there; for example, look at your own profession, the utterly segregated universities, medical schools, residency training programs, psychoanalytic institutes—why don't you study all that! Then, I had to contend with my great teacher Dr. W. C. Williams, to whom (1961, 1962) I'd sent some drafts of my psychiatric reports. "For God's sake," he told me once, "try to find a cure for that passive voice you use, for the third person, for all that highfalutin technical language—it's a syndrome!" My apologies and chagrin and self-pity only elicited this: "Take your readers in hand, take them where you've been, tell them what you've seen, give them some stories you've heard. Most of all, write for *them*, the ordinary folks out there, not for yourself and your buddies in the profession of psychiatry." I can still recall my sense of futility and inadequacy as I thought about those admonishing remarks. I had always known that Dr. Williams could be irritable with people he knew and wanted to help (I'd seen him be so with patients), but now I felt critically judged, and unable to do anything in keeping with the advice given me—lest I lose my last link with my medical and psychiatric and psychoanalytic life: my capacity to write articles that would earn me (not to mention the work I was doing) a hearing, some acceptance.

What Dr. Williams urged, my wife, a high-school teacher of English and history, also urged. She began listening to the tapes we'd collected (she and I worked together, full-time, until our sons were born in 1964, 1966, and 1970). She marked up certain moments in the transcripts which she found interesting, pulled them together, and wrote from memory some descriptions of the scenes in which those comments were made: times, places, details such as the weather, the casual talk exchanged, the food so generously served us, the neighborhood excursions we took—to churches, to markets, a world explored with the help of embattled people who knew that if we were really to understand them, we had to go beyond those clinical questions that I wanted so much to ask them. In time Jane had assembled "moments," she called them, for me to read: a mix of descriptive writing and edited versions of interviews, with suggestions for what she called "personal reflection" on my part. "You'll have some old-fashioned essays," she wrote. "Nothing to be afraid of!"

Plenty to be afraid of, I thought. It took me a couple of years to overcome that apprehension and worry. I was taught and rallied and reassured by Jane, badgered by Dr. Williams, until he died (March 4, 1963), challenged by some of the friends I'd made in SNCC, who kept telling me I should "tell their stories," not try to "shrink" them, and encouraged by Margaret Long, a novelist who worked for the Southern Regional Council, an interracial group long devoted to standing up in many ways to segregation. In 1963 the Council published my first nonprofessional piece (as I thought of it back then) on the work I was doing: "Separate But Equal Lives." The very title signified a break for me, a departure from the heavyweight jargon I'd learned to use as an expression of professional arrival. With this new kind of writing, I began to think differently about the very nature of the work I was doing. The point now was not only to analyze what children said, or the drawings they made, but to learn about their *lives*, in the hope of being able to describe them as knowingly and clearly as possible to anyone who cares to read of them rather than to my colleagues in child psychiatry.

In 1970, well along in such writing, I heard this from one of my old supervisors at the Children's Hospital in Boston, George Gardner: "You're doing documentary work, documentary child psychiatry, I suppose you could call it." I was pleased, though also worried—haunted by the judgmental self, its appearance often a measure of careerist anxiety. When I told my wife what Dr. Gardner had said, she laughed and said, "When Dr. Gardner settles for 'documentary work' alone, you'll be there!" But where is her "there"? We never discussed that question at the time. I was almost afraid to think about what she had in mind, even as I know in retrospect what she was suggesting—that I try to respond more broadly (less clinically) to these children, give them their due as individuals, as human beings, rather than patients. After all, they weren't "sick," or coming to me in a hospital or a clinical setting for "help"; they were "out there," living their lives, and I had come to them in an effort to learn how they "got along." Those two words increasingly became my methodological description of intent, my rationale of sorts: to try to ascertain as best I could the character of particular lives, the way they are lived, the assumptions held, the hopes embraced, the fears and worries borne—in Flannery O'Connor's felicitous phrase, the particular "habit of being" that informs *this* person's existence, *that* one's. To render such lives requires that one take a stand with respect to them—that of the observer, first and foremost, so that they can be apprehended, but that of the *distanced* observer, the editor, the critic (not of them, but of them as the subject of a story). What of their lives to offer others, and in what manner of delivery? As I asked that question I could hear one of Dr. Williams's refrains: "the language, the language!" Williams was forever trying to do justice both to what he heard from others, and to what he heard in his own head: the narrative side of documentary work, the exposition of a particular effort at exploration.

Documentary work, then, ultimately becomes, for most of us, documentary writing, documentary photographs, a film, a taped series of folk songs, a collection of children's drawings and paintings: reports of what was encountered for the ears and eyes of others. Here we weed and choose from so very much accumulated. Here we connect ourselves critically with those we have come to know— we arrange and direct their debut on the stage, and we encourage and discourage by selecting some segments and eliminating others. Moreover, to repeat, some of us add our own two cents (or more); we work what others have become to *us* into *our* narrative—the titles we give to photographs, the introductions we write for exhibitions, the statements we make with films. Even if our work is presented as only about *them*, we have been at work for weeks, for months, discarding and thereby concentrating what we retain: its significance mightily enhanced because so much else has been taken away.

It is not unfair, therefore, for an Oscar Lewis or a Studs Terkel or a Fred Wiseman to be known as the one who is "responsible" for what are supposedly documentary reports about all those others who were interviewed or filmed. Those others, in a certain way, have become "creations" of Lewis, Terkel, Wiseman—even if we have no explanatory comments from any of them about what they have done, and how, and with what purpose in mind. The stories such documentarians tell us are, in a way, the surviving remnants of so very much that has been left aside. We who cut, weave, edit, splice, crop, sequence, interpolate, interject, connect, pan, come up with our captions and comments, have our say (whenever and wherever and however) have thereby linked our lives to those we have attempted to document, creating a joint presentation for an audience that may or may not have been asked to consider all that has gone into what they are reading, hearing, or viewing.

I remember, a wonderfully enlightening afternoon spent with labor economist Paul Taylor in 1972, while I was working on a biographical study of Dorothea Lange. Jane and I sat in Taylor's spacious, comfortable Berkeley home, the one he and Dorothea

Lange occupied together until her death of cancer in 1965. He took me, step by step, through their work together, the work that culminated in *American Exodus* (1939). We examined many of Lange's photographs, some of them prints that were never published or shown. We were looking at an artist's sensibility, as it informed the selections she had made—which picture really worked, really got across what the photographer intended for us to contemplate.

I studied her iconic "migrant mother," a picture known throughout the world, a visual rallying ground of sorts for those who want to be reminded and remind others of jeopardy's pensive life (Fig. 1). There she sits, her right hand touching her lower right cheek, the lady of Nipoma, caught gazing, in March of 1936, one of her children to her left, one to her right, head turned away from us, disinclined to look at the camera and, through it, the legions of viewers with whom it connects. The three figures seem so close, so "tight," it would be said in the South, yet each seems lost to the others: the children lost in the private world they secure by hiding their eyes, the mother lost in a look that is seemingly directed at no one and everyone, a look that is inward and yet that engages with us who look at her, and maybe with her, or through her, at the kind of life she has been living. But only minutes before Lange took that famous picture, she had taken others. At furthest remove (Fig. 2) we are shown the same mother and her children in the makeshift tent that is their home; two others, a bit closer, show her with another child who has just been suckling at her breast and now has settled into a sleep. In one picture (Fig. 3) the mother is alone with that child; in the next, (Fig. 4) another of her children has come to her side, its face on her left shoulder. I return to the picture Lange has selected: now the older children are alongside their mother, but her appearance commands our attention—her hair lightly combed, her strong nose and broad forehead and wide mouth giving her face authority, her informally layered plainclothes, her worker's arms and fingers

Figure 1

Figure 2

telling us that this is someone who every day has to take life on with no conviction of success around any corner.

Dorothea Lange has, in a sense, removed that woman from the very world she is meant, as a Farm Security Administration (FSA) photographer, to document. The tent is gone, and the land on which it is pitched, and the utensils. The children, in a way, are gone, their backs turned to us, their backs a sort of screen upon which we may project our sense of what is happening to them, what they feel. But one child's head is slightly lowered, and the other has covered her face with her right arm—and so a feeling of their sadness, become the viewer's sadness, has surely seized so many of us who have stared

Figure 3

and stared at that woman, who is herself staring, and maybe, as in a Rodin sculpture, doing some serious thinking: struggling for a vision, dealing with an apprehension, experiencing a premonition or a nightmarish moment of foreboding. We are told by Lange that she is a "migrant mother," because otherwise she could be quite another kind of working (or nonworking) mother, yet she has been at least somewhat separated from sociological clues, and so she becomes psychologically more available to us, kin to us. A photographer has edited and cropped her work in order to make it more accessible to her anticipated viewers. As a documentarian, Lange snapped away with her camera, came back with a series of pictures that narrate a kind of white migrant life in the mid-1930s—and then, looking for one picture that would make the particular universal,

Figure 4

that would bring us within a person's world rather than keep us out (as pitying onlookers), she decided upon a photograph that allows us to move from well-meant compassion to a sense of respect, even awe: we see a stoic dignity, a thoughtfulness whose compelling survival under such circumstances is itself something to ponder, something to find arresting, even miraculous.

Another well-known Lange picture that Paul Taylor and I studied was "Ditched, Stalled, and Stranded," taken in California's San Joaquin Valley in 1935. Taylor first showed me the uncropped version of that picture (Fig. 5), with a man seated at the steering wheel of a car, his wife beside him. He has a wool cap on, of a kind today more commonly worn in Europe than here. He has a long face with a sturdy nose, and with wide eyes he stares past his wife (the right car door open) toward the viewer. The woman's right hand is in the pocket of her coat, which has a fur collar, and she is looking at an angle to the viewer. She has a round face, and seems to be of ample size. A bit of her dress and her right leg appear beyond the bottom limit of the coat. My dad, politically conservative, had seen that version of the picture years ago, and had pointed out to me that he was not impressed by Lange's title: here, after all, in the middle of the 1930s, at the height of the Great Depression, a worldwide phenomenon, were a couple who seemed well-clothed, well-fed—and who had a car. Did I realize, he wondered, how few people in the entire world, even in America, could be so described at that time? An automobile and a fur-collared coat to him meant something other than being "ditched, stalled, and stranded."

Lange chose to crop that photograph for presentation in various exhibitions and books (Fig. 6). She removed the woman, save a touch of her coat (the cloth part), so the driver looks directly at us. Like the migrant mother, his gaze connects with our gaze, and we wonder who this man is, and where he wants to go, or is headed, and why he is described by the photographer as so thoroughly at an impasse.

Figure 5

The photographer, in turn, tries to provide an answer. The man's left hand holds lightly onto the steering mechanism just below the wheel, and he seems almost an extension of that wheel, the two of them, along with the title given them, a metaphor for a troubled nation gone badly awry: whither his direction, and will he even be able to get going again, to arrive where he would like to be? Once

Figure 6

more, Lange turns a photograph into a melancholy statement that embraces more than the population of a California agricultural region. She does so by cropping (editing) her work, by denying us the possibility of a married couple in which one spouse seems reasonably contented, by reducing a scene to a driver who is readily seen as forlorn, and also as deeply introspective, eager for us, his fellow citizens, to return the intensity of his (moral) introspection.

I remember Paul Taylor gazing intently at the migrant mother and the man who was "ditched, stalled, and stranded"—a return on his part to a 1930s world, but also a moment's opportunity to reflect upon an entire documentary tradition, in which *American Exodus* figures importantly. No question, Paul and Jane reminded me, social observers and journalists have been journeying into poor neighborhoods, rural and urban, for generations, and in so doing have connected their written reports to a visual effort of one kind or another. Henry Mayhew's sensitively rendered *London Labour and the London Poor*, which describes nineteenth-century London, was accompanied by the drawings of Cruikshank, the well-known English illustrator—an inquiry that included a pictorial response. When George Orwell's *The Road to Wigan Pier* was first published in 1937, its text was supplemented by photographs, poorly reproduced, their maker unacknowledged—yet surely some who read Orwell's provocative and suggestive text were grateful for a glimpse of the world this great essayist had visited.

By the 1930s, under the auspices of the Farm Security Administration, and especially Roy Stryker, who had a keen sense of the relationship between politics and public awareness, a number of photographers were roaming the American land eager to catch sight of, and then, through their cameras, catch hold of a country struggling mightily with the consequences of the Great Depression—in the words of President Franklin Delano Roosevelt (1937) "one-third of a nation ill-housed, ill-clad, ill-nourished." So it is that Russell Lee and Ben Shahn and Arthur Rothstein and Walker Evans and Marion Post Wolcott, and, not least, Dorothea Lange became part of a significant photographic and cultural moment—the camera as an instrument of social awareness, of political ferment.

Though some photographers place great store by the titles they attach to their pictures, or write comments that help locate the viewer, help give him or her a sense of where the scene is or even provide a bit of context (how the person taking the picture happened to be at a particular place at a particular time), most photographers are content to let their work stand on its own, a silent confrontation of us all-too-wordy folk, for whom language (in the form of abstractions and recitations) can sometimes become an obstacle rather than a pathway to the lived truth of various lives. But Dorothea Lange's work in the 1930s, quite able, of course, to stand on its own, became part of something quite unique and important; and that connection (her photographs and the statements of some of the men and women whose pictures she took, joined to text written by Paul Taylor) would become a major achievement in the annals of field-work, of social-science research, of public information as rendered by a photographer and an academic (who in this case happened to be husband and wife).

It is possible to take much for granted as one goes through the pages of the 1939 edition of *American Exodus* (it was re-issued in 1969 with a foreword by Paul Taylor). The pictures are still powerful, even haunting, and some of them have become absorbed in an American iconography of sorts—the one titled "U.S. 54 in Southern New Mexico," for instance, or the one taken in the Texas Panhandle in 1938 that shows a woman in profile, her right hand raised to her brow, her left to her neck: a portrait of perplexity, if not desperation. That woman is quoted as saying "If you die, you're dead—that's all," and we, over half a century later, are apt to forget that in the 1930s there was no solid tradition of interviewing the subjects of a photographic study, linking what someone has to say to her or his evident circumstances as rendered by the camera. Again and again Dorothea Lange asked questions, wrote down what she heard (or overheard). Her sharp ears were a match for her shrewd and attentive eyes, and she knew to let both those aspects of her humanity connect with the people she had tried to understand.

Meanwhile, her husband was daring to do an original kind of explorative social science. As he accompanied her, he learned about the individuals, the locales she was photographing: how much workers got paid for picking crops, how much they paid for living in a migratory labor camp, and, more broadly, what had happened in the history of American agriculture from the earliest years of this century to the late 1930s. This was a study, after all, of a nation's fast-changing relationship to its land, of a major shift both in land usage and population: from the old South and the Plains states to California and Arizona, and from small farms or relatively genteel plantations to so-called factory-farms that now utterly dominate our grain and food (and animal) production. A combination of the economic collapse of the 1930s and the disastrous drought of that same time dislodged hundreds of thousands of Americans, some of whom sought jobs in cities, but many of whom embarked on the great trek westward, the last of the major migrations in that direction. For Paul Taylor, such an economic disaster was also a human one, and he knew how to do justice to both aspects of what was truly a crisis for humble small-farm owners or sharecroppers or tenant farmers or field hands. Taylor wanted to let his fellow citizens know the broader social and economic and historical facts and trends that had culminated in the 1930s "exodus"; Lange wanted us to see both the world being left and the world being sought, and to attend the words of the participants in a tragedy (for some) and an opportunity (for others).

Although these two observers and researchers concentrated on the largely white families that departed the plains because a once enormously fertile expanse had become scorched earth, we are also asked to remember the Delta of the South, parts of Mississippi and Louisiana and Arkansas, and, by implication, the especially burdensome life of blacks, whose situation in the 1930s, even for progressives, was of far less concern than it would become a generation later, in the 1960s. The New Deal, it must be remembered, was very much sustained, politically, by the (white) powers-that-be of the South, and black folk, then, as now, on the very bottom of the ladder, were not even voters. Nevertheless, Lange and Taylor paid them heed, and did so prophetically—took us with them to the cities, to Memphis, to show us another exodus, that of millions of such people from the old rural South to its urban centers, or, more commonly, to those up North.

Also prophetically, these two original-minded social surveyors were at pains to attend what we today call the environment—what happens to the land, the water, that human beings can so cavalierly, so insistently take for granted. In picture after picture, we see not only human erosion—people becoming worn and vulnerable—but the erosion of the American land: farmland devastated by the bad luck of a serious drought, but also by years and years of use that become abuse. It was as if the prodigal land had been deemed beyond injury or misfortune. But suddenly the parched land said no to a people, to a nation, and suddenly the roads that covered that land bore an unprecedented kind of traffic: human travail on the move.

But Lange and Taylor go further, give us more to think about than the tragedy of the dust bowl become a major event in a nation already reeling from the collapse of its entire (manufacturing, banking) economy. Some of the pictures of California (the promised land!) tell us that new misfortunes, even catastrophes would soon enough follow what had taken place in Oklahoma and Texas and Kansas and Nebraska and the Dakotas. The lush Imperial Valley, where thousands came in hope of using their hands, their harvesting savvy, to pick crops and make a living, was already in the 1930s becoming a scene of litter, a place where the land had to bear a different kind of assault than that of a succession of plantings that aren't rotated, aren't planned in advance with consideration of what the earth needs as well as what it can enable. The debris, the junk that covers some of the California terrain was no doubt shown to us by Lange so that we could see how disorganized and bewildered and impoverished these would-be agricultural workers had become, see their down-and-out, even homeless lives: the bare earth all they had in the way of a place to settle, to be as families, at least for awhile. Yet today we know how common such sights are across the nation—how those who live under far more comfortable, even affluent circumstances have their own ways of destroying one or another landscape, defacing fields, hills, and valleys that might otherwise be attractive to the eye, an aspect of nature untarnished.

These pictures remind us, yet again, that tragedies have a way of becoming contagious, that one of them can set in motion another, that the temptation to solve a problem quickly (let those people cross the country fast, and find much-needed work fast) can sometimes be costly indeed. There is something ever so desolate about the California of Lange's pictures—even though that state welcomed the people who flocked to it by providing jobs, and the hope that goes with work. Environmental problems to this day plague parts of the western states, problems that have to do with the way both land and water are used. Half a century ago, Lange and Taylor more than hinted at those problems, just as when they followed some of the South's black tenant farmers into the ghettos of a major city, Memphis, they gave us a peek at the urban crisis we would be having in a decade or two.

Also prophetic and important was the manner in which this project was done: informally, unpretentiously, inexpensively, with clear, lucid language and strong, direct, compelling photographs its instruments. For some of us, who still aim to learn from people out there in that so-called field, this particular piece of research stands out as a milestone: it offers us a guiding sense of what was (and presumably still is) possible—direct observation by people interested in learning firsthand from other people, without the mediation of statistics, theory, and endless elaborations of so-called methodology. Here were a man and a woman, a husband and a wife, who drove across our nation with paper, pen, and camera; who had no computers or questionnaires or "coding devices," no tape recorders, or movie cameras, no army of research assistants "trained" to obtain "data." Here were two individuals who would scorn that all-too-commonly upheld tenet of today's social-science research, the claim to be "value-free." They were, rather, a man and a woman of unashamed moral passion, of vigorous and proudly upheld subjectivity, anxious not to quantify or submit what they saw to conceptual assertion but to notice, to see and hear, and in so doing, to feel, then render so that others, too, would know in their hearts as well as their heads what it was that happened at a moment in American history, at a place on the American subcontinent. Here in Lange's photos, finally, the camera came into its own as a means of social and even economic and historical reflection. These pictures, in their powerfully unfolding drama, in their manner of arrangement and presentation and sequencing, in their narrative cogency and fluency, tell us so very much, offer us a gripping sense of where a social tragedy took place and how it shaped the lives of its victims. This is documentary study at its revelatory best—pictures and words joined together in a kind of nurturing interdependence that illustrates the old aphorism that the whole is greater than the sum of its parts.

American Exodus was not only a wonderfully sensitive, compellingly engaging documentary study; it challenged others to follow suit, to do their share in taking the measure, for good and bad, of our nation's twentieth-century fate. Dorothea Lange was an energetic, ambitious photographer, but she also was a moral pilgrim of sorts, ever ready to give us a record of human experience that truly matters: our day-to-day struggles as members of a family, of a neighborhood, of a nation to make do, to take on life as best we can, no matter the obstacles we face. And so with Paul Taylor, a social scientist who dared pay a pastoral regard to his ordinary fellow citizens, even as he mobilized a broader kind of inquiry into the forces at work on them and on their nation. We can do no better these days than to look at their book, over half a century after it appeared, not only as an aspect of the past (a remarkable social record, an instance of careful collaborative inquiry), but as a summons to what might be done in the years ahead, what very much needs to be done: a humane and literate kind of social inquiry.

Speaking of such inquiry, Paul Taylor was quick to mention *Let Us Now Praise Famous Men* to Jane and me. He reminded us of Walker Evans's genius for careful, sometimes provocative cropping and editing of particular photographs—his ability to sequence his prints, look at their narrative momentum, and choose particular ones for presentation: the exactly memorable, summoning, kindling moments. Taylor made reference to Evans's photograph in *Let Us Now Praise Famous Men* that introduces one of the tenant farmers, a young man in overalls, his head slightly tilted to his right, his eyes (set in an unshaven face topped by curly hair) confronting the viewer head-on with an almost eerie combination of strength and pride on the one hand, and an unavoidable vulnerability on the other, or so many of us have felt (Fig. 7). That picture, now on the cover of the latest (1988) paperback edition of the book, signals to us the very point of the title, of the entire text as Agee conceived it: an ode to those hitherto unacknowledged, a salute to this man and others like him, this man whose fame has awaited a moral awakening of the kind this book hopes to inspire in us, just as the writer and photographer themselves were stirred from a certain slumber by all they witnessed during that Alabama time of theirs.

In the picture of this "famous man," as with certain of Lange's pictures, the viewer is given no room to wander, to be distracted.

Figure 7

Figure 8

This is eye-to-eye engagement, a contrast to other possibilities available to Evans of the same man sitting at the same time in the same position. That farmer's daughter was actually sitting in a chair beside her father; one negative gives us a full-length portrait of him and her both, with the door and part of the side of their house and a portion of the porch also visible (Fig. 8). But Evans is struggling for an interiority, that of his subject and that of his subject's future viewer/visitor: let us not only praise this man, lift him to the ranks of the famous, but consider what might be going on within him, and let us, through the motions of our moral imagination, enter his life, try to understand it, and return with that understanding to our own, which is thereby altered. This is a tall order for a single picture, but then Evans and Agee were ambitious, as evidenced by their constant citation of the inadequacy of their project (vividly restless dreamers fearing the cold light of a morning).

Taylor also wanted us to look at a sequence of Evans's photographs of a tenant's daughter, bonneted, at work picking cotton. We who know the book remember her slouched, bent over the crops (Fig. 9). We don't see her face, don't really see any of *her*; she *is* her clothes, as if they were perched on an invisible person who is beyond our human approximations, who is of no apparent age or race. She is huddled over the fertile, flowering land to the point where she seems part of it, only barely above it, a lone assertion of our species and, too, a reminder of our incontestable dependence on the surrounding, the enveloping world of plants and shrubs. Yet, other negatives taken of that same scene at that same time reveal the girl standing upright (Fig. 10), looking in profile at the surrounding terrain (Fig. 11), or hunched over a part of it that hasn't the abundance of crops that we see in the picture Evans chose to show us (Fig. 12). There is one photograph, taken from above (Fig. 13), that shows only the girl's straw hat, immersed in the foliage—an "arty" picture, an "interesting" one, a pretty image. With the circularity of straw (another crop!) imposed, so to speak, on the cotton field, the girl becomes a mere bearer of that hat (only a hump of her is evident).

Evans resists the aesthetic temptations of that last picture and of others in the series; he picks and chooses his way through a narrative sequence that might be titled in various ways: Alabama child labor; a young harvester; a girl at work picking cotton; or, drawing on Rupert Vance's wonderfully literate 1930s work at the University of North Carolina, an instance of a white child's connection to the "cotton culture." A photographer is carving out his own declaration based on his own survey research. He wants us, finally, to face facelessness, to see a child who isn't looking at us or at the nearby terrain (despite the fact that he had pictures of the girl doing both), but whose eyes were watching a row of plants, and whose body,

Figure 9

Figure 10

Figure 11

Figure 12

Figure 13

whose very being, seems scarcely above them, tied to them, merging with them.

There is, to be sure, an appealing beauty to the picture Evans selected from this sequence for the book: a graceful curve to the body, an elegance, a consequence of a learned, relaxed capability to pick and pick, as I saw in a migrant worker I once knew, who tried to teach me how to harvest celery. As I watched him look carefully, then make this cut, then the next one with his knife—swiftly, adroitly, with seeming ease and authority and exactitude—I caught myself thinking of his dignity, his full knowledge of a particular scene, while at the same time I worried that I was being a romantic: I was struggling with my own obvious lack of skill by ennobling his hard, tough, ill-paid labor (as, arguably, Orwell did when he went down into those mines in 1936). And so, perhaps, with this picture of Evans: we attempt to contemplate people's strenuous exertions even as we try to rescue them, at least partially, from those exertions. A miner can have his nobility, or be seen in a noble light by an observer, and that migrant can extract from his terribly burdened life moments of great, knowing competence, and this girl whom Evans noticed so painstakingly can also have her times of agility, balance, suppleness, the mystery of a lithe, enshrouded form as it "works on a row." Or are we to think of her only as an example of exploited child labor? When, that is, does our empathy and compassion ironically rob those whom we want so hard to understand of their loveliness, however tough the circumstances of their life? (I recognize the serious dangers, here, of an aesthetic that becomes a moral escape, a shameful avoidance of a grim actuality, a viewer's flight of willful blindness—hence, I think, Evans's refusal to let us dote on that hat, with its "interesting" setting.)

Walker Evans, in his own way, addressed the broader question of documentary expression in a lecture at Yale on March 11, 1964. He was sixty-one then; he had spent a lifetime traveling with his camera, planning and then executing various photographic expeditions. At Yale he said this: "My thought is that the term 'documentary' is inexact, vague, and even grammatically weak, as used to describe a style in photography which happens to be my style. Further, that what I believe is really good in the so-called documentary approach in photography is the addition of lyricism. Further, that the lyric is usually produced unconsciously and even unintentionally and accidentally by the cameraman—and with certain exceptions. Further, that when the photographer presses for the heightened documentary, he more often than not misses it. . . . The real thing that I'm talking about has purity and a certain severity, rigor, simplicity, directness, clarity, and it is without artistic pretension in a self-conscious sense of the word. That's the base of it."

So much there to applaud, especially the descriptive words "inexact" and "vague" and "grammatically weak": the difficulty we have in doing justice to the range and variation of writing and photography and film that a given tradition embraces. The word "documentary" is indeed difficult to pin down; is intended, really, as mentioned earlier, to fill a large space abutted on all sides by more precise and established and powerful traditions: that of journalism or reportage, those of certain academic disciplines (sociology and anthropology in particular), and of late, a well-organized, structured approach to folklore and filmmaking (as opposed to an "unconscious" or "unintentional" or "accidental" approach)—university departments of "film studies" and "folklore studies." Evans's three adjectives are themselves meant to be scattershot, if not "inexact" and "vague"—a means of indicating a style, a manner of approach, or, in his friend Agee's phrase, "a way of seeing," and also a way of doing: the one who attempts documentary work as the willing, even eager beneficiary of luck and chance, the contingent that in a second can open the doors of a craftsman's imaginative life. Academics have their well-defined, carefully established, and ever so

highly sanctioned (and supported) routines, procedures, requirements, "methodologies," their set language. Journalists are tied to
the news closely or loosely. Nonfiction writing deals with the consideration of ideas and concepts, with ruminations and reflections
of importance to a particular writer and his or her readers. Certain
photographers follow suit, address *their* ideas and concepts: light,
forms, the spatial arrangements of objects—lines, say, rather than
lives. In contrast, even the word *documentarian* (never mind the nature
of the work done) may be imprecise, hard to pin down, at times
misleading—in fact, no "documents" need be gathered in the name
of authenticity, in the name of moving from a suspect (to some)
"oral history" to a history of affidavits and wills and letters, the
older the better. But that is the way it goes—and there are advantages: no deadline of tomorrow for the morning edition, or three or
four days for the Sunday one; no doctoral committee to drive one
crazy with nit-picking scrutiny of a language already sanitized and
watered-down and submitted to the test of departmental politics, a
phenomenon that is surely a twentieth-century manifestation of original sin.

Instead, as Evans suggested, the doer of documentary work is out
there in this world of five billion people, free (at least by the nature
of his or her chosen manner of approach to people, places, events)
to buckle down, to try to find a congenial, even inspiring take on
things. Evans celebrates a lyricism, and defines aspects of it nicely:
a directness and a lack of pretentiousness, a cleanness of presentation
that he dares call severe and pure. It is a lyricism, be it noted, that
proved worthy (in its expression by Evans) of companionship with
Hart Crane's *The Bridge*, a lyricism that in general bridges the observer,
the observed, and the third party, as it were, who is the second
observer—a lyricism, Dr. Williams would insist, of "things," a broad
rubric for him that included human beings, and a rubric meant to
exclude only the rarefied, the insistently abstract. The document in

mind (mind you) can for a while be hungrily, ecstatically abstract—the dreaming, the planning, the thinking out of a project—but down the line, somehow, in some way, we have to get to "the thing itself."

Here is Evans being ambitiously abstract, as well as impressively industrious, aspiring, enterprising: "Projects: New York Society in the 1930s. 1. national groups 2. types of the time. (b. and wh.) 3. children in streets 4. chalk drawings 5. air views of the city 6. subway 7. ship reporter (this project get police cards)." He continues, "the art audience at galleries, people at bars, set of movie ticket takers, set of newsstand dealers, set of shop windows, the props of upper class set, public schools faces and life." Those notes were, appropriately enough, scribbled on the reverse side of a Bank of Manhattan blank check in New York City during 1934–35. Another series of notes: "the trades, the backyards of N.Y., Harlem, bartenders, interiors of all sorts—to be filed and classified." A letter to Roy Stryker of the FSA in 1935: "Still photography, of general sociological nature." The point was to dream, to wander from topic to topic, and then, finally, to find the specific place and time, so that the eyes were free to follow the reasons of heart and mind both: a lyrical sociology; a journalism of the muse; a dramatic storytelling adventure that attends a scene in order to capture its evident life, probe its secrets, and turn it over as whole and complicated and concrete and elusive as it is has been found to those of us who care to be interested.

In a handsomely generous and affecting tribute to his colleague, his friend, his soulmate, James Agee, written in 1960 for a fresh edition of *Let Us Now Praise Famous Men*, Evans describes James Agee in 1936 as one who "worked in what looked like a rush and a rage." He also refers, in that vein, to Agee's "resolute, private rebellion." I do not think Evans himself was immune to this virus—an utter impatience with, even outrage at a sometimes stuffy and often callous world. As I read Evans or Agee I think of a motley assortment of others who fit in to this odd, cranky crowd—Studs Terkel and Oscar Lewis and George Orwell and Dorothea Lange and Paul Taylor, to name again some whom I've been calling in witness. Once, as I tried to get down to the specifics, a documentary mind preparing for a task, I remembered Evans's comments on what he hoped to do on, of all places, New York City's subways:

> The choice of the subway as locale for these pictures was arrived at not simply because of any particular atmosphere or background having to do with the subway in itself—but because that is where the people of the city range themselves at all hours under the most constant conditions for the work in mind. The work does not care to be 'Life in the Subway' and obviously does not 'cover' that subject.
>
> These people are everybody. These pictures have been selected and arranged, of course, but the total result of the line-up has claim to some kind of chance-average.
>
> The gallery page is a lottery, that is, the selection that falls there is determined by no *parti pris* such as, say, 'I hate women,' or 'women are dressed foolishly,' or '———.' It *is* an arrangement, of course, as is the rest of the book, but the forces determining it have to do not only with such considerations as page composition, tone of picture, inferential interest of picture or face in itself.
>
> Speculations from such a page of sixteen women's faces and hats remains then an open matter, the loose privilege of the reader, and whoever chooses to decide from it that people are wonderful or that what America needs is a political revolution is at liberty to do so.

There he is, difficult and ungovernable for others, for his viewers and readers even, prepared to make substantial, maybe overwhelming demands on them. He'll have no truck with the most inviting and, alas, the most banal of titles for his work, even though one suspects that the abstraction "Life in the Subway" crossed his mind more than once as he thought about what he intended to do, its rationale, never mind its locale. He distances himself from all that is implied by the verb "cover," lest he be charged with the sin of inclusiveness, let alone that of a devouring topicality—as in a report or story that "covers" an issue by covering it with all sorts of facts, figures, opinions. Phrases like "chance-average" and "loose privilege" tell of the writer's venerable experience with both our language and this century's toll on our values. Who in the world today will settle for such informality, such a casual and relaxed attitude toward what is (or is not) an *average*, or a *privilege*? "Chance" and "loose" bespeak sipping whiskey in an armchair, with one of the big bands, Tommy Dorsey, maybe, playing "Whispering": a time before computer printouts arrived, or cocksure polls that have a plus or minus accuracy of—God knows what number. As for his concluding challenge (to himself, to all of us), it is one that laughs at ideology, that announces a sensibility contemptuous of singular interpretations, and that gives all of us splendid leeway to do as we damn please in what is volunteered unashamedly as an earnest, persistent, highly personal "visit" with some folks traveling underground.

There is evident discomfort in Evans's message, meant for himself above all; it never appeared in the foreword to the book showing his subway pictures. He wanted to define himself and his pictures so that they were not considered photojournalism, or part of yet another attempt to survey people or expose some (detrimental, damaging) aspect of their life. He was *there*, looking at men and women and children on their hurried way someplace. As the trains roared and sped, he presumably tried to catch hold of himself and others— literally as well as figuratively, a still moment in a quickly shifting scene of entrances and exits, a passing parade of technological and human activity. "I was pretty sure then, yes. I was sure that I was working in the documentary style. Yes, and I was doing social history, broadly speaking"—a cautious embrace at a point in a life's spectrum. But Evans would always qualify, circle around a purported professional location for himself, rather than hone in, dig in, *declare* without reservation. Here he is in a splendidly qualified and edifying further approach: "When you say 'documentary,' you have to have a sophisticated ear to receive that word. It should be documentary style, because documentary is police photography of a scene and a murder . . . that's a real document. You see, art is really useless, and a document has use. And therefore, art is never a document, but it can adopt that style. I do it. I'm called a documentary photographer. But that presupposes a quite subtle knowledge of this distinction."

A struggle there—to grasp, to adopt a style while reserving the artist's right of freedom to roam and select as he wishes. Others (in no way is this matter hierarchical) have their important and necessary obligations (the police photographer and, by extension, a host of people who work for or have joined a variety of institutions: newspapers, magazines, schools, universities). Evans's documentarian draws, in spirit, upon the earthy practicality of a police photographer, and also on the social and political indifference of an artist who, at a certain moment, has to be rid of all ideologies, even those he otherwise finds attractive, lest he become someone's parrot. The "style" he mentions here and elsewhere is nothing superficial; it refers to the connection an artist wants to have with, again, "human actuality," be it that of a police station, a subway, Alabama tenant farmers, Havana's 1930s street life—wherever it is that a Walker Evans imagines himself being, or ends up visiting. The rock-bottom issue is not only one's stated attitude toward "art" in general, but one's sense of oneself.

Once in a discussion at Dartmouth College in the 1970s, Evans took offense at questioners who wanted to know the mechanical details of his work, the kind of camera he used, and, beyond that, the way he developed and printed his photographs. He pointed out that what mattered to him was his intelligence, his taste, and his struggle for what such words imply and convey. Other photographers might have been eager to reply to such inquiries, men and women who are vitally interested in the technological possibilities of the machines they own and use, and who can get from them certain "effects": light or shadows amplified; appearances given new shape; the distortions, the "play" available to skilled men and women who, like Evans, are trying to be artists, photographic artists, but not artists and photographers in the "documentary style" or tradition, for which reality, however shaped and edited and narrated, has in some way to be an initial given. Hence the apprehension, the sorting of that reality in what Evans acknowledged to be a sociological manner, and hence his constantly moving presence in accordance with the demands of such a reality rather than those of a technological artistry, which certainly doesn't need central Alabama or the New York City subway for its expression, an artistry that can even confine itself to one room where the light arrives, moves about, and departs, all the while touching, in various ways, objects, human or inanimate.

William Carlos Williams was among Evans's admirers; he followed his work closely, wrote about it. He struggled, as Evans did, to be almost austere at times in his dispassionate insistence upon seeing many sides to whatever scene he was exploring—even as his big and generous heart could not help but press upon him as he sat at the typewriter, hence his gruff, tough moments followed by his fiery, exclamatory ones. In *Paterson* he struggled in that respect, struggled for a stance: the detached spectator, the informed but reserved onlooker as against the spy, the voyeur (and Evans, along with Agee, uses such imagery to indicate that side of himself: someone who has a lot at stake in what he's trying to do). Like Evans, Williams tried to come to grips with that word *documentary*, and made no bones about his belief that location and time mattered enormously: where one chose to stay and for how long, but also (he kept saying so in dozens of places and ways) the "language—and how it is used," by which he more broadly meant the relation of the watcher to the watched, of the one listening to those who fill his ears with words.

Williams was forever exploring in his mind the nature of a writer's, a photographer's, a filmmaker's dealings with those being called to what he once suggestively described as a "tentative alliance," one that might "fall apart at any minute." I asked for an explanation of that imagery (aware that in 1953, the Second World War and all the horror that preceded it, the pacts and agreements, the duplicities and betrayals, were still very much on his mind), and he was not loath to give it a try:

When you're a doctor seeing a patient you're there by permission: the two of you have an agreement (or if it's a kid, the parents have signed you up, and the kid knows it). You can poke around; no other person in the world can poke around like that. You look and you listen and you poke some more, then you talk to yourself, you remember what you know and you compare notes with what you've seen in other patients (this silent talking, this recalling), and then you've made up your mind, so you start talking. Now, you're telling someone something, rather than asking; you're giving advice—orders, really. But the whole thing [the relationship] is based on that agreement: you can explore this body of mine, and you can ask me any damn thing you want, because that's who you are, a doctor, and that's who I am, a patient.

"Now, when I'm walking down the street there [in Paterson, where many of his patients lived] I'm trying to do another kind of "examination"—I'm still poking around, but I'm not doing it under the same terms. I'm hoping people will give me some access—talk with me and help me figure out what's going on around here [we were in Paterson]. I'm trying to look and listen, just as I do with the sick kids I see and their parents. I'm sizing up a place, a whole city, you could say: what is

OK, what's working fine, and what's no good, and what "stinks out loud." A guy I know, I'll be standing there in the drugstore with him, and he's telling me "This positively stinks out loud," and I want to hear more. I'm excited, hearing him sound like he's Jeremiah's direct-line descendent. He can't do much more than sign his name. He has trouble reading the newspaper. He has to work to figure out those headlines. It's the radio that tells him everything. He hunkers down with it. He calls it his "friend" sometimes; [and] once I heard him call it his "source." Source of what, I wanted to know. "Everything," that's how specific he could get! "What, for instance?" I asked, and he said, "The Guiding Light," and "Vic and Sade" [two soap operas], and then he said "the local news," he keeps up with it, and if he had another life, he'd like to be a "radio guy," he called it—he meant an announcer, the one who gives people the news. Then, he said: "Only I'd like to go see what's happening out there, and I'd know the people, I'd really know them, before I'd say anything about them. If you talk about people on radio, you should know them, otherwise it's not fair!"

I couldn't get him, what he said, out of my mind for a while. Days later, I'd think of him. It's not so easy to know people! I guess he'd find that out; he's ready to go try, in another life, if he could have it. But when I try to get him going more, about his own life, there's only so far he'll walk with me—and why should he? If you start thinking of yourself as a doctor examining a city, a diagnostician walking the streets, looking for people who can talk to you openly enough, so you can figure out what the illnesses are, the social illnesses, and what's "healthy" about it all—then you've got to *work* to get people to "sign up," to give you the trust you need for them to level with you, really level. Otherwise, you've got formality; you've got off-the-top-of-my-head stuff; you've got a quickie news story on that guy's radio, or the headline he struggles to make out. I feel like saying to him: save your energy, forget the damn headline and keep listening to that radio, if you can find something good on it, a big "if."

I've long felt that such "top-of-the-head" ruminations, testy and splenetic, sometimes plaintive (if only it could be easier to learn what Williams so much wanted to learn about the "local pride" that was Paterson!) are themselves texts on documentary work for us to contemplate. Williams was anxious to connect his own thoughts to those of others, to let so-called ordinary people become his teachers, just as his patients all the time taught him. His profound distrust of all aestheticism ("The rest now run out after the rabbits") was prompted by his intuition that solipsistic art was not a suitable haven. He simply wasn't able to be indifferent to social reality in the ways that some of his poet friends found quite congenial. He knew the difficulties of apprehending that social reality, and, too, of finding the right words, the rhythms, the beat that would make his music somehow worthy of the music his ears picked up in Paterson: street music, tenement tunes, soul music and jazz and polkas and the tango and country music. He was always talking about the "American vein," which he tried to tap throughout his writing life—and to do so, he didn't only sit in his study and muse (though he wasn't at all averse to that kind of exploration). "Good luck to those who can keep their distance from the howl, the yell of things," he once said. Later, I'd wonder whether, by chewing out those writing colleagues every once in a while, he wasn't trying to exorcise his envy. But in the end he was who he was, and he more than settled for that existential fact. He built up, he wrote a *Paterson* that whispered and shouted, in good faith, stories of the chaste and bawdy Paterson, his witness to that city and its engagement with generations of needy seekers of all sorts: the words of honor spoken; the covenants abandoned; the people sold down the river; the victories won and lost; the folks who earned good dough, got a leg up; the folks who fell by the wayside. He gave us a chronicle, of course, but also a call to arms—and for him, the war was a struggle, against substantial odds, for a consciousness that isn't blunted and warped by the thousands of deceptions everywhere around. His version of Evans's "documentary style" was a vernacular not showily summoned out of a craving for distinction, but earned in the daily and various rounds of his several working lives (the doctor, the social observer, the historian and chronicler of the nearby, the poet and novelist and essayist, the painter even) whose simultaneity was a constant source of amazement to any of us lucky enough to catch sight of it all.

A precise definition is probably the last thing Walker Evans or William Carlos Williams would suggest for us today who want to consider, yet again, the nature of documentary work. Those two large spirits were unruly enough to scoff at the fantasy of control that informs a pretentiousness which won't allow for indefiniteness— that last word, for the documentarian, a necessity: the arm and leg room of exploration that has to take place, once one heeds the call, the refrain of "outside/outside myself/there is a world to explore," and the further instrumental refrain of "no ideas but in things." The one time I got Dr. Williams to consider the specific subject of "documentary research" or "documentary fieldwork," he laughed, and echoed Evans's wary refusal to get pinned down. He was more curt and gruff than, I suspect, Evans had ever desired to be, and so he dismissed the word documentary, in a way, by asking a rhetorical question, mimicking those who love to give themselves names, the more the better: "Would you want me to tell folks out there that I'm a documentary poet—and are you doing some documentary child psychiatry, now that you're visiting homes of people who haven't got the slightest interest in taking their kids to a clinic, and they don't need to?" He then laughed, to break the tension partially created by his remark, but also initiated by my floundering perplexity, and offered this, in a more gentle mode: "Lots of streets to walk, lots of ways to walk them"—a brief whistle, meant to signal the virtue of an elusive melody as about the best he could do.

To take Dr. Williams's hint, to remember the words of an Apocrypha rescued for our American century's time by James Agee and Walker Evans, let us praise the many "famous people" we can get to meet as we pursue a "documentary style," rather than keep trying to spell out authoritatively various essential characteristics; let the doing be a big part of the defining. Let us, that is, recount and depict, and thereby embody what we're aiming to do and, yes, to be. Let us think of those observers of their fellow human beings who have tried to hug hard what they also know can suddenly escape them, to their apprehending peril. Dr. Williams: "I'll be standing at the store counter talking to that loud-mouthed pest who is trying to con me into buying something stupid that I'll never need, and I should be enjoying the fun of hearing him out—what a *line!*—but instead I demolish him in my mind with *ideas*, ethnic and sociological and psychological, and pretty soon it's no fun for me, or for him either. I've forgotten him; he's disappeared under the withering fire of my clever thinking. I've left him for another ball game!"

To be less exhortative, more declarative, they are of many "sorts and conditions," documentarians (if that is what they want to be called—and we oughtn't be surprised if lots of people decline, say no to that word, maybe any word, any combination of words: "not the letter, but the spirit"). I think of writers or photographers or filmmakers, of musicologists who spend their time enraptured up Appalachian hollows or in Mississippi's Delta, of folklorists (Zora Neale Hurston was one) crazy for wonderfully wild stories told in odd and loony ways. I think of documentary work that is investigative or reportorial; that is muckraking; that is appreciative or faultfinding; that is pastoral or contemplative; that is prophetic or admonitory; that reaches for humor and irony, or is glad to be strictly deadpan and factually exuberant; that knows exactly where it is going and aims to take the rest of us along, or wants only to make an impression—with each of us defining its nature or intent. In a way, Orwell, in *Wigan Pier*, showed us the range of possibilities as he documented the life of the Brookers (and blasted them sky-high) and documented the life of certain miners (and put them on a tall pedestal), and, in between, wondered about the rest of us, himself and his buddies included: wondered about the way a study of others comes home to roost. In a way, as well, Williams was being more enlightening and helpful than a young listener of his comprehended when he jokingly referred to the documentary side of his prowling, roaming New Jersey patrol, and when he posed for me a consideration of how a clinician ought to think of the documentary work he is trying to do—home and school visits in which he talks with children who are of interest not because they have medical "problems," but because they are part of one or another larger (social or racial or national or economic) "problem." Journalists cover those children in their way; a documentarian will need to put in more time, and have a perspective at once broader and more detailed, one that is, maybe, a follow-up to the first, difficult, sometimes brave (and costly) forays of journalists.

How well, in that regard, I recall conversations with Ralph McGill of the Altanta *Constitution* during the early years of the civil-rights struggle (1961–63). He had no small interest in the fate of the nine black students who initiated (high school) desegregation in Georgia's capitol city during the autumn of 1961, even as my wife, Jane, and I were getting to know those black youths and their white classmates (Atlanta had managed to prevent the kind of riots that had plagued other Southern cities, such as Little Rock and New Orleans). The three of us would meet and talk, and from him, through his great storytelling generosity, Jane and I learned so very much. Often we discussed what Mr. McGill referred to as "the limits of journalism." He would remind us that "news" is the "commodity" his reporters go everywhere to pursue, their words worked into the "product" that gets sold on the streets and delivered to stores and homes. But those reporters (and photojournalists) are also great documentary teachers and scholars: they know so very well how to go meet people, talk with them, take pictures of them, right away take their measure, decide when and how to go further, look for others to question. They know how to make those utterly necessary first steps (find contacts, use them) that the rest of us can be slow in realizing will make all the difference in whether a particular project will unfold. They know, many of them, and they know well, how to pose the toughest, most demanding and scrutinizing questions, at times utterly necessary questions, and ones that naïfs such as I have certainly shirked entertaining, let alone asking. "How did you learn to do your work?" students ask me all the time. I reply: from the great reporters I was lucky to meet and observe, from Pat Watters of the Atlanta *Journal*, from Claude Sitton, the Southern correspondent of the *New York Times*, from the ubiquitous and sometimes riotous Maggie Long, who edited the *New South*, but called herself "an old newspaper hand," and from Dorothy Day, who edited the *Catholic Worker* when I first met her, but who had worked on journalistic assignments for newspapers for years (in the 1920s) before she turned her life so radically around upon her conversion to Catholicism, and who, as she often reminded us, was the daughter of a newspaperman and the sister of two of them.

Yet, as Mr. McGill sadly had to aver: "At a certain point we have to stop"——meaning that a documentary inquiry ends, in favor of the requirements of another documentary initiative. It is then, he explained, that "the magazine boys take over"——his way of referring to the greater amount of space magazines allow, but also, of course, to the more leisurely way of exercising Evans's "documentary style." We never got into specifics, but because of his comparison, I began to think of the essays I read in various magazines (including those published by newspapers) in a different way: began to see the relative degree to which the author turns to people other than himself or herself as fellow bearers of a story's burden, and the degree, as well, to which such people are allowed (encouraged) to teach us by giving of themselves. Today, I think of Truman Capote's *In Cold Blood*, of Ian Frazier's pieces, short and long, of Alec Wilkinson's efforts with migrants in Florida, of his remarkable *A Violent Act*; and I remember *The New Yorker* of William Shawn as very much, at times, given to a "documentary style." Among photographers we can go back to Matthew Brady and the devastation of war that he made a lasting part of our knowledge, if we care to remember; to Lewis Hine and those children through whose condition he aroused our moral sensibility (again, if we care to take notice); to, of course, the FSA men and women; and today, Wendy Ewald, with her many brilliantly ingenious, spiritual explorations of childhood, aided by the children to whom she gives cameras, and whose photographs and words she shares with us. Photographers Alex Harris and Eugene Richards and Susan Meiselas and Gilles Peress and Danny Lyon and Robert Frank and Thomas Roma and Helen Levitt and Lee Friedlander; filmmakers Robert Flaherty and Pare Lorentz and Fred Wiseman and Robert Young and Michael Roemer and Ken Burns and Buddy Squires— all of these men and women are deservedly famous in the way Agee and Evans meant to signify for their Alabama teachers, known to the world as tenant farmers: humble by various criteria, but learned in ways any documentary tradition worth its name would aim to detail, to corroborate.

At a certain point in his research on Gandhi's life, Erik H. Erikson became dissatisfied. He had read many books and had spent a long time talking with a variety of scholars, historians, and political scientists, not to mention his psychoanalytic colleagues. He had obtained access to various library collections; he had attended a number of conferences; he had reviewed, courtesy of microfilm, journalistic accounts of Gandhi's various deeds and evaluations of the significance of his life. Nevertheless, this would-be biographer felt himself at an impasse. Why? I had no answer, despite the fact that I was teaching in his course then, helping him run a seminar, and trying to write about him, even as he was "struggling" with Gandhi (the phrase he often used)—almost as if the two were personally at odds, I sometimes thought.

We are sitting in Erikson's Widener study and I am interested, at the moment, in his work on Luther (my favorite of all his writings). He doesn't want to talk about that; he wants to talk about Gandhi's moral virtues, and, just as important, his flaws, if not vices: "I don't know whether I can proceed without in some way having it out with him [Gandhi]—how he fasted so honorably, risked his life for a just and merciful and fair political settlement, how he developed a decent and civilized manner of protest [nonviolence], and yet how he behaved as a husband and a father." Eventually, Erikson would write his well-known "letter," a breakthrough moment both in *Gandhi's Truth* and in psychoanalytic and historical thinking generally: a direct confrontation, a "having it out" with the spirit (the psychological "remains") of a figure who has left the living yet will endure through the ages. I listen, nod, try to steer us back to the fifteenth century, to *Luther's* contradictions—it is, after all, *my* interview that we are conducting! Few of my attempted subtleties miss my teacher's notice. Why am I now so interested in *Luther*? Well, Erik, why are *you* now so interested in Gandhi? That is the "line" of our reasoning together: mutual irritation expressed through a reductionist assault, by implication, on one another's motives, all under the dubious protection our shared profession provides. Finally, Erikson tells me, in annoyance at someone *else*, what he'd recently heard said by a distinguished cultural critic (and political philosopher)—that his *Young Man Luther* was a "marvelous novel"! I am taken aback; I keep silent; I worry about what my face wants to do, smile; I worry about what my voice wants to say (that such words are a high compliment), for I feel sure he wouldn't agree. He can sense, though, that I don't share his apparent chagrin. He puts this to me:

"What do *you* think?" Lord, *that* question, the endlessly recurrent one of the late-twentieth-century, psychoanalyzed American *haute bourgeoisie!* I gulp. I feel my lips holding on tight to one another. I feel the inquiring openness of those wide blue eyes of this almost awesome figure. I find myself glancing at that shock of white hair flowing backward. I plunge: "Erik, it's a high compliment." I pause. I know I need to amplify, but I'm not prepared to, I'm afraid to. I settle for two more words, "the highest." He stares back at me. His face is immobile. I plead silently for the descent of compassionate understanding upon both of us. Continued silence; seconds become hours. I'm ready to speak, though I don't really know what I'll say— a dangerous situation, people like Erikson and me have long known: random conversational thoughts are a grist for an all-too-familiar (these days) mill, a gradual presentation by the unconscious of various unsettling thoughts.

But suddenly, amid a still persisting silence, the great one's face yields a broad smile. I immediately return it without having any prior thought that I should or would. He ribs me: "I know why you said that." I then pour out my explanation: that "novel" is not a pejorative word, certainly. I then make a statement about the revelatory nature of stories, not unlike the one I have tried to write here and elsewhere. I remind him that no one can know for *sure* what "young man Luther" thought and felt; that his story has to do with speculations, with informed guesses as well as facts, all told persuasively if not convincingly; that imagination is at work in such an effort; and that sometimes, in those "gray areas" or moments, the imagination appeals to or invokes the imaginary—a Luther who becomes more in a writer's mind that he can possibly be with respect to anyone's records, recollections, or reports. I tell him about a question I once heard William Shawn ask of an about-to-be *New Yorker* writer: how would you like us to present this piece? What did Shawn mean? As a factual piece, a profile, or a short story? But, the writer said, it's about someone who was real, who lived! Yes, it certainly is, the distinguished, knowing editor acknowledges, but he could imagine it being presented, with a few narrative changes, as a *story*, with that "someone" as a character in it. Erikson now goes beyond smiles; he laughs heartily and tells me that I seem to be "enjoying all this," and he goes further: "Now, you see why I want to go to India and interview those people who knew Gandhi and worked with him! You see why I want you to show me how you use your tape recorder!"

He stops; it is my turn to laugh. I tell him he'll become a "field worker." He gets irritated, and justifiably so; he reminds me of his expeditions to Indian reservations (the Sioux, the Yurok) in the 1930s and 1940s, trips I well know to have been brave and resourceful (and, yes, imaginative) actions, given the prevailing psychoanalytic orthodoxy then settling in on his generation in the United States. I apologize. He tells me he isn't asking that of me; he wants us, rather, to discuss the nature of those trips, of his forthcoming "visit" to the Indian subcontinent. I call them, cautiously (following his lead), "field trips." He wonders about the adjectival addition of "anthropological." I demur. I say that these days any conversation with a child or adult on one of our Indian reservations gets connected to the discipline of anthropology—an outcome that needs its own kind of historical inquiry, because conversations by Erikson or anyone else (who isn't an anthropologist) in this country ought not be so reflexively regarded. We sit quietly thinking—one of the joys, always, with him: a capacity, a willingness to put aside mere chatter, to endure those lulls which, after all, sometimes fall for a good reason. Finally, he smiles, asks me this: "What would your friend Agee call those 'trips'—or the one I'm going on?"

I have been teaching Agee in my weekly section of Erikson's course, and I have introduced the professor to some of the more compelling passages of *Let Us Now Praise Famous Men*. I smile; we banter. I observe that I don't know what Agee would say, because he's so hard to pin down on such matters, even in connection with his own Alabama trip, but Erikson asks me to surmise. I reply that whatever Agee would say, it would be long, constantly modified, and perhaps hard to fathom without a good deal of effort. Erikson laughs, and tells me that I need to learn to "speak on behalf of Agee," whom I admire and whose values and work and thoughts interest me. No way, I say.

Now I feel him headed toward his own research, toward our earlier discussion, and we get there with the help of his jesting self-criticism, meant also to put more bluntly on the record a perception of mine, maybe even a felt criticism of mine with respect to his work: "You don't seem to want to do with Agee what I may do with Gandhi, and did with Luther: try to figure out what was more or less likely to have happened in someone's life, and then say it—with the knowledge on your part, and [on that of] your readers, that we're not talking about letters or diaries or conversations recalled by someone, but that it's someone today doing the best he can with what *is* available." I think and think, let his words sink in. I take a stab: I say yes, maybe so. But then I try to embrace what I've hitherto kept at arm's length. I use the word *documentary*, and say that in the 1930s that word had a common usage among certain photographers and filmmakers, including Agee's friend Walker Evans. Perhaps, I suggest, Agee, were he to be "sent back" here by his Maker, might oblige us with that word—might allow Erikson's search for a first-hand *documentary* exposure to Indians here, and now Indians abroad, in the hope that what he saw and heard and then described would, in sum, be informative.

He likes the word *documentary*. I've seen him savor English words before, he who spoke German as his native language for over two decades, and who learned to speak such excellent English and write a beautifully flowing, even graceful and spirited English prose. He looks the word up in his much-used Oxford dictionary. I tell him that a dictionary "doesn't always help." Quickly he replies, "What does?" I'm slow in replying: "A word can gradually emerge in its meaning—can fill a gap." "What gap?" We're on to an extended discussion now, one that anticipates by a long three decades these lectures, this book. We speak, especially, about "seeing for oneself," as he keeps putting it—the importance of "making a record that you the writer can believe, before you ask someone else to believe it." I remember that way of saying it, will keep going back to those words, will regard them as helpful, as greatly "clarifying" (a word Erik loved to use): the documentary tradition as a continually developing "record" that is made in so many ways, with different voices and visions, intents and concerns, and with each contributor, finally, needing to meet a personal test, the hurdle of *you*, the would-be narrator, trying to ascertain what you truly believe *is*, though needing to do so with an awareness of the confines of your particular capability—that is, of your warts and wants, your various limits, and, too, the limits imposed upon you by the world around you, the time allotted you (and the historical time fate has given you) for your life to unfold.

When Erikson returned from that voyage to India, he was full of new energy, excited by what he'd been told, what he'd witnessed. He loved being back in his Widener study, but as often happens to us when we have gone on a long and important and memorable journey, he was finding it hard to "settle down." He was full of memories of what he'd experienced; he was trying to do justice to those memories; and he was recounting them, fitting them into a narrative, one the rest of us would soon read; he was speaking of his "colleagues," now not professors in a big-shot university, but rather hitherto (for him) nameless, faceless fellow human beings who would soon become (for us readers) developed characters with something to put on "record." He was, indeed, doing documentary work.

And so it goes, then—doing documentary work is a journey, and is a little more, too, a passage across boundaries (disciplines, occupational constraints, definitions, conventions all too influentially closed for traffic), a passage that can become a quest, even a pilgrimage, a movement toward the sacred truth enshrined not only on tablets of stone, but in the living hearts of those others whom we can hear, see, and get to understand. Thereby, we hope to be confirmed in our own humanity—the creature on this earth whose very nature it is to make just that kind of connection with others during the brief stay we are permitted here.

four

❧❧❧

A Range of Documentary Inquiry

I would like to return to the efforts of Dorothea Lange and her husband, Paul Taylor, for the larger questions their explorative studies pose with respect to documentary work. Lange, especially, was a feisty soul, determined to establish the camera as a means of systematic social, cultural, and psychological investigation; so in a sense, her photographs lend themselves to a kind of argument, even as they can be regarded with a skepticism that shadows all photography meant to render the world's reality.

I would also like to glimpse a range of documentary work—descriptions of studies of particular places—and, lastly, to offer a course of sorts: a list of books, photographic work, and films that, in their sum give the reader plenty, I hope, to ponder about this ever so concrete yet ironically elusive tradition of documentary inquiry.

Dorothea Lange and Documentary Argument

Back, then, to Dorothea Lange. One of Lange's best-known photographs of the Depression era was taken in late 1932 and is known to a wide public as "White Angel Bread Line" (Fig. 14). The photograph can be regarded as the product of mere chance; no grant was made to the photographer, no project had sponsored a documentary effort so that the poor, the hungry of San Francisco might be caught visually, their misery thus made the property of countless other Americans. Rather, Lange found herself (maybe in a couple of senses of the expression) taking photographs of people on a bread line near her studio—one established by a wealthy San Franciscan woman known as the "White Angel." Lange left the confines of the studio for the street, left a controlled situation (and a reliable job) for the potential chaos of a crowd of the indigent. She had no clear idea at the time what she meant to do "out there," her camera all too embarrassingly in her hands. Worried by the possibility of resentment, if not violence (look at that one, snapping away at us!), she asked her brother to come along. But the unhappy people standing there, waiting for a handout, waiting for bread, waiting for a moment's kindness, apparently had other things on their minds than the wish to put rage and envy and suspicion into words or action.

Who will ever know what, if anything, crossed the minds of those bewildered souls at that moment when, arguably, a significant career of documentary photography—one meant to collar the world with respect to just such moments in the life of mankind—had its onset? The central figure seems lost in another world, that unshaven old man with the tattered hat, his arms not so much holding as enveloping a tin cup. The light hits the fedora's felt brow, not the shrunken face. Other hats, a couple of caps such as one sees so often among English and Irish working men, seem to announce themselves: we are all that is left; the men who wear us have disappeared, have

Figure 14

become lost. Hats queued for an anonymous lady's achievement of visual grace. Bodies folded into the shadows of winter coats. At least the bodies have them, have enough clothing to stave off the pain of exposure. Nevertheless, these are exposed individuals, vulnerable, needy, acquiescent recipients of charity. And we, by looking, are asked to leave our own "studios" for a moment, consider what such scenes were doing not only to those men but to others, warm and well-fed, and to this country as well.

Dorothea Lange has spoken of her complex response to that moment, the first in a long succession of situations that she would end up entering more and more frequently: a participant by proxy for so many of us, the viewers of her pictures. Her words reveal, yet again, the mystery of art and of psychological motivation alike:

> I can only say I knew I was looking at something. You know there are moments such as these when time stands still and all you do is hold your breath and hope it will wait for you. And you just hope you will have enough time to get it organized in a fraction of a second on that tiny piece of sensitive film. Sometimes you have an inner sense that you have encompassed the things generally. You know then that you are not taking anything away from anyone: their privacy, their dignity, their wholeness.

Lange was, of course, looking back, hoping for an acknowledgment, from herself, of the "dignity" and "wholeness" of an effort. Put differently, she was trying to affirm the worth of a particular working life. Not all photographers, journalists, or writers of factual pieces wish to speculate on the moral significance of their various exertions. In any event, documentary writing and photography are essentially a response of the mind and heart to a given state of affairs; after a certain point, one has to go along with one's limitations and transparent or potential flaws in the hope that some redeeming intelligence and aesthetic competence will assert itself. In late 1932 and 1933 Dorothea Lange was mentioning "pictures of people" that she had taken. In 1934 she was referring to "photographs of people." They were not the "people" she had hitherto spent time with, a group of wholly privileged men and women who had taken themselves to a studio. They were, increasingly, those she had seen in the course of walking, driving, looking here and there in the West of California, Utah, Nevada.

She had even come across a motto, a statement that got to the heart of what she wanted to be about: "The contemplation of things as they are, without substitution or imposture, without error or confusion, is in itself a nobler thing than a whole harvest of invention." Francis Bacon wrote these words centuries ago. Lange kept them posted on her darkroom door. For a photographer they amount to a more controversial message, it can be argued (it *has* been argued), than a quick pietistic reading might suggest. The picture offers the "contemplation" of a "thereness" that existentialist philosophers such as Heidegger or Marcel make so much of—and yet, inevitably, a degree of "invention" takes place. Who is imposing (with how much claim to "truth," with how much "substitution" or "imposture") on what particular human scene, or on what aspect of the earth's landscape? This question began occurring to Dorothea Lange just as she embarked on a career as a documentary photographer, and the asking, obviously, was a measure of a particular person's sensitivity and thoughtfulness.

In the summer of 1934 Lange met Paul Taylor, the man who would soon become her second husband, and whose interests, energies, and concerns would connect powerfully with her artistic life. One has a hard time imagining Dorothea Lange's career without the arrival in her life of Taylor, even as her work gave an enormous lift to his aspirations as a socially minded economist, a morally alert citizen alive and active during one of the more confusing, if not tragic, decades of American history. Paul Taylor came to California from Iowa. He had studied at the University of Wisconsin and had become, early on, a committed populist. He became interested in the problems of Mexican migrant workers during the 1920s, well before the Great Depression, well before white families from the drought-struck Midwest would, in their hard if not desperate travels, add a new dimension to what formally gets called the question of migratory labor.

In Mexico, Taylor observed the world left behind by so many agricultural workers: the wretched poverty, the mix of Indian and Spanish culture, the necessary but reluctant departure (in the face of virtual starvation) north to California, Arizona, Texas, and points beyond. As he amassed his statistics and did his interviews, he found himself wanting to record what he saw. He took snapshots, lots of them. He was trying to capture evidence rather than take "interesting" pictures. He was a social scientist with a strong conscience, not quite the same sort of person as a photographer anxious to respond artistically, dramatically to a given scene. An article of Taylor's on the migrant labor problem of the American Southwest was published in *Survey Graphic* (1931), and the editor, Paul Kellogg, commissioned Ansel Adams to take some photographs to accompany the text. Kellogg had previously commissioned Lewis Hine for the same purpose: to show readers the visual referents of the words, numbers, and percentages on a magazine's paper. But so-called documentary photography was not known as such until the mid-1930s. And many claim that Dorothea Lange, in her work with Paul Taylor, which began in 1934 and 1935, was the first documentary photographer.

What was she trying to do? And Taylor—what exactly were his purposes? When my wife and I talked with him (he was well over eighty) in the Berkeley home he had shared for so long with Dorothea Lange, he could still remember the response of any number of his fellow social scientists to the collaborative work he did with his second wife. Photographs are "irrelevant," he was told, or, worse, "subjective," even "inflammatory." The point should be dispassionate, detached analysis, not polemical statement or propaganda. Nor would Dorothea Lange be allowed to pursue her intellectual and moral instincts, her particular inclinations as an artist, without a similar kind of reaction from certain colleagues who objected to what they saw as art demeaned, art as an instrument of indoctrination, of partisan ideological persuasion. In his fine, extremely helpful biography *Dorothea Lange: A Photographer's Life* (1978), Milton Meltzer does well to quote in full the written remarks of Willard Van Dyke, inspired by a small number (five) of Lange's photographs, all published in *Camera Craft* (1934). Here is Van Dyke's early, precise, wonderfully suggestive, insistently open-minded attempt at a definition of what Lange's career would be all about—and no one has said it better:

Dorothea Lange has turned to the people of the American scene with the intention of making an adequate photographic record of them. These people are in the midst of great changes—contemporary problems are reflected on their faces, a tremendous drama is unfolding before them, and Dorothea Lange is photographing it through them.

She sees the final criticism of her work in the final reaction to it of some person who might view it fifty years from now. It is her hope that such a person would see in her work a record of the people of her time, a record valid of the day and place wherein made, although necessarily incomplete in the sense of the entire contemporary movement.

One of the factors making for this incompleteness is the camera itself. It must make its record out of context, taking the individuals or incidents photographed as climaxes rather than continuity. In approaching the subject or situation immediately before her she makes no attempt at a personal interpretation of the individual or situation. Neither does she encompass her work with in the bounds of a political or economic thesis. She believes or depends more on a certain quality of awareness within herself. This awareness although perhaps inarticulate through herself (in words) is apparent in her adherence and approach to certain subject matter. She is not preoccupied with the philosophy behind the present conflict, she is making a record of it through the faces of the individuals most sensitive to it or most concerned in it. Her treatment of this type of human subject shows her in turn sensitive to and sympathetic to the uncertainty and unrest apparent at the present time.

Naturally the range of human emotions which Dorothea Lange now photographs are not those which a sitter expects in a portrait studio. Sixteen years as a portrait photographer have shown her that the subject of a commission rarely sees himself as the camera does, even at its best, and is unlikely to be convinced of the objective truthfulness of the camera. Sitters mistake the lens for a mirror wherein they are wont to see themselves colored by the glamour of their romantic ideas. Of course, in order to please patrons, one must make concessions and this limitation led Dorothea Lange to photographing people with or without their knowledge, outside the studio.

Most photographers under similar circumstances would have turned to photographing other subject material, or away from photography entirely, but Miss Lange's real interest is in human beings and her urge to photograph is aroused only when values are concerned.

For equipment she uses two cameras. On any given trip she takes one or the other of these with her, never both. One of these is a 3¼ x 4¼ Graflex equipped with a 7½ inch focal length anastigmat lens and magazine film holders, the other a Rolleiflex which she considers to have a general advantage in that it is less obtrusive and can be operated at closer quarters. The latter, of course, by virtue of the smallness of the film does not permit of as great a degree of enlargement. She also uses a Weston exposure meter to test the general light conditions once or twice during the expedition.

Miss Lange's work is motivated by no preconceived photographic aesthetic. Her attitude bears a significant analogy to the sensitized plate of the camera itself. For her, making a shot is an adventure that begins with no planned itinerary. She feels that setting out with a preconceived idea of what she wants to photograph actually minimizes her chance for success. Her method is to eradicate from her mind before she starts, all ideas which she might hold regarding the situation—her mind like an unexposed film.

In an old Ford she drives to a place most likely to yield subjects consistent with her general sympathies. Unlike the newspaper reporter, she has no news or editorial policies to direct her movements; it is only her deeply personal sympathies for the unfortunate, the downtrodden, the misfits, among her contemporaries that provide the impetus for her expedition. She may park her car at the waterfront during a strike, perhaps at a meeting of unemployed, by sleepers in the city square, at transient shelters,—breadlines, parades, or demonstrations. Here she waits with her camera open and unconcealed, her mind ready.

*   *   *

Perhaps we can arrive at a better evaluation of her record in terms of a future observer than as contemporary critics. We ourselves are too poignantly involved in the turmoil of present life. Much of it is stupid, confused, violent, some little of it is significant, all of it is of the most immediate concern to everyone living today—we have no time for the records, ourselves living and dying in the recording.

We can assume the role of that future critic by looking back to the work of Matthew Brady, who in the dawn of photography made a heroic record of another crisis of American life. Brady and Lange have both made significant use of their common medium—they differ mainly in terms of the technical advancement of the medium itself. Lange can photograph the split-seconds of the dynamic surges of the scene about her— Brady, carrying a complete darkroom about with him through the northern battlefields of the Civil War, sensitizing his own plates before each shot, making twenty-minute exposures, had to wait for the ample lulls between engagements. The implications of his record are retrospective, the scene after the battle, the dead that were once living, the ruins that were once forts, faces still and relaxed. Both Lange and Brady share the passionate desire to show posterity the mixture of futility and hope, of heroism and stupidity, greatness and banality that are the concomitants of man's struggle forward....

It is now over sixty years since those words were written. What kind of record did Dorothea Lange give us? How does her work stand up—as art, as a kind of social analysis, as a reflection of certain values, sentiments, beliefs? How correct is Van Dyke when he says that "her subjects became unaware of her presence"? How successfully did she "eradicate from her mind" the various "ideas" Van Dyke mentions? Was that mind really "an unexposed film"? Did she actually, *could* she psychologically, make "no attempt at a personal interpretation" of the given person or predicament she happened to be photographing? Did she, in truth, "act as if she possessed the power to become invisible to those around her"? Could she, in daily point of fact, manage "to completely ignore those who might resent her presence"?

Who will ever know the answers to such questions? Even Dorothea Lange herself, were she with us today, might not be able to give us completely satisfactory replies. But her photographic statements are terribly revealing; they leap at us with their earnest claim of objectivity, their declaration of scrupulous anonymity and reticence, their insistence upon a calculated, controlled distance on the part of the observer. Moreover, they make an interesting distinction between those (largely well-to-do) who come to sit for photographic portraits in a studio and those (largely poor, dispossessed, badly down-and-out) who are presented on the road, on the farm, in the factory, in front of the neighborhood store or school. We see the narcissism, the self-centeredness and vanity of the former and the pronounced helplessness of the latter, with its implication of a cleansing virtue. Are hobos and tramps, not to mention newly up-rooted farmers or suddenly jobless working-class people, without their own kind of what Van Dyke refers to as "romantic ideas"?

The idea of "objective" observation remains a dubious one. We still could send an Agee or a Walker Evans (if only persons of their caliber were available for the project!) down South, or, for that matter, into various Northern spots, and expect a report no less dismaying, and heartbreaking than *Let Us Now Praise Famous Men*. But such a book was the product of more than two individuals. Agee and Evans were sent by a magazine—one not all that likely, even then, to take a great interest in American poverty. They were sent in a national climate of urgency and despair. They went as citizens of that nation. Those who received them were fellow citizens. All of which is to say that in the 1930s the lucky few were no less caught up in the Great Depression than the "famous men" (and women) who ended up familiar to many of us *there*, in those pictures, and *there*, in a different way, through the magical mediation of a writer's words.

Not even at the height of Lyndon Johnson's "war on poverty," however, did the federal government acknowledge a need for spon-soring the kind of photographic expeditions Roy Stryker subsidized under the auspices of the Farm Security Administration. For one thing, of course, the television networks had arrived: "Christmas in Appalachia," for instance, a documentary of the early 1960s, set a lot of hearts beating faster with those well-known liberal virtues of empathy, compassion, concern, social responsibility, and political ac-tivism. Moreover, speaking of liberalism, the government of the 1960s had, as a kind of social or political capital, so to speak, the consensus that the New Deal under Roosevelt (with Stryker as one among many participants) had aimed to create. It was by no means taken for granted during the years 1934–39, despite two strong Democratic electoral victories, that a major part of the American electorate was prepared to raise its fists with indignation, or shed tears of sympathy, if told of the hard and mean circumstances that many other American citizens had to accept as an inevitable, fixed lot. The so-called FSA photographs, well known to us—indeed, an ironic fixture of a well-to-do sensibility—were commissioned almost surreptitiously, by a man who was worried that the taxpayer's dollar might have better or, certainly, more conventional uses. But Stryker also worried that without the vivid, wide-ranging observations of the FSA documentary photographers, the New Deal reforms would be a bit more vulnerable, likelier victims of voter apathy, boredom, incredulity.

That last word had best be examined in connection with Lange's work of the 1930s, the body of photographs for which she is best known. Their power, their arresting visual presence, commanded what Roy Stryker wanted: a growing consciousness of a kind of life that had hitherto, for many, been safely out of sight, and, moreover, beyond imagining. In the 1960s, a television program here, or an article or book there, had a lot to stand upon—a previous decade's political struggles, among them the artistic ones. Not all photographers, of course (and not necessarily out of selfishness or heartless indifference), liked the idea of their colleagues spending time and federal money on a constant search for only one side of American life, the "human erosion" that Dorothea Lange and Paul Taylor mention in *An American Exodus*.

Lange and Taylor's intentions were unmistakably on the table. They show the waste, the cheapness and meanness of life in the South, in the Central states, in the West. They offer a predominantly visual kind of social geography. The titles of the sections in *An American Exodus* go from east to west, following the exodus but also the historical referents of the Old South: Plantation under the Machine; Mid-Continent; Plains; Dirt Bowl; and finally, Lost West.

We wince now, aware that there have clearly been other Wests, because the kin of the individuals whom Dorothea Lange portrays, once white "Okies," no doubt now live in Southern California quite comfortably. Maybe (there is a good chance) such individuals have strong conservative convictions and want no part of any scheme to awaken, yet again, a concern for any "human erosion" that may be taking place (that some photographer might record taking place) in, say, the barrios of Los Angeles, or among the migrant workers of the Imperial Valley. What I have heard, in California and elsewhere, from the descendants of the kinds of people Lange photographed in the "Plains" and the "Dirt Bowl" goes like this: leave us alone; stop looking for trouble; stop playing with emotions such as sentimentality and pity; stop being a predator anxious to find and use "scenes" for political purposes.

Of course, to go back in time, nineteenth-century England's romantic poets, especially Wordsworth, worried themselves (and their readers) constantly about the predatory nature of the writer, even the appreciatively pastoral poet. Nature has its own integrity, Wordsworth and Tennyson insisted, and ought not to be the subject of violating inquiry, an effort that immediately changes what is being regarded; that is, turns the truth of God's world into mere words, however well-assembled. Not that Wordsworth or Tennyson were inclined to stop writing. They may have been self-critical enough to declare themselves inevitably corrupt, no more successful at escaping Victorian capitalism and colonialism than the child laborers in Birmingham and Manchester. They may have had their strongly visionary moments—the God of undefiled Nature calling for atonement, restraint, and the acknowledgment of heinous, accumulated errors. But these writers were sinful human beings rather than souls nearing Purgatorio, or far enough along to be on the verge of witnessing Beatrice. So they kept on writing, committing their small, exemplary thievery. With smoke defiling the sky and the land, with bodies chained by the many thousands to sweatshops, surely no one in God's scheme of things would mind a nature poem or two, a small, well-intentioned intrusion: the writer's greed feeding off something meant to be pure, untouched.

When Susan Sontag, in *On Photography* (1977), uses words such as "aggression," "imperial," and "capture"; when she talks about photography as a "tool of power"; when she declares that photographs enable people to take "possession" of the past, of space, of experiences, she is echoing a Victorian scrupulosity that was, of course, inadequate. In whose name, in what name, are her moral misgivings, and outright condemnations handed down? She worries about "consciousness in its inquisitive mood," and tells us that the camera facilitates such a psychological process. No doubt cameras do enable observers to grasp, snap, and then hold on tight and keep: slides can be stored, filed, trotted out occasionally, and put back in safekeeping, ornaments of the sighted bourgeoisie. But we are given no comparisons, no connections, no effort to put in perspective what has been said about a particular artistic and social medium of expression—an especially interesting absence in a writer whose ideological affinities are clearly historical in nature. Writers can be charged with every sin Sontag calls upon in the course of her sharp look at photographers and their work. Writers are full of the lusts she keeps referring to, the cannibalistic desire to absorb the world, to make it the property of a given sensibility, then offer it back, shaped in accordance with the requirements of the man or woman whose pen and computer, like the buttons and meters of a camera, are agents of a will.

As for "aggression," it is a part of everyone's life, certainly including writers'. Sarcasm, satire, parody, the meanness and nastiness of the literary world are much more than a match for the photographer's sallies upon man, nature, society. Sontag worries that we have become sated by images; meanwhile, books by the thousand pour upon us every year—billions and billions of words, all of them meant to seize control of our consciousness, direct our thoughts, and shape our imaginative life, if not usurp the authority of our consciences. In that last regard (the way we look to others, utter strangers, for elementary ideas of right and wrong), my own wordy profession, so sure and full of itself, so much a part of the literary sensibility and now, alas, making serious and wrong-headed inroads upon the realm of history, is a major culprit. These days psycho-analysts are all too heeded; their authority is tiresome, expansionary, and, not least, wordy. It was Jung, no stranger to words, who pointed out that dreams are predominantly, often exclusively, pictures—the mind's evening camera at work, flashing on the cerebral screen those various images a given life has collected. Yet, we can take those pictures and turn them into a spoken narrative. Some neurophy-siologists speculate that immediately upon rising we convert these tableaux into verbal accounts for ourselves ("Last night I dreamed that . . ."), or later, for others ("Doctor, I had a dream, and in it . . ."). Why such a conversion? One of my psychoanalytic supervisors, Eliz-abeth Zetzel, a student also of the "fine arts," a collector of paintings and long interested in photography, once pointed out to a group of us that we were constantly taking the visual experiences of others or ourselves and turning them into "verbal abstractions." She called our deeds, interestingly enough, "a triumph of one medium over an-other." Her military imagery converges, one has to think, with Son-tag's: a paradox showing the helplessness of the visual, for all its colonialist aspirations.

A Hopi youth, a young woman of fourteen, once gave me a lecture on the camera that Susan Sontag would have enjoyed, but only so much:

We don't need cameras here; we have enough trouble controlling our eyes! I waste my time looking and not seeing. If a camera helped us to see, we would be better off—but it would not be *us, seeing*. A camera distracts you. It makes you less of a person. Words are even worse; they make birds fly away, and they make us dizzy with noise. Who can pay attention to the world while someone chatters? The books of the Anglos are as noisy as their planes overhead. My mother says that the books fill up our head with words, and take over our eyes, too. We end up seeing what the words told us about. We *stop* seeing; the noise of the words takes over. I have a cousin who is a New Hopi; he went to a BIA school, and lived with the Anglos in Albuquerque. He came back to us and said that he doesn't look at the mesa anymore. He doesn't watch the clouds, see them meeting, leaving each other, doing a dance for us. He *thinks* about them; he talks to himself about them. He wishes his head could be quiet, the way it used to be. Stick with the Anglos, and you have a noisy head!

But apart from photographers and their sensibilities, there is the matter not only of what a photographer chooses to heed, but what is, in fact, there to be seen. And one does also wonder about the America that Lange herself approached. Which aspects of it are *not* familiar to us today—"eroded" from our sense of how it went back then precisely because of the persuasive strength of certain photographers, not to mention a particular social and political thinking that we bring to bear as we look at those pictures? To ask in another way, what did Dorothea Lange see but *not* photograph? What did she photograph that we don't get to see—pictures unused, pictures not well-known? What point of view was Lange proposing, what narrative argument was she trying to construct and sustain, picture by picture, as she took and then assembled her many photographs? As a result, what is overlooked in this apparently unsparing documentary effort?

The consequences of historical irony or contradiction can bear down on anyone's work, however bravely and honorably done. Lange and Taylor were investigators in a remarkable tradition nurtured at the University of North Carolina at Chapel Hill during the 1920s and 1930s. It is no accident that Rupert Vance is quoted several times in *An American Exodus*. Vance and Howard Odum and their colleagues were social scientists who had no infatuation with jargon; they favored clear, pungent prose mobilized for the purposes of direct, careful observation, with theoretical speculation kept under watchful tether; and, not least, they had every interest in reaching a broad public, readers of general magazines and newspapers, in the hope that obvious inequities, not to mention injustices, would be addressed. Put differently, the North Carolina social scientists were unashamedly subjective and announced one or another moral position without hesitation. They abandoned even the pretense of being "value-free"; and they never tried for a language that announced neutrality or emphasized the secret, cabalistic, guarded world of the academy.

The black people who figure in *An American Exodus* are extremely hard-pressed men and women, and their misery is no fictive matter, no mirage conjured up by a camera at the beck and call of a Washington bureaucrat anxious to stay on the federal payroll. The same goes for the Oklahoma and Texas farm and small-town people whom Lange caught in all their complex relationship to the midwestern land, never a completely reliable provider due to the unpredictability of the weather. In the best of her pictures, individuals appear harassed, yet determined; humbled, yet proud; uncertain, yet quite clear about their misfortunes and about what (hope against hope) must happen to forestall a complete disaster. In other words, life's contradictions and inconsistencies have a way of demanding their due, no matter the particular, honorable intent of an observer who was quite properly horrified at the sight of the human loss, at the sight of a community's decline ("erosion"), and who was anxious to portray such a development so that others would know and, as citizens, be inclined to act.

Nevertheless, a "record" is commonly less clear-cut than some of us observers might wish. The best tribute a victim can obtain from an outsider who comes, watches or listens, and then abruptly leaves is some acknowledgment of the kind of strain implied in the edited remarks of a Delta farm hand—a strain connected to negotiating an exceedingly difficult *apologia*, it can be called:

> We want help. We need a lot of help. But we don't want to be looked down on, and called a new bunch of names, to replace the old ones. I'd rather be someone's son-of-a-bitch, than someone's beaten-down goner, about to disappear from the face of the earth! I'd rather be neither; I'd rather be myself, only better off. How do you get better off? And when you are better off, how do you get to be "yourself," and no copycat of everyone else?

Not a bad kind of existentialist questioning. Not a bad kind of human observation and self-scrutiny. Not a bad mandate for the rest of us to remember the divergent aspects of subjectivity and objectivity alike as we compile our various "records," state our "conclusions." I am not arguing that Lange failed in that regard. I rather suspect that many who have had her level of moral earnestness have, in fact, succeeded, though not necessarily because of (and often in spite of) the presence of that particular quality of mind and heart. Certainly *An American Exodus* is not only a tale of woe. Some of the photographs show desolation; show a collapsing agricultural order; show perplexity or a contained but unmistakable resentment. But even those black-and-white representations of human reality turn out to be—just that: inescapably ambiguous, in keeping with the strange contradictions of this life. For example: those Texas "displaced ten-

Figure 15

ant farmers" seen here in a cropped version, so well-known to us through the Lange photographs (Fig. 15). They are fixed in time, of course: June, 1937—down to the day of the week, Sunday morning. The oldest is thirty-three, we are told. They are native Americans, we are also told, and white, we don't have to be told, rather than with skin that belongs to other "Native Americans." Not one of them, we read, is "able to vote because of Texas poll tax." They are "all on WPA." Each supports "an average of four persons on $22.80 a month." The message is clear: this quintet of white Anglo-Saxon Americans isn't doing well at all. Not only are they economically in trouble; they aren't even exercising their rights as citizens. And they are only the *evidently* harmed; their wives and children, out of sight but no doubt near at hand, who are doing just as badly.

In case we hope to get nearer the spirit of an occasion, Lange and Taylor supply words, and they amount to five questions—presumably to balance the five standing men. "Where we gonna go?" "How we gonna get there?" "What we gonna do?" "Who us gonna fight?" "If we fight, who we gonna whup?" We didn't know, needless to say, who asked what, and in which context, under what conversational auspices. We don't know whether the farmers volunteered anything on their own or whether they were asked questions that in turn prompted questions of their own. But the quotation marks tell us that they said those words, and when they are added up, so to speak—placed one underneath the other—they amount to a decidedly quizzical sum: what in hell is going on, and what in hell do we do in order to change it?

Yet the men do not appear especially alarmed or agitated. They aren't lined up, or ready to take on somebody or something *en masse*. They keep their distance from one another. True, there is a heaviness to them, but it is a measure, arguably, of their substance, rather than their collective sadness or despair. The dry, hot winds of America's central states may have ruined and blown away some good and necessary topsoil, creating a "dust bowl," but these men do not appear anything but *there*—stolid, stoic maybe, yet also relaxed in their informality, in their readiness to make do under most circumstances, however rough.

Nor is there a uniformity to their posture or attire. Their hats vary. Their pants do, too. A suit jacket stands out. One pair of hands rests in pockets; another seems to hold onto or work on a hidden object; a third does so with less tautness; two men fold their arms, thereby hiding their hands, yet the faces of those two don't seem especially grim. Nor, to repeat, are the men emaciated. They are solidly built, and they have a lot of strength in them.

Are we frivolous or absurd to regard their questions as "existentialist," as well as pointedly economic or political? Are we indulgent to think of Gauguin's mighty Tahiti triptych, painted just before his attempted suicide (1897), on which one sees three questions asked by the rich and poor alike? Where do we come from? What are we? Where are we going? Ridiculous, one begins to say—the rhetoric of transcendence, as against the concrete agony of a particularly difficult immanence. Yet anyone who has met the individuals to whom such social investigators as Oscar Lewis, Studs Terkel, or Theodore Rosengarten have introduced us in recent years—the very best of oral history—will surely remember the constant recourse to meditative speculation on the part of those impoverished men and women. To be poor, more desperately so even than Lange's five Texans, is still to be human—to connect one's questions about work and politics and the problems of a given region or nation to those personal yet universal questions, the asking of which makes us the particular creatures we are.

No one will ever know all that went through the minds of those five American farmers in the early summer of 1937. We aren't even told whether they just happened to be standing there, or whether they were asked to do so; whether they obliged immediately, or dragged their feet a bit through that Panhandle dust. But in facial appearance, in general manner, in attire, these men resemble the Appalachian yeoman, the so-called mountaineers my wife and I came to know in the 1960s and early 1970s. They too were impecunious, many of them, with small prospects as far as good jobs go. They too asked questions, and in doing so offered a listener, a documentary fieldworker a number of opportunities:

It's true, we don't have much in the way of cash. For me, the sight of a dollar bill is something special. We mostly raise the crops we can, provided the Lord cooperates and sends good weather. And we do our hunting and our fishing. We could move, of course. We could go to a city. My brother went to Dayton, Ohio; and he's sorry as can be. He traded being here, our home, for a welfare check—after losing a job he was hoping to keep.

They came here last year, with cameras. They were television people. They said they wanted to show the whole world how we live, and we thought it would help us out, if they did. They said we should just go about being as we are; but they wouldn't let us be as we are. How could we—with them snapping their little cameras and running their big cameras, and asking us to go here and go there and try to look this way and look the other way? Finally, my oldest boy came to me and said he was tired of all of them, and he was going to leave and stay in the woods, up the hollow, until it was quiet here, and they were all gone.

They left, finally. They kept on trying to get us to say we're in bad shape. They kept on pointing out how we don't have this and we don't have that. They took pictures of us doing everything—well *almost* everything! But, I ask you, what will the people who see the pictures think? They'll think bad of us, I guess—sorry for us. They'll pity us. I'd like to talk with every one of them. I'd like to tell them that we're in trouble, sure; we don't have the easiest life. But we're not the way they want to point us out to be. We're God-fearing people, and we have pride in ourselves, and we're going to meet the Lord with our heads up high, and that's the most important thing in this life. Sure, if we could have a more comfortable life, we wouldn't object! But we're put here for a short stop, and we have to do the best we can, and there's no point in us crying, or in someone else being asked to cry for us, or someone being made to feel better, because they're not us, or being told they've got to help us, fast, because we're so low, low down.

The man who was the head of the television crew, and the newspaper man with him—on the day they left they asked me: what would you want, if you could wish it right now, and the wish could come true? Damned if I didn't draw a blank. The only thing that crossed my mind was something I couldn't say—that they'd leave, real fast. I kept looking down the road, and I couldn't find the answers for them. Then they asked me if there was something I was looking at! I said no, but they got suspicious. Lord, they were suspicious. Lord, they wanted to see everything under the sun and the moon, and then some more! When they were gone, finally, I took a big breath in, and I unbent myself. We all started smiling and we had a good laugh. For a few minutes we looked around: they might still be there, picturing us one more time! But no, they were truly gone! My wife said to me: too bad they didn't get us this time, having some fun for ourselves! But if they'd been about, we wouldn't be the way we are with ourselves when we're alone.

A man who was, who still is, quite poor. A man who has gotten a raw deal out of life: much illness in the family, extreme poverty, even hunger and malnutrition as continual threats. Yet a man whose mental, moral, spiritual life does not deserve to be circumscribed by "socioeconomic indicators," by exclusive reference to "the culture of poverty," or "marginality," or "deprivation," or "disadvantage." He turns out to be thoughtful, keenly observant, graced by a lively sense of humor. He turns out to have a fine sense of his own worth, of his own rights as a human being. He spotted in an instant what others wanted from him, but also what they would deny him: "I knew they want it to be better for us; but they don't really look to see who we are!"

This danger threatens all of us who leave one world, spend time in another one, then return to our original point of departure. None of us armed with cameras and tape recorders, no matter our conviction of empathy and sympathy, can be quite sure that we aren't inadvertently falling into some of the pitfalls rather tactfully but knowingly suggested by that Appalachian yeoman. No account of documentary work should be without some self-scrutiny that responds to the spirit of his remarks—which were not meant, of course, to defend the status quo, or to be ungrateful in the face of proffered help. What aspect of any given reality do we want to comprehend, those of us who make it our work to travel, to enter one community, then another, in the hope of bringing back information? How ought we best state our purposes, hopes, objectives? To expose inequity? To expand a given (sociological, anthropological, legal, economic, and on and on) body of knowledge? To inform one or another kind of reader? To obtain "material" for a particular viewpoint? And, not uncommonly, to further a writing career, a photography career? Moreover, how ought we state what we have seen and heard? To what degree, if at all, should we qualify our observations or conclusions, lest they be misinterpreted or misused?

A black minister in Greenwood, Mississippi told my wife one summer day in 1963 that he'd been hearing more and more about documentary work. He thought it good that such work was being done—except for a risk or two.

I worry about who's doing the "documenting," and what a person has in mind to see—before they even get here to take a look or take a listen! I say to myself: will they "document" our tears, but not our smiles? Will they "document" our rough times, but not show us having a good time, now and then—no matter how poor we be, and how down-and-out it gets for us, and how bad the treatment we receive from Mr. White Man? I know we need outsiders to lend us a hand. The people who run this country won't budge, unless they're pushed, and no one hereabouts who's got dark skin is going to push very long, without getting a bullet through the heart, or being pushed right into the Mississippi River!

But if people come here, and they want to help us, and they try to help us—but they end up thinking of us as only in trouble, and only in pain, and only persecuted—then we'll end up with the world getting the wrong picture about us. We'll end up appearing the way the Klan people want us to appear—as bad off as animals, and all the time whining, like a cat or a dog. The truth is, we've got bad troubles, but we're children of God, and we know how to hold our heads up high, and we're not always slinking around like animals do, and we can pray and we can look ourselves straight in the eye and not be ashamed, and we can sing— oh yes, we can! I told some people who came by last week—they be from New York City and California—that I saw those records in their cars, the jazz and the spirituals: it was all *our* music, and if we can make that music, it's a sign of God smiling on us—amazing Grace! They should "document" that part of us, too, you know.

I'm not sure I did know! I feared I knew otherwise: the awful circumstances that I felt more and more people in distant cities and states ought to be persuaded to comprehend and try to change. But no matter how earnestly one cautions oneself against romantic idealization or inadvertent lapses into a defense of blatant injustice, one doesn't easily avoid the ironies that minister pointed out. Certainly, Dorothea Lange as a documentary observer managed to pay her respects to the minister's message—to a message, one suspects, that her own sharp-witted intelligence insisted upon heeding. The people of her 1930s "dust bowl," her Southern tenant farmers, her migrant American men, women, and children are all indeed in bad straits, are dazed and suffering a great deal. But in picture after picture, they are also able to demonstrate various virtues and strengths: patience, determination, resourcefulness, tenacity, even a touch of wry humor.

True, one is asked to consider, in these photographs and textual comments, the brutishness of a given social order, the low wages, poor working conditions, a fiercely competitive climate, the indifference of certain employers, and the willingness of many sheriffs or policemen to do the bidding of those with money and power, as if "the law" is, in truth, a handmaiden of any town's, any state's bigshots. One is asked, as well, to extend quite openly a large measure of concern for a citizenry caught in a specific crisis: the dislocation of thousands of Americans as a result of that terrible coincidence of bad weather and an especially persistent economic downturn. We are shown, that is, the 1930s in all of their misery. On the other hand, Lange's photographs give us people working; people ready to go far indeed in order to work; children playing; men having a chat; women with not only pain on their faces but character, poise, a sense of purpose, of dignity.

As for the American land, it is clearly injured and ailing, or it is the property of a mere handful who share precious little of their agricultural profits with the harvesters. But throughout *An American Exodus* and all of Lange's work from the 1930s, indeed all of her work in underdeveloped countries, one sees a vitality in people, a richness and promise in the artifacts pictured, in the countryside singled out for the magazine buyer's or the book buyer's attention. Even those extremely well-known FSA photographs of hers, linked for good reason in our consciousness with the social sorrow of America's Great Depression, lend themselves to other, less sociological or polemically political interpretations.

Two strong photographs, known as "Ex-slave, Alabama," taken in 1937 (Fig. 16), and "Woman of the Plains," taken in 1938 (Fig. 17), do not exactly show destroyed human beings. On the contrary, the elderly black woman appears as tough as can be. Her hands hold on to a stick rather well. Her chin is notably strong. Her eyes are intent on taking in what the world offers. Her clothes are simple, neatly worn. The white cloth on her head obviously dominates the picture, if not her—a solid covering, a swath of light, a reminder of old-fashioned country ways among the South's black women, and, yes, a reminder that this woman wants to protect part of her face and hair from dust and dirt: "I put on a bandanna during the week so there will be less trouble on Sunday making myself respectable for church!" That explanation, offered to my wife by an Alabama

Figure 16

black woman, the granddaughter of slaves, twenty-five years after Dorothea Lange's journey through the same state, may offer a possible clue to the way we outsiders ought to think of such people— men and women who are hard-pressed, unquestionably, and in def-

Figure 17

inite need of many things, but with a cultural tradition to defend, with ideas, ideals of their very own to uphold, with strengths and assets of personality and family to call upon.

Nor is Lange's aesthetic response to such a woman without interest. The Alabama ex-slave is given to us as, arguably and ironically, a study of black and white, darkness and light. An ordinary bandanna becomes a cloth of grace, a luminous presence telling us that here is a long life, lived under duress, to be sure, but lived honorably. The last thing we are asked to offer is pity—a self-important emotion that the supposedly strong can use to take a slap at the supposedly weak, often enough with absurd and ironic consequences:

> I look at the Mister and the Missus, he drunk so much of the time, and her pretending to be helpless, and wanting to kill her own husband— you can tell by her look, and she told me so once—and I don't think it's so bad being their maid. They both told me last year that I'm the strongest one in the house, and I said no, to be polite, but I'm not sure the answer isn't yes!

Just another ever so tactful, knowing, thoughtful, compassionate, and sensitive "servant." Just another Alabama black woman, a great-granddaughter of slaves, and no fashion plate, no high school graduate even. Just what her important, well-educated, rich bosses say she is, just what William Faulkner described her kind as: resourceful and enduring.

And the "woman of the plains," without question an inhabitant of the lower socioeconomic orders, 1930s vintage: how is she presented to us? A big woman. Not fat, but sturdy and long-legged. A distinct neck. Arms folded with a mixture of strength and agile but unaffected poise. The nose is far from weak. The hair is simply there—not put up, not arranged with any affectation, but not without a certain compact, neat quality. There is a depth to the eyes.

Figure 18

The forehead acts as a helping visor of sorts. The mouth is shut, but not with thin-lipped anger. The lower legs are plain: no effort to assert what Madison Avenue has called "femininity," a notion tied to a given period of time, to a certain class and level of "culture." The shoes reinforce a particular woman's practical appearance; again, there are no preposterous, self-demeaning, plaintively painful "spikes" and tight-fitted, shiny leather to negotiate, a burden that makes each step an obliging surrender as well as a curse. As for the plain dress, it is finely unpretentious, powerfully and commandingly blessed by a uniformity of light. One has to work hard indeed to find this robust, angular, unbowed, straightforward, even elegantly linear woman worthy of our transient, potentially shallow, and affected sighs of condolence.

As for the "Plantation Owner and his Field Hands" (see Fig. 18), who lived in the Mississippi Delta and were captured by Lange in an unnerving picture in 1936, one hesitates to call that scene anything but emblematic of the old, rural South: Coke and suspenders and Panama hat and country store and Mississippi license plate, with the big man, white man, out front, foot on the car, and the humble black "property" behind him—a frightened, silent mainstay. The picture was cropped for Archibald MacLeish's *Land of the Free*, a documentary narrative of that decade, meant to remind a nation beleaguered by unemployment and unremitting poverty what its purposes were supposed to be: "all men created equal," under a "government of the people, by the people, for the people." But what do we know, really, about this particular plantation owner's moral life, his character? If the same man were standing in the same position near a car whose license plate read MASS rather than MISS, what would we be inclined to think of him? Is it the presence of blacks that decides for us? If we saw that white man and five other white men, or, for that matter, five black men or Indians or Chicanos, in a northern or western setting, and were told that somehow the older man had helped the others out, would we find the picture credible?

There is a distinct possibility that our "plantation owner" was a grumpy, mean-spirited, arrogant racist; that he patronized, intimidated, maybe even terrorized, and certainly exploited his "field hands"; that the blacks to his rear had put up with a lifetime of nasty remarks, brazen insults, peremptory orders, and small, small paychecks. Perhaps they were living in a barter economy, their hard work, from sunup to sundown, not to mention their apparently unquestioning obedience, given in exchange for some food and a dismal kind of housing, namely, shacks with no electricity and no adequate sanitation. Still, there are other possibilities, and they require mention, not as apologies for segregation or the class structure of the plantation South, and not in some effort to spin a yarn of rural sweetness and light, as against the supposed coldness and anonymity of Yankee, urban life. But one can be white, old, fat, and wrinkled, with glasses and semi-tropical hat and suspenders, and be rather personal, if not friendly and decent, with black men who are by no means receiving their due but are not necessarily much worse-off than others like them, *today*, in the South and the North, who are ordered around and robbed and cheated and even killed by men who, in my experience, have been young, thin, without glasses, dis-inclined to hats of any kind—and black. I refer, alas, to crew leaders who lead across this country's land thousands of migrant workers or field hands, a population that interested Lange very much. Life in the rural South is more complicated than some of us care to admit; our own attitudes can require very careful sifting and sorting.

Dorothea Lange, in a sense, defied the FSA. Her New Deal em-ployers, for the best of reasons, wanted her help in educating a nation, in teaching its citizen-voters what was wrong, sorely wrong, with an economy by showing them how much wretchedness had suddenly come upon an advanced industrial nation. Yet her Amer-ican people, her American land, her barns and stores and road scenes attest to a vitality, a perseverance, a willfulness of purpose. One even finds beauty in all that injury and perplexity, in strong, handsome faces, vigorous bodies, and attractive buildings, and a grace and gran-deur in the countryside, even in its ailing parts. An artist has asserted herself, it can be said, no matter how strong her interest in polemical statement, in argumentative portrayal. In her later, international work, the same tension, of course, persists: Lange as the pained observer, herself reasonably well-off, yet terribly cognizant of, re-sponsive to the demeaning situation of so many others, versus Lange as the visual person, the one whose sensibilities are extremely broad and whose representational faculties are awake, energetic, stubborn, and refined. In Ireland, in Nepal, in Egypt, and in Korea, Lange saw extreme poverty. She also saw objects to admire, scenes to record in all their striking charm or symmetry: the faces of men, women, and children whose dignity, whose inviting loveliness simply could not be denied, overlooked, or put under wraps in the interests of a strictly propagandistic or one-dimensional evocation of the miserable side of things.

Nor is it altogether forcing matters in connection with Lange's work to think back to William Carlos Williams and Walt Whitman, even to those decidedly aristocratic, wonderfully astute observers of America, Alexis de Tocqueville and Henry James. The last of these may have summarized it all—what any of us who try to do documentary studies can only hope to do with a small quota of his brilliantly penetrating success: "the manners, the manners," his terse mandate of what must be seen, what must be set down for others to see. Whitman was more celebratory, less dispassionate. Williams was a fiery enthusiast, a mordant critic if not a vigorous combatant. The French visitor de Tocqueville was less literary than James, more systematic in his elegant nineteenth-century prophesy not only of America's coming history, but of a new division of intellectual activity—the so-called social sciences. Lange reveals elements of all those observers in her work. In the Jamesian tradition, she can concentrate on the distinctive appearance of a woman's neck, on the complementary splendor of two shoes, on the extended power of a particular barn's sloping roof. She can also roam America, follow its various roads, large and small, and marvel at the variety and robustness of our people in the tradition of Whitman: a gentle and loving but also tough, willful, and resourceful traveler, determined to return home with productive, inspiring memories. She can shake her fists as W. C. Williams used to do at the stupidity of so many, the needless injuries of people who deserve better; and, like him, she can summon a kind of redemptive, celebratory music in response to what she has seen others experience and, through them, experienced herself. She can even be the careful analytic student de Tocqueville was, giving us those hands, those tools, those clothes, those signs;

in sum, those physical aspects of existence that tell us so much about a given people's aspirations and difficulties.

Dorothea Lange was, finally, yet another restless visionary artist. Again and again she was anxious to be a moral witness; she used photographs to make the point that novelists and poets and painters and sculptors all keep trying to make: I am here; I hear and see; I will take what my senses offer my brain and try to offer others something that will inform them, startle them, move them to awe and wonder, entertain them and rescue them from banality, from the dreary silliness inevitably pressed upon us by the world. She failed at times; failed personally, as she herself acknowledged, when she discussed the many leaves of absence from her home, from her young children; failed artistically, when she lapsed into the photographer's version of coyness, rhetorical overstatement, and repetitive posturing. But she succeeded repeatedly—gave us our rock-bottom selves: a clear and full-bodied and trenchant portrait of any number of this earth's twentieth-century people.

Instances

Others have also succeeded, have accomplished particular documentary projects in a way that brings the rest of us closer to places, people, situations, events. A city, a state, an aspect of human experience, human expression, a kind of life, a person's story (or that of a community)—such are the various excitants and provocations, the range of subjects that have prompted an observer's, a narrator's attention, a commitment of aesthetic, intellectual, moral energy. What emerges, of course, is a "them" or an "it" turned into one person's idiosyncratic, responsive statement—words or pictures (or both) or film footage assembled to characterize, convey, and connect an audience of readers and viewers to a scene, a life or lives, a moment of infinite time, a patch of infinite space, a *here* chosen (and attended) out of all that is out *there*.

Stories and Voices

In the early 1970s, the United States Army Corps of Engineers set about constructing yet another of its dams, this one to restrain Caesar's Creek, a tributary of the Little Miami River. The project required the sacrifice of the 200-year-old Ohio farming village of New Burlington, which was south of Dayton and just north of Cincinnati; the town occupied the site of the reservoir that the dam would create. During the sad final year in the life of this Midwestern rural community, John Baskin, a young writer and woodcutter, came to live in it, in an abandoned farmhouse, and came to know its inhabitants. Mr. Baskin, who had recently graduated from Mars Hill College, in North Carolina's western mountain country, is himself the son of farming people. He turned the experience he had in New Burlington into an excellent book, *New Burlington: The Life and Death of an American Village*, a book that is hard to classify. It is certainly not a study by a social scientist; the author has no interest in conducting interviews, accumulating data, and coming forth with "findings." In fact, in his brief but lively introduction, Mr. Baskin refers to the "bleak treatises" of sociologists and says that he wants no part of them.

Instead, he simply wants to describe what he has witnessed. He wants to set down the words he has heard, to tell us what the people of New Burlington have to say about themselves and their lives. He realizes that these people have managed to gain access to us only through him—the wanderer, the listener, the visitor—so he begins the book with an account of the "accidents" of his life that led to his encounter with the dying town. Soon after Baskin arrived, he learned from the villagers that before long they would be gone. Their children and grandchildren would be water-skiing over their corn-fields, some of which were nearly as old as the nation itself. "Full of complaint," the author says, describing his reaction to the news he heard, "I thought...I would *restore* New Burlington." He would do so, he hoped, by writing something that breathed life into the statistics and the abstract reports on the village that the Corps of Engineers had relied upon in making its decision about the dam. He would try to write what he calls at one point the town's "obit-uary." Before "the world (engineers) crashes in to obliterate the past (the village)," Mr. Baskin tells us, he wanted to take notice, to give us "a book of stories and voices in which the characters ponder some of their time on earth." In this respect, he says, he "perceived New Burlington as a *gift.*" The book, too, is a gift: it is an excellent social history, strong on personal statement and deliberately weak on what the author calls "noise" and "messages."

A prologue tells us, on a rather broad temporal scale, about the town's origins: "New Burlington, Ohio, in the Paleozoic Era was very largely limestone, at the bottom of the sea. Later the ice came, so heavy it depressed the spine of the continent, and after the ice, cranberry bogs prepared the ground for the great hardwood forests." Some fifteen thousand years ago, Baskin tells us, the Indians found their way to this area. After the arrival of white men, it became known first as the Northwest Territory, and then, in 1803, as the State of Ohio. The whites had made their way west in increasing numbers. The Indians retired farther west. Settlements like New Burlington grew. A decade or so after the Civil War, Mr. Baskin tells us, the town consisted of "one sawmill, two churches, one school, one hotel, three groceries, one wagon shop, two dry goods stores, two doctors, one carpenter, one cobbler, one undertaker, three blacksmiths, and one chicken thief. Population: 275. Real estate: $16,281."

Nearly a century later, in 1973, just before the moment of extinction, the town had not grown very much. Its single street offered farmers a brief, intimate, tidy stretch of stores and churches. These farmers, along with the people who healed them, ministered to them, and taught their children, were those in whom Mr. Baskin was most interested. Their lives unfold in all their strangeness, banality, drama, and dreariness. One family, the Haydocks, originally came to New Burlington from Yorkshire, England. Their very name connects them to farm life. Sarah Haydock Shidaker, then in her eighties, obviously reminisced with Mr. Baskin a good deal, and from what she told him he reconstructed old conversations and events: "At the school commencement in 1913, Sarah meets Edwin Shidaker. They have known each other forever but this time they regard each other differently. Edwin drives Sarah home in his buggy. She invites him in but he says no. 'My horse is rather fractious and I should get him home,' he says."

Throughout the book Mr. Baskin has thus woven the past and present together, mixing old photographs and new photographs, quoting old letters and excerpts from diaries and church records and notebooks, and reproducing fragments of remembered songs, poems, and sayings. The author often uses the present tense to bring the reader closer to the kind of existence that is being described. Mr. Baskin collected more than enough material to sustain this novelistic-factual mode of presentation; at various places in the text, Sarah and others are allowed to speak at considerable length without interruption. When the author takes the liberty of acting as commentator or chronicler of events, he does so with directness, immediacy, and verve. He begins a section called "Light" this way: "In the late Twenties electricity comes to New Burlington. A traveling man comes to do the wiring and boards on a nearby farm where he milks a cow to pay his keep. His work goes slowly because the cow kicks him and breaks his leg. Finally, curious neighbors gather outside a lower New Burlington home and watch a porch light switched on.

The bare bulb hangs from the porch ceiling on a long cord. When the light goes on the people think they see the darkness shaken as if it were dust settling."

The paragraph immediately following that one indicates how skilled Mr. Baskin is at connecting the general to the specific, the historical to the personal: "Lights in the village make Sarah happy. Light dispels mystery and she too would have it. An old villager explains to her how it works: 'You pull a cord,' he says. 'On and off, you see.' For the Christmas of 1939 electricity lights the Shidaker Yule tree. Sarah buys lights for the tree, the table, the ceiling, a floor lamp, and a radio. When Edwin turns on the radio a voice is singing."

Sometimes Sarah and her fellow townspeople seem informative and dignified—tough, hardworking men and women who have endured. At other times, they show eloquence and wit. Sarah tells us, "I have always liked the stars. I was born under Libra. Justice, you know, is blind. And erasers are on lead pencils to take care of the wrong we do. The signs have an effect upon our dispositions. If the moon can change tides, why not dispositions?" She provides no answer and moves quickly away from metaphysical speculation: "My, but I am old. This was once a dimple. Now it's a crack. I have trouble with my feet and my conscience. First one pains me, then the other." Then, continuing her almost contrapuntal expression of the straightforward and the rhetorical, she gives this general account of her habits and her thoughts: "I do not smoke, drink, or drive an automobile. There's nothing left for me to do but play the piano. Lay not up your treasures on earth where moth and rust corrupt. But if I married an old man I would want him to have $90,000 and a very bad cough. . . . I am the last leaf on the tree and I believe I am outliving everyone else. My love for my people has been very strong. I am root and branch New Burlington."

Near the conclusion of the section about Sarah, Mr. Baskin adds

an ironic word or two of his own: "The old villagers are mostly gone now and Sarah's grandchildren study science in distant universities. A young man lives in the upstairs which she rents out. He is training to be a psychologist. Sarah listens carefully to his definitions. An interstate highway slices in front of the old Shidaker homeplace and she is the last of the family to own any of Preserved Fish's land. New Burlington itself is mostly gone. The rest waits for the waters of the new reservoir."

There are others besides Sarah, from somber Quakers to lively Methodists. They have memories of their own, but they also remember their parents and grandparents remembering, and we are thus carried back almost to the earliest days of the Republic. One man, John Harlan Pickin, recalls hearing about the Spanish-American War and about Grover Cleveland's election, when his great-aunt exclaimed, "The country is finished!" (A Democrat had not been elected President in twenty-eight years.) John's mother was a grown woman before she laid eyes on a Catholic, and she knew only one Jew in her lifetime. John offers us particularly vivid descriptions of farm life, which, he tells us, was "hard on everyone": "There were horrible stories of people going through manure spreaders, of tractors rearing up and crushing the driver, ragged cuts that led to lockjaw. My aunt felt sorry for the women because they had no one to talk to. They spent their lives looking at the backside of a cow."

We learn that Charles Dickens passed through New Burlington, and that it was a stop on the Underground Railroad. We learn that men and women left the town, year after year, to go farther west. They sometimes wrote back home, sometimes lost touch. And they sometimes came back. We learn that drink was a "secret passion" in the village, that it was considered "more shameful than illegitimacy." At Quaker meetings, drinkers were prayed for, long and hard. The man who speaks of these matters—of the secret lusts and shames of his neighbors—is one Joshua Scroggy, who at ninety-two

can still recall the essence of H. L. Mencken's definition of Puritanism: "The suspicion that somewhere someone might be having a good time." There were also what Joshua refers to as "mental problems" in New Burlington, illnesses that used to be regarded as a "curse." And there were suicides. "We had all these things," Joshua says in summary, "all manner of pride and gluttony, and sins real and imagined, but the village life caused a tolerance among us. It had to. Everyone came face to face each day."

No one in the town from whom Mr. Baskin seeks "answers" comes across as a sage. On the contrary, the people of New Burlington for the most part tether their comments about life to the shared, familiar experiences or occasions of everyday life. " 'Never saw a family tree that didn't need spraying,' " one old-timer remembers hearing. "A good hot egg is a small miracle," another person declares. Speaking of the Great Depression, Mary Robinson, a woman of seventy-five, recalls, "After the commotion on Wall Street, a farmer down the road came home and said, 'The stock market has crashed!' His little boy heard him and asked, 'Was any cows hurt?' That's all the stock market meant to any of us."

Still, New Burlington did suffer during the Depression, for a long time and badly. Many proud families were reduced to a barter economy. But they never went hungry, as did many who lived in crowded, and thus more vulnerable, cities. "We grew what we ate during the Depression," Mary says, "and husked corn in the flat land for six cents a shock." For all that, the people of New Burlington did not take very kindly to the New Deal or to President Roosevelt; Mr. Baskin gives us a limerick that was current in New Burlington during the Depression:

> There once was a lady of fashion
> Who had a very fine passion.
> To her boy friend she said

As they jumped into bed,
"Here's one thing Roosevelt can't ration."

The people of New Burlington watched the seasons come and go with special care and were prepared to take advantage of any generosity that nature offered. The author is keen and lyrical in a section called "Syrup." He learned from his friends all about the technique of syrup-making and the patience they brought to this enterprise. The style that Mr. Baskin uses in this section surely makes some readers hope for a second book from him in this genre, and a third: "When the trees are scratches against the surly February sky Charles McIntire goes into the woods where his breath hangs in balloons as if momentarily the balloons might fill with language. He drills small holes in the maples which he recognizes by the dignified bark which looks like marbled slate. And waits for the precarious succession of freezing nights and warm days which makes the sap rise in the irresolute veins of the maple. There is no clue that inwardly the maple seethes in the breaking up of winter. The world seems still and vague. It is as though color and motion have never existed except in the imagination. For Charles to come here is an act of faith in a dead season. The woods could be etchings."

These men and women may have experienced many hard times, but they were, by and large, stoic, and they maintained a robust sense of humor. The Quakers among them, Mr. Baskin tells us, knew that "human equilibrium is poor and the fall from grace constantly imminent." Severely tested people, even austere people, can manage a smile, or at least develop a certain wry, amused perspective on themselves. Mr. Baskin cites a man named Carl Smith, who at the age of eighty-six acknowledges his luck in having lived a long life and waits patiently, expectantly, for the end: "A long life is partly care, more mystery. Providence watches over fools and children. And I'm no kid." In a grimmer vein of humor, the author tells us about

the man who went mad during one of the floods that have peri-
odically devastated or threatened the countryside. He was found
splashing in the kitchen sink by the rescuers who entered his house.
"You'll all drown," he warned them. "Only I am safe. When the
water rises up to me, I'll pull the plug." Another spoke of a time
when there were five-party and ten-party telephone lines—ten different rings in each house! "Farmhouses sounded like fire stations,"
Della Wilson recalls—and she is only forty-six.

The older people cling tenaciously to the past but stumble during
the slow wait of the present. A good number of them are in their
eighties—survivors, who did without antibiotics and all sorts of
medical technology, who never dieted or took vitamin pills or had
their cholesterol measured or their emotions analyzed. Elizabeth
Beam, at eighty-five, acknowledges that she knows "more people
underfoot than above." She goes on as best she can, even though
her faculties are failing: "With fading eyesight [she puts] Jell-O in
the skillet thinking it is liver." The widow Jemima Boots goes to
sleep easily and stays asleep, but she has her secret worries and keeps
a cowbell under her pillow, just in case. Her neighbor Ellen Jenkins,
also a widow of advanced age, "puts on her best dress when expecting the telephone to ring."

The town of New Burlington is gone now, but in a way it will
never be gone. Its landscape, its people, and their traditions and
customs, their experiences, victories, defeats, and abiding moments
have been given new life in this rare moral document, written by a
young and imaginative observer. John Baskin now lives on a farm
in Wilmington, Ohio, not far from where many of his New Burlington friends, whose ideals and manner of endurance he obviously
admires and wants to uphold, settled after their town died. Mr.
Baskin's book—which resembles James Agee's *Let Us Now Praise Famous Men* in spirit as well as in subject matter—demonstrates that
he is also not far from what Agee called "human actuality."

The Manners, The Manners

Until the nineteenth century, those who made it their business to observe the way people get along with one another had to rely in their reports upon the printed word, and the best of them—such as Arthur Young, the English author of *Travels in France*, a carefully detailed description of French society in the eighteenth century— were called "vivid writers"; that is, observers who evoked such clear and lifelike mental images that they made their readers practically see things. By the middle of the nineteenth century, "vivid" was not quite enough; when Frederick Law Olmsted's firsthand accounts of the South were published, in the 1850s, James Russell Lowell and Edwin Lawrence Godkin applauded Olmsted's writing not only for its "vividness of description" but for its "photographic minuteness." The camera had already opened up new possibilities, and writers were beginning to worry: could they demonstrate not only "minuteness" but the peculiar power of a photograph to be at once thoroughly accurate and powerfully suggestive?

There are times in *Let Us Now Praise Famous Men* when Agee seems in honest, unenvious awe of the power that another kind of artist can command. With words he tries to make a picture, but it is hopeless: "This is why the camera seems to me, next to unassisted and weaponless consciousness, the central instrument of our time." This is not to say that photographs without words are always sufficient. Dorothea Lange knew this when she gave titles to some of her most unforgettable pictures: "On the Great Plains, Near Winner, South Dakota," "One Nation Indivisible, San Francisco," "Funeral Cortege, End of an Era in a Small Valley Town, California." When Robert Flaherty covered the same ground, he, too, found the camera—even a motion-picture one—not quite enough. *The Land* is considered by many his least successful documentary, and he himself labored hard over the script in an effort to give his always brilliant film footage coherence and plausibility.

Wright Morris, writer and photographer, combines in his one person the spirit of artists like James Agee and Dorothea Lange and Robert Flaherty, who tried to make those who read see, and those who see well-informed and humanely literate. *God's Country and My People* is his third and, I believe, most effective attempt to walk back and forth between words and pictures in such a way that his readers will feel themselves on a voyage of their own—to the American past that he tries to recapture, and in particular to our mid-continental Nebraska farm country. Wright Morris was born in Central City, Nebraska, in 1910, and though at the age of nine he started wandering the earth, the scenes of his first nine years appear and reappear in his novels and essays. In the mid-forties, he returned to those scenes with not only his mind's eye but his camera. In 1946, the first of his three volumes of "photo-texts" appeared, entitled 'The Inhabitants," which contains fifty-two full-page photographs, each one facing a text—statements, poems, bits of dialogue, descriptions, exclamations, lamentations; it is hard to classify them all. The author wants to know, as others before him have wanted to know, as others do now, what it means to be an American, to inhabit this great big nation of regions, states, peoples, races. He has a highly developed sense of history, his own and his country's, and the two match: he left the family farm and the small town that catered to men who work the land, and in his lifetime hordes of Americans have also said good-bye to all that and sought the cities, where they have been redeemed at last or betrayed rather sooner but are still mindful of the old days—the past we neither forget completely nor remember accurately. The nation's pulse may be in its cities, but its soul is, or should be, elsewhere. Morris may not believe this, but he recognizes that it is a sentiment shared by millions of Americans whose ancestors not so long ago left farms here and abroad for tenement flats and factories and crowds of people who ignore and suspect and resent one another. The past is gone, the statistics say, but statistics don't quite tell the whole story. We yearn for other days and ways. We have reveries. We have heard tales that are perhaps merely the wistful stuff of nostalgia, yet they live on in us, ready to respond to a slogan, a candidate, or a turn of events, as American history continues to demonstrate.

In 1948, Mr. Morris resumed his look backward and inward with "The Home Place." Again he offers photographs, but now they accompany fiction. Nebraskans who long ago moved East return "home" and are enchanted and made sad and brought up short and in the end left (by their experiences as well as by the author) neither here nor there, unable to decide where they ought to or want to belong. The farm boy become city slicker glares at his aunt:

I looked right straight at Clara's good eye, which is blurred and a little faded—not so good, really, as the strain has worn it out. This is the kind of nerve, the kind of calm, the mean in heart have. You get it after ten or twelve years in the city—it's the kind of spunk that makes good alley rats, Golden Gloves champions, and successful used-car salesmen. It doesn't take much nerve to sell used cars, but I always like to bring in used-car salesmen, all of them, when I have reference to something pretty low. With this kind of nerve I stared at Aunt Clara, and after a moment it occurred to me that I—we, that is—had her buffaloed. She had never seen the like of us before. She had never seen a woman, with two children, throw a well-rehearsed hanky-tantrum while her husband looked on, admiringly. Simple folk don't know how to deal with vulgarity. They're puzzled by it, as real vulgarity is pretty refined. You don't come by it naturally. Maybe you can tell me why it is that simple folk are seldom indelicate, while it's something of a trial for sophisticated people not to be.

So we leave in search of a destiny, find it in business offices and law offices, and eventually stop thinking about ourselves because it is too painful. We have sold out to "the coming thing;" let us forget about our Aunt Claras.

But in *God's Country and My People*, Wright Morris seems to have concluded, twenty years after *The Home Place*, that forgetting is impossible: the more we try to push things out of our minds, the more they gnaw at us. It is best, then, to go back—not simply to conduct a "survey" and so be done with the whole problem, not to cull another novel out of the effort, but to say yes, I know about all that, I lived in it, and I will rejoice at the chance of a homecoming. Along with that Yes, though, comes the feeling that one just can't take the scene for granted anymore. Nor, for that matter, can one try to deny its presence in one's mind. So the situation is tense, a mixed bag, and maybe good on that account, because sympathy won't become sticky with sentiment.

Nebraska is the God's Country of Wright Morris: the Nebraska that Willa Cather first saw at age nine, that Morris left at age nine, and that both wrote and wrote about and fled from and never could quite shake off. Morris uses his camera as Ansel Adams does, to look closely at the texture of things we see so often but never really notice; at the same time, he is after the larger look that goes by the name of "social comment" or "social analysis." He wants us to see the contours of the land, the quality of the soil, and the details of man's artifacts. He wants us to know what man and his works and the prairie and its God-given possibilities have amounted to in the years since 1843, when John Frémont took the Indian word *nebraska* ("flat water") and applied it not only to the Platte River but to the broad territory that river dominates, feeds, and drains. The Platte Valley *is* Nebraska; well over half the state's eighty thousand square miles are in the drainage basin of the river and its tributaries. During the nineteenth century, Easterners followed the Platte across the plains, sure that it would lead to mountain passes. Traders and trappers, missionaries and fugitives, Mormons and gold-seekers passed through or stopped for good, challenged by the rich land that seemed to have no bounds. Nebraska, Morris constantly emphasizes, is a great, gently undulating land that slopes gradually from the northwest to the southeast. To the west are the high plains, the tablelands, broken by deep canyons. Eastward come sandhills, and finally the plains. The land grows abundant crops and furnishes fine grazing, for it is rich and fertile. Yet it can suddenly seem old, weathered, and abandoned; to the west, buttes almost without vegetation rise hundreds of feet above the countryside, and the slopes of the sand-hills are wind-raked, pitted, and creviced. All this Morris shows in his photographs.

God's Country and My People is divided by its concerns: God's Country, Nebraska, a land of valleys, lakes, rivers, and farms that only happen to be of human significance, or so it seems when the photographs are viewed apart from the text, and My People, the kin that still live in the minds of Morris and many others, rather than the men, women, and children who are living today as citizens of the God's Country that persists. (Not all of Nebraska's sons leave.) Morris has us see old clapboard houses whose angular roofs point toward the vastness of the prairie's sky. One house is newly painted; another is about to collapse; a third is little more than a cabin in the endless snow; and others are alone and a touch eerie, or alone and merely drab, or part of a settlement, a small town. There are churches flourishing and decrepit, stores open and abandoned, water towers and windmills and barns and outhouses and a marble-like bank and a huge grain elevator and a grandstand and a railroad station, still waiting for Willa Cather's train whistle—"that cold, vibrant scream, the worldwide call for men." There are things that bring the viewer closer to the everyday habits of people: chairs patched but still sat upon, porches and windows and doors and mailboxes, mirrors and pictures on flowered wallpaper; trees that stretch their arms toward a chimney or raise fingers at a power line but that also support a swing or rim a road or shelter a waiting place; pieces of wood joined together, spoked wagon wheels, a saddle and stirrups, a barber's chair, a barber's sign—without those flashy lights, just a red-and-white column beside a hydrant.

So it goes in God's country. Wright Morris assigns no captions to his photographs, but many of them speak—to the point where one can almost hear voices pointing things out as the pages turn. An egg is waiting to be gathered. The water pump still works. Half the chimney is painted white, but there's just no reason to paint the other half. The old clock in the barbershop will still do, and so will the mug and the brush. Letters from way back deserve keeping, and the same goes for those old receipts and stubs. And those kerosene lamps—well, it's a foolish man who relies on electricity. The old city hall is fine with us; a bigger one will only encourage more officials who don't work for a living themselves and want to interfere with those who do. Telephones and Western Union are fine, but not in a bad winter storm. That's our stove, and I'm just as happy with coal as with the new kind of fuel. There's nothing like a clean, nicely made-up bed. I know where every bucket in this house is, and I never misplace my hat. Do you remember those old cars? Well, we have them still. Sit and be comfortable. I want my children to read a lot, and I have the books for them here, and they're good books. Kids, kids—they're always marking things up. Oh, in there they have the big new record machine—the latest kind, I hear.

Wright Morris's camera just about says all that; his text is reserved for more personal comment on the people he knew when he was growing up. Each page brings us closer to the way they were, the boy who would later write and take pictures, and his mother and his father and his uncles Harry and Verne and his friends. Who are all these people, and what have they to tell us? It depends, Morris seems to conclude. They may seem quaint and stubborn and mistrustful and secretive and provincial, but they are also patient, clever, stronghearted, strongwilled, sensible, decent, and kind. They live in Holdrege or Sidney or Beatrice, and a lot of their kinfolk are gone to the cities—to Chicago, to Milwaukee. And as for the smart young ones, there's Harry in Washington, D.C., and Calvin in New York, even if their brother Jim is happy teaching back home in Lincoln. Morris names the people he knew, but he wants the reader to experience on his own a spate of recollection, which this book, if any book can, will certainly inspire. Nor does a hard look back toward childhood have to be a strictly psychological (or therapeutic) effort. A mind set upon recall, upon fresh intimacy with its origins, ought to seek out not solely the doctors who study free associations (which lead back to only one part of the past) but social historians and writers and photographers like Wright Morris, who is merely a literate, sensitive observer of the people.

The words in *God's Country and My People* struggle to convey irony and seriousness and complexity, yet they come across as direct, natural, clear, and even playful. In *The Territory Ahead*, his book of literary criticism, published in 1958, Morris never gets far away from the question he is still asking: what do neighborhoods do to people over a span of time, and people to neighborhoods? Space, place, and time are abstractions whose concrete expressions surround our lives and make them what they are, and the titles of Morris's novels show how much these abstractions concern him: *One Day, In Orbit, The Field of Vision, The Huge Season, The World in the Attic, The Man Who Was There.*

More than once, to be sure, Morris has wanted to be done with all of that—with the Nebraska in him, in us, and in the entire world. He admires D. H. Lawrence, who had the courage and brilliance to break with the past and strike out for "the territory ahead"; he sees Lawrence as having been constantly threatened by both the past and the present, his own and his country's. He sees little room in our time for more T. S. Eliots (can there possibly be a *Fifth* Quartet?). The great exception, for Morris, is Henry James. Writers like Mark Twain and Thomas Wolfe and Hemingway got caught in the traps of nostalgia; they allowed the past to define the present, to narrow their vision of what is in store for us, and ultimately they paid the price as writers. Henry James certainly sought out the past, and even left his native land to find it, but, says Morris, "We have had hundreds of exiles, and many of them talented. . . . Among all of these exiles, he alone is not a captive of the past." James knew that a person's character and temperament, even his deepest thoughts (as we put it these days), can only be *approached*, not defined or labeled or—in the case of a novelist—dramatically submitted to the turn of a phrase or to a particular plot. The job of analysis and portrayal is a lifelong one, for those who want to try. Freud knew that, knew that anything he saw in people was only part of the story. (If he has now been turned into a caricature of himself, a man with all the answers, that is another matter.) For James, too, there could only be the attempt, each approximation a beginning, each of his "impressions" an endless challenge to him as both observer and writer. "On the evidence, and on nothing else," Morris declares, "it is possible to say that no other book contains so much of the American scene, since no other book has so much to give out." (He is referring, of course, to *The American Scene*.) Of James the expatriate come home, Morris remarks, "He is consciously self-conscious; the impressions he records are not those of a traveler but those of a native who is finally aware of what it is he feels. In James, the American scene becomes articulate." The great, proud, discreet man would no doubt smile appreciatively at such praise, but he might be even more grateful for *God's Country and My People*. "The manners, the manners: where and what are they, and what have they to tell?" Wright Morris, paying heed to those words of Henry James (which one wants to keep summoning), has done a fine job of giving us yet another answer to that demanding, exhausting question.

Mississippi

During the early 1960s, at the height of the civil-rights movement in the South, even the tough-minded, daring young activists of SNCC were given pause by the state of Mississippi. Mississippi had a reputation as the final bastion of segregation, the place where a last stand would occur on behalf of the racial status quo—hence the "Mississippi Summer Project" of 1964, meant to "go for the heart, go for the jugular," as some young men and women kept putting it at the time. Sometimes, cardiovascular imagery yielded to the neuro-psychiatric kind, and we were told, in those "orientation sessions" that preceded the onset of the Project, that Mississippi was not only a scene of fear and terror but "a state of mind," or a place where "a war of nerves" was constantly being waged.

Now, of course, Mississippi has substantially changed politically and, to a certain extent, socially and racially. Yet its formidable notoriety and singularity persist in the memories of those old enough to have known what was: the parents, for instance, of Anthony Walton, who left the state for the North before he was born and who return there with him as he tries in his documentary to comprehend their past, which is also his, and ours as Americans.

Fiefdoms fall in this book, *Mississippi*—all those academic and intellectual delineations of proper terrain. The author wants us to know about a state's history and geography, its ecology, its cultural and economic past. He has us following its roads and rivers, attending its music, its literary tradition, its terrible stories of hate, betrayal, murder. He gives us his parents' experiences and those of his kin and their friends. And he gives us his own experiences as he moves across the state in this last decade of the twentieth century, noticing, musing, listening, engaging with various others in various locales and situations. The result is a narrative of great strength, variety, and authority: social history mingling with musicology; literary criticism keeping company with political analysis; contemporary reportage giving way to moral reflection; extended passages of prose interrupted by poems and, too, by the extraordinary photographs taken by FSA photographer Marian Post Wolcott, which, in their dramatic, telling way offer silent witness to an American colonialism all too readily available for visual scrutiny.

At times, the author gets caught in the inevitable tug between the past and present, between the South and the North. Some of his informants remember not "the good old days" but their own honorable efforts to live decent lives no matter the hardships, the suffering—and contrast all of that with today's somewhat improved political and racial and economic climate, which has not, however, prevented drugs and crime and sexual promiscuity from taking serious hold. Nor has the trek toward freedom, to Chicago and Detroit and Cleveland and the cities of the Northeast, spared former Mississippians a similar jeopardy: ghetto life, with all its threats to a people's family life, its spiritual legacy and traditions. Such ironies are put squarely before us by men and women uninterested in "resolving" (that cool, slippery word) this life's inconsistencies, paradoxes. Still, they worked hard, prayed hard, sang hard, a tenaciously proud struggle to make do, to stand up to the constant threats, the terrible injustice imposed by a caste system whose grip was only loosened a generation ago, and then only after a strenuous fight.

Although that story is by no means over, this book is a reminder of what has recently changed. After all, the author is a man whose parents were born into the Mississippi tenant-farmer world, but who now moves with no great difficulty into all realms of that state. He is a guest in the homes of the wealthy, the socially prominent, and the well-educated even as he talks with candor to the working people of both races. His knowledge of the past, energized by his parents experiences and recollections, can give him pause every once in a while, even prompt a moment of apprehension as he makes his way across haunted, blood-drenched territory—counties where lynchings took place, where all the time one race lorded it over the other in every possible way. Yet, out of that extended time of exceptional vulnerability came a stoic dignity as well as wounds, and it is the achievement of this book that both sides of that moral as well as racial story get told.

At times, Walton's subject matter and his compelling, lyrical, ironic voice bring Agee to mind. Like Agee, Walton is an author of Southern ancestry who has gone back to the homeland, as it were, to explore and then assemble an account for others. Like Agee, Walton stretches and challenges the confines of the conventional essay. He dares long takes and short riffs on a variety of subjects: places, highways, foliage, individuals. He gives us biographies of Richard Wright, Robert Johnson, Medgar Evans, Emmet Till. He tells us about cotton and schoolteachers the way Agee did—with detailed description, fluidly and invitingly presented. He does special honor to jazz and the blues and even, in "A Sort of Chorus," bows out of the picture altogether so that we may meet novelists, ordinary people, musicians, and poets, look at photographs, and contemplate passages from our constitution, or from the Bible—let a whole history come at us from different directions, with the author a behind-the-scenes conductor of sorts.

All through this marvelously evocative book we are graced with interviews; people of all sorts and conditions tell us "how it used to be," how it goes now, how they hope things will turn out in the years ahead. But it is Anthony Walton's voice that ultimately wins us over, carries us the distance he himself has traveled, carries us from places afar right to the Delta, to its melancholy music, to the backbreaking toil of the people who have lived there, to the soul-wrenching effort of so many to stay afloat morally and spiritually against such high odds. With his help we arrive at the destination he had in mind for himself as well as for us—a landscape of understanding that enables a coming-to-terms with nightmares all too commonly overlooked, nightmares refused the instructive scrutiny they deserve and demand. The book's subtitle is more than earned: a private look into a family's past becomes "An American Journey," a tale of one state's fate become a great moral lesson for all of us, wherever we live.

Dakota and a Cloister Walk

"Grace is everywhere," the French novelist George Bernanos has his dying curé exclaim in *The Diary of the Country Priest*, and in recent years the American poet Kathleen Norris has been developing a similar point of view. She began to do so in *Dakota* (1993), which she called a "spiritual geography." *Dakota* is a lyrical, documentary homage to a place but also a modest, telling insistence on immanence: God as present in the things of this world, the daily rhythms of our particular lives. In the prairie land of our late-twentieth-century upper Midwest, an observant writer finds a stoic, introspective dignity, an abundant moral energy. She gives us the voices of people still at a substantial distance from our big cities, our confident centers of money and learning. She attends with knowing devotion a social and moral landscape; pays grateful respect to the individuals who have clung to it, often against great odds; and renders what she had witnessed with a meditative intensity and originality worthy of James Agee's response over half a century ago to Hale County, Alabama, or William Carlos Williams's extended examination in verse of Paterson, New Jersey—a tradition of watchfulness and evocation that in form defies literary conventions and in content mixes concrete description with spells of soulful inwardness suggestively put to word.

In a second book, *The Cloister Walk*, Norris persists in her wonderfully idiosyncratic ways. The book is the result of an "immersion into a liturgical world" begun five years ago when Norris became closely connected to St. John's Benedictine monastery, in Minnesota. Five years earlier, she had already become a Benedictine oblate; that is, she had professed monastic vows (modified, in accordance with her secular life as a married woman, a writer, and a sometime lecturer). Raised a "thorough Protestant" and not especially knowledgeable about religious orders, Norris soon enough experienced in full panoply the "solemnities and feasts" of the various saints in a monastery that became for her a spiritual home, even as she left it rather often for her life in Lemmon, South Dakota, and her worshipping commitment there to a Presbyterian church.

As a Benedictine oblate Norris was, really, a vigorous participant in a world all its own, one devoted to continual reading, singing, praying—"a school for love" was the phrase St. Benedict used. Such a world is at a jarring remove from that inhabited by the rest of us, who clock into our jobs and rush headlong from one day's hurdles and tasks to the next day's. The author reminds us that "liturgical time is essentially poetic-time, oriented toward process rather than productivity, willing to wait attentively in stillness rather than always pushing to get the job done."

Nevertheless, monks and nuns and oblates in monasteries are our fellow human beings, and much of this book chronicles the yearnings, the worries, and, not least, the lusts to which these men and women are heir. Even the saints, the author comes to realize, are not the "impossibly holy people" she once thought them to be. They are, she nicely calls them, "witnesses to our limitations," even as, of course, they affirm "God's vast possibilities." All the while, more prosaicaly, these men and women, like the rest of us, struggle for balance and proportion—best supplied, they seem to have learned, by an earthy humor. In that regard, one day at the monastery's noon prayer time the author heard that St. Thérèse of Lisieux "detested the pious trivialities which find their way into religious life," and she noticed that Thérèse's own description of her convent sisters as a 'fine bunch of old maids' broke everyone up."

These are people who live close to the bone, materially; who every day try hard to become part of a community, to relinquish aspects of the very egoism that the rest of us spend our lives trying to enhance. Put differently, these are cloistered ones—with whom, as she describes it in her title, Norris was privileged to "walk": alongside them, but not fully one of them. Her primary vow was, after all, matrimonial; theirs was to a celibate life, a willful surrender of some pleasures on behalf of, we begin to understand, certain important (and sensual) satisfactions. The author is subtle and shrewd on that subject; she shows us how these men and women put themselves, mind and body and soul, into a community's demanding but fulfilling life—one that we today, unsurprisingly and all too instructively, try to understand through resort to the psychiatric word *sublimation*. But as the author points out, there is "a classic conflict between a psychology that emphasizes individual development, and the Benedictine charism of life lived in community." She refers to "a strong, cultural prejudice against celibacy." In her words, "to channel one's sexuality into anything other than being sexually active is highly suspect; it leaves celibates vulnerable to being automatically labeled as infantile or repressed" (even though some most distinguished psychoanalysts, among them Anna Freud, knew well such a manner of living, one Freud himself was trying to comprehend, without pejorative intent, in his *Group Psychology and the Analysis of the Ego*). These Benedictines have long known that celibacy can be a kind of sexuality: a passionate offering of self to others, and with them, to the great Other, all accomplished through rituals and procedures, through spoken and sung avowals, through (in a phrase of Dorothy Day's) "the work of the body, the work of the heart."

Such a life—one's time offered to God, to a community whose religious ideals and activities are meant, finally, to acknowledge Him—is obviously not meant for most of us. Yet, over the centuries many individuals of great moral courage have lent their voices and their enthusiasm to the furtherance of such communities; or have put themselves in intellectual or personal jeopardy, even lost their lives, out of convictions that have radically challenged the materialist assumptions, the secular authority and norms of this or that place or time. These are the companions of sorts who figure prominently in this book: the Hebrew prophets Jeremiah and Isaiah, who dared take on "principalities and powers"; the early Christian martyrs, whom the author knows well, and whose stories she conveys with a vivid, compelling charm; the anxious and melancholy psalmists who proposed a soaring, complex wisdom both joyous and tragic; the self-effacing pastoral sage St. Benedict, whose levelheaded modesty of phrasing barely concealed the complex emotional canniness he strived to communicate; the powerfully prophetic St. Augustine, whose confessional asides and polemical broadsides make many twentieth-century psychologists and psychiatrists seem hopelessly naive; and, not least, Norris's fellow poets, upon whom she poignantly calls, now and then, as guiding spirits—Keats, Emily Dickinson, Yeats, Czeslaw Milosz, and Thomas Merton.

Most of all, naturally, these pages offer the voice of Kathleen Norris, a plainswoman and an essayist, a documentary writer who has published two volumes of poems, a person of modern sensibility who dares leap across time and space in order to make the interests and the concerns of any number of reflective thinkers her own and, by virtue of her direct, engaging prose, the reader's as well. Feisty and moody, stubbornly her own person, she nevertheless has her soul brothers and sisters. Her writing is personal, epigrammatic—a series of short takes that ironically address the biggest subject matter possible: how one ought to live a life, with what purposes in mind. She is one of history's writing pilgrims, as in Pascal's *pensées* or Simone Weil's diaries, which after her death became books. She is, though, a contemporary American pilgrim, boldly willing to forsake any number of cultural trends and preoccupations in favor of this "walk," this searching expedition within herself, courtesy of her Benedictine friends.

Fortunately for the rest of us, Norris is not completely alone. Her fellow Midwesterner Ron Hansen gave us, a few years ago, the novel *Mariette in Ecstasy*, another knowing journey into monastic life; and we have the novelist Reynolds Price, who (in *A Palpable God* and in his more recent gospel translations) has dared explore Biblical stories, the reasons for their still-gripping hold on us. In these last years of the second millennium, when whirl and whim rule, when there is so much snide and sneering cynicism around (in politics, in the arts, in criticism), these talented visionaries of ours point us in another direction: toward an embrace of moral and spiritual contemplation—of a kind blessedly free of the pietistic self- righteousness increasingly prominent in our present-day civic life.

A Photographer's Brooklyn Find

In *Paterson*, the long, lyrical examination of the American experience which William Carlos Williams began offering us in the late 1940s, the reader is immediately confronted with the three words "a local pride"—the poet's defiant response (by implication) to those many fellow artists who have chosen to leave behind the world they knew growing up for fancy, important (and self-enhancing) worlds elsewhere. Dr. Williams would have none of this shift in residence (and the accompanying shift in focus of energy, attention, concern). A distinguished poet, well along in his career, was making his major statement, and doing so resolutely on familiar territory. He had been born in Rutherford, New Jersey; he had practiced medicine there and in nearby Paterson; and he would die in the house, 9 Ridge Road, where he had kept an office and seen patients for almost half a century. His was a fiercely insisted, unrelenting loyalty to certain neighborhoods, to the people who inhabited them, to their habits and customs and traditions, and especially to the words and thoughts, the aspirations and worries, of the families who lived on streets he regularly visited. He was the busy doc, of course, hurrying from here to there, but he was also (as some of us who got to meet him, know him, soon enough realized) the ever watchful and listening observer, one moment very much connected to individuals, to whole families, the next moment removed enough to take note, take stock—a prelude, of course, to what his mind would do, later, as it directed his fingers to work as they did on that typewriter that he summoned in the evening and early morning in exchange for the day's stethoscope.

I thought of him as I looked at Thomas Roma's (*Found In Brooklyn*) pictures, and I remembered that high-pitched poet's voice, now cranky, now singing with excitement, enthusiasm. Once, after a doctoring visit to Paterson, he spoke in a way that I think Roma would appreciate:

I can't always say I love it here. I'm not interested in being sentimental! These folks—they'd smell that rot [of sentiment] in a second. I'm interested in them because they are the people I've known all my life—and they're the kind of people who *made* this country, worked and worked to build it up, turn its natural wealth into its industrial wealth. They came here from everywhere, and made this place, right here, their somewhere. Not without plenty of regrets—who leaves a place and doesn't think back and yearn for what it was, with all the pain and disappointment! But they had no choice, really—they had to come [here], if they were going to stand a chance. I was in this home the other day, and that's what a man said to me—I was seeing his girl (she had pneumonia): 'I had no choice. I knew that when I got on that boat, it was Italy and no hope, and a living death, then an early death, or coming across to America.' Don't think he dreamed of [finding] gold on the streets; hey, these people knew the score, knew they were headed for a damn strange place, where it'd be a big fight to keep their heads above water. But they had a chance, they knew that; they had a chance to swim, to break away from a dead-end life, and maybe, just maybe, land themselves on another kind of territory, where their kids might find a big boost, a chance to *take off*, to get an education and make a living, to be a somebody, not a big shot, not a fat-cat, but a person who could say at night, not bad, not bad.

Across the Hudson from the flatlands of New Jersey stretches Flatbush, a Brooklyn close kin to Paterson, a Brooklyn that is a place of "all sorts and conditions," a borough of one of the world's greatest cities but also a huge city itself, a city within a city, and a place where people are born, live, and die without much interest in or reason to go elsewhere, even via the bridge or two that would take them to Manhattan, to Staten Island, to the Jersey shore that lines the Hudson. Thomas Roma both is and is not one of those people. To be sure, he has traveled beyond New York (the city and state both) but he has resolutely stayed home as a worker (and I suspect he's the kind of artist who wouldn't at all mind being called that name: an honor for any of us, rather than something to be lived down, or left behind on one's way up). He has stayed home, of course, for his own private reasons—but in so doing, he has also made us viewers a part of that decision: we are his students, and he is our guide, our teacher, the one whose eyes are intent on helping us see a given world.

Right off, in the first photograph, this alert, knowing, keen-eyed instructor puts his cards on the table. He is going to give us a glimpse of a particular world, all right—a world that is modest and unpretentious, a world of clothespins and clotheslines and towels hanging outside in search of the sun, towels now become curtains to a drama. Next come the play's several acts, the stories—the homes, of all shapes and sizes, the streets, the parked cars, the fences, the religious artifacts. In one picture a tree stands up front, a link, perhaps, to the well-known *A Tree Grows in Brooklyn*. In another picture, fences and a scraggly bush merge into a hodgepodge of lines and patterns: either an ugly, distracting mess or a modern aesthetic moment worthy of a museum's notice. Flowers, here and there, try to assert themselves. Venetian blinds abound, often closed tight. After a dozen or so street pictures with no one in sight, a boy appears, leaning on a fence, his head lowered. He seems to have been given pause. He seems to be remembering something. He seems to be wondering: where and why? A portrait of the artist as a young man? A teacher takes a step in a discourse: you have walked the streets with me, seen the quiet, even desolate side of a city usually regarded as teeming with people, as virtually uninhabitable because of their constant, fractious presence, and now I will move from the inanimate to your own kind, to one, solitary person who is doing what we human beings distinctively do, thinking, trying to figure something out, stopping himself in his tracks so that his mind can exert *its* musculature. Near him a ladder stands in mute witness— to what? A boy's dreams and aspirations, his worries and fears— these we can only imagine, or attribute to another out of our own lives: a ladder of expectations, of escape, of limited access.

We move on, turn from one picture to another and encounter, in an unlikely place, in a postage-stamp backyard filled with chairs for sunning, a graceful pair of statues, two women who lift their left arms to hold cisterns. Whence these sculptured objects, which might have stood in ancient Rome or Greece? This story won't be told us, but it is actually given us in the picture: life's surprises and incongruities await us around any corner, even in someone's backyard. Graffiti also awaits us—not the accomplished, chalked humor that Helen Levitt noticed for us in Spanish Harlem half a century ago, but not a muddled or mean defacement, not a provocative eyesore, not a visual confrontation analogous to the urban cacophony so many of us have learned to endure; rather, a row of spiritual symbols, a declaration to the world (beside a garbage pail!) that love and faith are within our grasp, no matter our humble circumstances—and indeed, on their account, such qualities of the mind and heart may flourish. The Jesus who was a carpenter and kept the company of fishermen, of peasants, and, too, the Hebrew prophets who railed against "principalities and powers"—those people might have walked these simple, unprepossessing streets, spotted a wall all too darkly bare, and shed on it the light (the Light) that a kind of graffiti can enable: a collective reminder to us passers-by, always on our busy way, of what is uniquely possible for us, the inwardness of taking stock, of seeking direction.

How gently, yet how pointedly, this morally energetic and intro-spective photographer moves us along, nudges us from the graffiti abstractions to our first "crowd," three youths huddled on a pave-ment, a fire nearby, cultivating their own kind of fiery inquiry. As I looked at that picture, I remembered my work with a fire-setting boy of nine. I was a resident in child psychiatry at The Children's Hospital in Boston. This boy, Patrick, came to the clinic because he had dared to be "fresh" with his schoolteachers; he had said "damn" (oh, the 1950s!), and he was seen setting a fire on the school playground during a recess, immediately dubbed an "arsonist," and sent to a school psychologist, who worried (in portentously opaque terminology) about his mind, his mental prospects. When I met him, he seemed quiet, but thoughtful, alert. Soon enough, I learned of his good sense of humor, his intelligent capacity to take the measure of others, his teachers included. I can still hear him saying this: "They thought I was out to cause trouble, but I just wanted to copy the cavemen. We talked about them in class." He stopped, and I was ready to fire away, as it were, to ask more questions of him in order to explore his "motives," his "personality"—but suddenly, I heard this: "You'd think they [his teachers] would be happy, because we were remembering what they told us [in class, about the use of fire by our distant ancestors] and we tried to imitate them [those ancestors]." All of us who "evaluated" this lad would come to see not only his obvious charm, but his originality of thought, his goodness, and, very important, his soundness of mind. He *was* a bit different; already, he had the explorer in him, the pilgrim even. Who will ever know what the three boys in this picture are thinking, are saying, as they stare at the magic, the heat, the glare, the promise and danger both, of that burst of light—in whose presence, surely, all the surrounding cement, whatever its apparent gravity, its extensive nearness, must have been as nothing, the utterly inconsequential backdrop to a breakthrough moment?

Next, two more boys, one casually asleep on the pavement, his patient dog at hand, watching (over) him, waiting for him; and another lad, who has climbed a not very tall or luxuriant tree in search of a view, a vantage place, a position of prominence: there it be, what moves, what can be seen thrusting into a particular cityscape. Now another house, more massive, perhaps, because uninterrupted by any human presence. Now, too, a young woman "under the el", as the painter John Sloan put it, pictured it—paying attention to herself, adjusting herself, so to speak. Now, the splendor and dignity and authority of the American automobile, perhaps our most defining instrument of expression in this century. Here is a picture, one thinks, that would be ruined by anyone's presence! Now, another "crowd," four young people this time, and another car, and more trash cans—and more mystery: what are they thinking, contemplating for the near future? For that matter, what is the man thinking who, in the next picture, leans against a street pole, his left leg folded, his left foot also up against that pole? Now, a more disorganized, turbulent world, a ramshackle wire fence, random, confusing graffiti, kids at play as houses, lined up, look on; a man drawing a puff as the kids play; a man with his hammer, the drawn sword of his daily living; another ladder; a covey of birds, saying goodbye, taking for the air, headed somewhere, elsewhere; and another fence, hidden by shrubbery so thick it hides the entire city and makes us think of the country; and the clutter of a back alley, the clutter of a backyard, the twin mystery of what once was and what now is.

Finally, the theme of departure: a cemetery; an older man nursing his wound, displaying his vulnerability; birds perched, ready to fly the coop; a man working on a car, so that it can do its job, move away; a beautiful woman, waiting and sunning, spreading herself over the front seat of an open car that will also soon move away; and love, love at last, unashamed love, no matter the modest abode that will house its daily, its nightly life, love that one can only hope will last, love that keeps company with another one of those towels out to sun itself, lose its wetness, give itself to the breeze. Perhaps that final picture conveys the spirit that the first picture promises us: enter ye this kingdom, push aside the curtains (towels), and eventually you will learn what takes place inside, what makes this world go around. A son (well, given their respective dates of birth, a grandson) of William Carlos Williams followed his lead: "Outside / outside myself / there is a world, / he rumbled, subject to my incursions." This poet of the camera, this localist poet, this poet, in Williams's phrase, "with the bare hands", walks, stalks his hometown, keeps us resolutely outside those homes, garages, stores, and schools, and yet in so doing brings us up close, indeed: we are shown what he "found," the soul of a place as it is, and as it gets lived daily.

Stripped Bare at the Follies

Over thirty years ago a man named Robert Rohner was riding his bicycle late at night when he was spotted by a policeman and stopped. He was in Stoughton, Massachusetts, and on his way to Boston, which was about twenty miles off. Mr. Rohner didn't feel that he should be questioned simply because he had selected an unusual time to travel. He protested vigorously, but he was arrested and charged with "vagrancy"—whereupon he became "belligerent in violent protest at his arrest." The next day he was brought into Stoughton District Court, still angry and still demanding to be released. The police had put him in a straightjacket, and the judge ordered him sent to Bridgewater State Hospital for the Criminally Insane for thirty-five days of observation. Those days turned into years. A psychiatrist recommended "permanent commitment," and Mr. Rohner, a poor man, had no lawyer to fight for him. Eventually, the Supreme Court of Massachusetts ruled that Robert Rohner, and all those who fall into his predicament, have a right to legal counsel, and to more than just a hearing (which is in fact an arbitrary administrative decision by those who run a state hospital).

Robert Rohner's fate at Bridgewater State Hospital was actually far better than Dominic Rosati's. While Mr. Rohner found himself virtually imprisoned for life because he didn't take lightly to gratuitous arrest, Mr. Rosati's stay at Bridgewater was suddenly terminated: he was found naked and dead in his cell, a victim of rat poison.

The hospital was investigated by a legislative committee. Both the Massachusetts Bar Association and the Massachusetts Medical Society expressed concern. Newspapers all over the state demanded action, changes, reform—as did the hospital's superintendent, Charles Gaughan, a very intelligent and compassionate man who pleaded year after year for more money, more personnel, better programs so that his patients would be treated like something more than caged animals living in an eighty-eight-year-old institution whose facilities and arrangements prompted one observer to compare it unfavorably to a "race-horse stable"; another, the brave superintendent himself, talked of a "hencoop." The hospital was charged with allowing dangerous criminals to escape, with providing little or no psychiatric care to its patients, and with keeping its inmates improperly or unfairly—that is, offering them no chance of release, no clarification of their psychiatric and legal status, and no right to a periodic public review of their case before a judge or other impartial authority in the presence of a defending lawyer.

Against such a background a young lawyer, Frederick Wiseman, began to plan a documentary of the Bridgewater hospital. Wiseman lived in Cambridge, and I suppose it can be said that he had his problems. He was not a member of a law firm. He did not spend his days studying the tax laws or helping (with dozens of other lawyers) this or that business solve its various corporate intricacies. He has never used law as a means of political advancement. After he graduated from law school he became interested in the fate of criminals and the poor: what do *they* do when they get into trouble? Who looks after them—that is, which of our distinguished law firms, so competitively pursued by aspiring members of the bar? Mr. Wiseman started teaching law students, and in 1958 he took them to Bridgewater State Hospital so that he and they together could see firsthand what American doctors and lawyers do for some of their fellow citizens.

Apparently that visit, and some others to similar places, "traumatized" Mr. Wiseman. He began to lose interest in 'the law as such. He started wondering about the reasons people end up in places like Bridgewater, never to leave. He started looking at some of our ghettos, too, full of desperate, wild, anarchic youths who don't consider the police their defenders, or lawyers and judges men of integrity and righteousness. He made the connection that others have: Bridgewater and sections of Harlem aren't all that different. Ghettos have walls as high as any the state of Massachusetts can build to confine its "criminally insane."

Perhaps the time had come for such a man to seek out psychiatric "care." Why was he forsaking a promising career on State Street or Wall Street? What made him "identify" or become involved with blacks or severely disturbed people? Why was he beginning to commit his energies, his life's work, to "them"? Did something in his past make him want to sacrifice, do the unconventional, work for the "deprived"? We all have our sympathies, but wasn't he going too far, becoming unusually and unrealistically worried about the fate of people who are notoriously poor "treatment risks"? In 1961, apparently still unable to "work things out" and become a "normal, self-respecting" lawyer, Frederick Wiseman decided to produce a film. He had read Warren Miller's *The Cool World* and couldn't get out of his mind the book's particular hellish view of Harlem. On an impulse—yes, unexamined—he went to see Mr. Miller, and he secured from Miller the rights to make a movie out of his book. In 1964 the movie was finished: *The Cool World*, produced by Frederick Wiseman and directed by Shirley Clarke. The reviews were excellent, both here and abroad, but the film lost money, much of it the producer's own savings.

Now Wiseman was *really* in trouble: his interests had led him into a new career. Working alongside Shirley Clarke, he had learned how to direct as well as produce a film; but he was nearly broke, and he had no idea what to do next. How long can an adult give himself free rein to live in a dreamworld, build fantasies, ignore a professional life, throw away money on "losing propositions," on celluloid? Moreover, the Bridgewater that Wiseman had seen in 1958 came back to haunt him—surely evidence that some kind of "conflict" was under way in his unconscious. He decided to try making a documentary of the place, one that would convey to the viewer what it is like to be sent there, to live there, to die there.

He had to find backers, no easy job in the precarious world of "educational" or essentially "noncommercial" films. Even more difficult, he had to gain access to Bridgewater, a state hospital under the ultimate jurisdiction of politically sensitive and vulnerable men. But Bridgewater's superintendent was desperately anxious for change, for the kind of exposure necessary to enlighten people and move them to action. He himself was pleading with and exhorting audiences all over the state, telling them how awful conditions were in his hospital, asking them for help. In 1965, Mr. Wiseman moved ahead in earnest and secured his shoestring budget for the film. In the spring of 1966 he started shooting at Bridgewater. It is probably fair to say that the hospital's superintendent encouraged his project, and so did the state's attorney general and former lieutenant governor Elliot Richardson, who was a distinctly superior public official. Both men would soon enough have cause to regret whatever help they gave Mr. Wiseman, whatever interference they ran for him against the bureaucrats of a state fairly well known for its colorfully vicious politics. Why? What happened to set Mr. Richardson and Mr. Gaughan against Mr. Wiseman?

When the film was finished, it attracted wide and enthusiastic critical acclaim. One audience after another was shocked, horrified and disturbed; but by court order, *The Titicut Follies* would not for many years be seen in Massachusetts, even though it was shown at New York's Lincoln Center Film Festival and won first prize in West Germany's Mannheim Film Festival. A look at the film itself is perhaps the best way to find out why it would inevitably stir up a political controversy. The Indians used to call the area around Bridgewater Titicut, so when the guards and inmates of the hospital put on a public benefit show, they called it "Titicut Follies." Mr. Wiseman's 16-mm black-and-white film, 84 minutes long, opens with a scene from that show: eight men in straw hats are onstage singing "Strike Up the Band." Behind them one reads the tinseled sign: Titicut Follies. From a long shot we go to close-ups, first of the performers' faces, sad despite the singing, and then of others, of the people "backstage" who spend their days and nights in the hospital as inmates, prisoners, guards, doctors, nurses, whatever. At the very end Bridgewater's temporary entertainers appear once again—so that if we wish, if we can, we may forget everything that went on in between, for that is the privilege of free men. Ironically, the film is so effective because it is not another *Snake Pit*, another brutal and unrelenting exposé of life behind the closed doors of a mental hospital. Yes, there are some scandalous and disgusting moments, but by and large they are not standard "backward" scenes, with their shrieks and groans and hilarious desolation or grim excitement. I have seen much worse in other state hospitals that Massachusetts maintains.

Something else is at work to give this film its power, and to unsettle its critics, many of whom objected to the nudity or demanded to know why the faces of inmates were used in clear violation of the right to privacy. (The legislators who were shocked that patients appear live and undisguised in *Titicut Follies* have yet to raise their voices against a book called *Christmas in Purgatory* by Burton Blatt, in which mental patients are also photographed and not always provided with black bands across their eyes. Mr. Blatt's descriptions of the hospitals located in several states, including Massachusetts, make *Titicut Follies* seem like a whitewash job.) If Frederick Wiseman has offended the sensibilities of his fellow citizens he has done it, I believe, by making them nervous about far more than nudity (in this day of bikinis and miniskirts) or the individual's right to privacy (in this day of wiretapping, of cleverly manipulative advertising, of espionage in so many settings that any number of people can reasonably doubt whose purposes they have served and with whose money).

After seeing *Titicut Follies*, the mind does not dwell on the hospital's ancient and even laughable physical plant or its pitiable social atmosphere. What sticks, what really hurts is the sight of human life made cheap and betrayed. We see men needlessly stripped bare, insulted, callously herded about, mocked, taunted. We see them ignored or locked interminably in cells. We hear the craziness in the air, the sudden outbursts, the quieter but stronger undertow of irrational noise that any doctor who has worked under such circumstances can only take for so long. But much more significantly, we see the "professionals," the doctors and workers who hold the fort in the Bridgewaters of this nation. We see a psychiatrist interview a new patient. We see another psychiatrist and his staff question another patient and then discuss him upside-down. In sum, we see ourselves. Even the most callous and cynical politician has a right to become uneasy and fearful when he sees the most respected, educated, and "rational" members of *his* world, his middle-class, professional world, behave as they do in this film.

"Why do you do this when you have a good wife?" asks the doctor of a youth driven to molest children. The questions pour out, one after another—crudely put, monotonously asked. The young man is told that he is sick, sick, sick. His frightened, searching face contrasts with the doctor's boredom, his weariness, his vulgarity, his lack of interest in the man he yet feels free to interrogate (feels he has the right and knows he has the power to interrogate). Then there is the staff meeting, where another heartbreaking encounter takes place. A young man feels himself driven mad by the hospital and pleads for a return to a regular jail. Again the questions shoot out at him and in a few minutes shred him to bits. He is given a label, a diagnosis. The faces, the professional faces, smile ever so faintly. They are satisfied. He can go. It is cruel of Mr. Wiseman to do this to us—to all of us who pin names on people in order to brush them aside.

In any event, the film's producer and director went to court, charged with violating the privacy of patients and with a "breach of contract." The documentary wasn't supposed to turn out like that, said the men who allowed it to be made. The politicians, who for years had ignored Bridgewater's problems, had someone to attack, a movie to vilify. The former lieutenant governor, Mr. Richardson, and Bridgewater's superintendent, Mr. Gaughan, had to run for cover, run for their lives. And the same politicians now had people to defend: the inmates whose privacy was invaded.

Titicut Follies is a brilliant work of art, and as such it did not go unnoticed despite its opposition. We are asked not to be outraged at others (a cheap and easily spent kind of emotion) but to look at ourselves, the rich and strong ones whose agents hurt the weak and maimed in the name of—what? Our freedom. Our security. Our civilization. Were men's "rights" violated, or do places like Bridgewater strip men of everything, of their "rights," their dignity, their humanity? Does a man like Frederick Wiseman have the obligation to say or show what he saw, or is the state entitled to *its* privacy? If so, how can we move the state to correct its wrongs, to end its evasion or corruption or worse? (A series of newspaper stories over the years had had only a limited effect.) How long will men like Mr. Richardson, Mr. Gaughan, and Mr. Wiseman be divided? They were all three caught up in a web of accusations meant to gratify some of the more seedy elements in American political life. Meanwhile, our Bridgewater State hospitals still stand; and the human beings in them bother us only rarely, when a film like this one comes along or a particularly scandalous story (like the two I mentioned at the beginning) breaks into the news. We can even shut out those bothersome reports. The inmates of Bridgewater know that, know the limits of our concern. When we see them, that knowledge of theirs, never stated but apparent, unnerves us. For a second *our* privacy is invaded, *we* are stripped bare. Then we compose ourselves, and we become angry. The rest is easy and perhaps has been best described by T. S. Eliot: "We demand a committee, a representative committee, a committee of investigation. Resign Resign Resign."

Senses and Sensibility

Alabama's Institute for the Deaf and the Blind was founded two years before the Civil War began. It is now a nationally known and respected institution located in Talladega, about fifty miles east of Birmingham. I remember Anna Freud mentioning AIDB, as it is known, during a discussion of the special challenges that fate puts to blind and deaf children as they grow up. She and her colleagues in child psychoanalysis were much interested in such children and had done some substantial work with them, especially blind boys and girls. Miss Freud asked about AIDB in the way foreigners often do when they come to a country with limited knowledge of its geography. She came regularly to New Haven and New York and was no stranger to certain other cosmopolitan cities, but the South was not her regular beat. With a certain wistfulness she looked around the Yale dormitory room where we had been sitting and then made a comment I can still hear: "I'd like to go visit that school [AIDB] one day."

She never realized that wish, but she would certainly be enthralled by the results of someone else's visit. Frederick Wiseman's four film documentaries on the AIDB run nine hours. They attempt to show how the blind, the deaf, or those blind *and* deaf (and perhaps impaired in other ways) manage at a residential school, how they become reasonably educated and even begin to make their way in the outside world. With such films, Wiseman has been directing a school, of sorts, for two decades: he has wanted to help us overcome our own versions of blindness and deafness.

After he had completed *Titicut Follies*, Wiseman turned his attention to one institution after another: a high school, a court, a department store, a hospital, a racetrack, a seminary, a city's welfare system, a place where young military recruits are indoctrinated, a slaughterhouse. Each film is meant to place us viewers in the midst of a particular social and institutional scene, in the hope that as we view people going about their chores, doing what they are paid to do or required by law or custom to do, and hear what is said (or shouted or whispered), we will know more about our large and complex nation.

Wiseman's four documentaries on AIDB amount to his most ambitious project yet. "Before I made these films my experience and knowledge of deaf and/or blind people was limited, practically nonexistent," Wiseman explained. "When I began to think about it I realized that I had never gone to school with anyone who was deaf or blind, nor did I have any contact in my work or social life with anyone who was without one or both of these basic senses." Of the four films, *Blind* and *Deaf* are the two basic texts. They aim to show how children make do without sight or hearing—how they learn to take care of themselves, to read and write, to get on successfully with others, to negotiate their way in a world where vision is taken for granted, as is the capacity to understand the spoken word. *Multi-Handicapped* and *Adjustment and Work* take us further along: to the more strenuous difficulties of those who are both deaf and dumb (or have, for instance, cerebral palsy as an additional disability), and to the adulthood of those who have attended AIDB and now hope to find work, to achieve a significant degree of personal and financial independence.

Each of the four films invites us, first, to the South, to Talladega, Alabama: the country roads, the fields with their crops, the Winn Dixie market, the homes, modern and Victorian, the courthouse, and, inevitably, a strip, with gas stations, honky-tonk stores, and fast-food restaurants. All four films present a Southern city's social life: the genteel white neighborhoods, the modest homes of working-class white or black families, the streets where impoverished blacks struggle for survival. All four also offer sights and sounds that many of the children who attend AIDB have missed: the well-known Talladega stock-car racetrack, with its zooming machines and boisterous crowds, the mock-elegant world of mall shopping, and, most affecting, the simple but powerful noise of the railroad engine—again, Willa Cather's "cold, vibrant scream."

Deaf and *Blind* essentially chronicle the way children in two quite unusual residential-school settings spend their time. Early in *Blind*, we notice one form of affluence: the sunglasses of those who can afford to dim their vision. Minutes later we meet boys and girls who are learning to feel their way along corridors, who follow voices, who brave their own kind of adventures. The students are black and white, boy and girl, quite bright and retarded. No matter—they hold hands and seem thoroughly at ease with one another, blind in a different sense of the word to differences that the rest of us are quick to regard as important, even when quite young.

Not able to notice skin color or clothes, they attend to the texture of cement or wood or glass—what it feels like when a cane (or one's hand) moves from one part of a building to another. They learn with the cane to "sight" an approaching door or set of stairs. They learn not so much to rely on the cane as to master it. With no embarrassment or sense of irony they and their teachers talk of going to "see" what is out there awaiting them—paths to trod, directions to pursue, choices to make. They "keep looking." They "watch for" landmarks. They listen hard. They find a water fountain and feel the obvious satisfactions of an important discovery.

They play sports. They learn braille. They let their fingers feel the way to a control of a needle and thread: they knit, they sew. They talk with their teachers about family troubles—a drunken father, a broken marriage, a disappointment experienced on a home visit. They feel low and hesitant at times. But they are constantly encouraged and complimented—in soft, Southern drawls that seem especially fitting for such occasions. Throughout the film the camera is kept busy, moving from room to room, activity to activity: children playing, cooking, learning to make change, creating messes, cleaning up after themselves, dancing, and, finally, getting ready for bed. As they pray before falling asleep, the film begins to conclude. The moon is out. The lights of the city are turned on. Soon, all will be darkness—though for these children there is, alas, no such transition.

Deaf (2 hours and 43 minutes) is half an hour longer than *Blind*. The structure of *Deaf* is similar to that of *Blind*—the camera's constant attention to the events of a school day. Children learn to sign, to read lips and, not least, to use their vocal chords, to talk—no easy task for someone who has not heard himself or herself speak, never mind anyone else. Gradually Wiseman's camera shows us the special technology that a contemporary school for deaf children requires—lights for a phone or a clock alarm, closed-caption television, a "minicom" typewriter that enables telephone conversation. But teachers matter more than those devices; only they can see what happens between them and their students as they try to comprehend each other. Some of the teachers are deaf themselves, and their earnest professional devotion obviously draws on reservoirs of personal experience.

The centerpiece of *Deaf* offers a family squabble (one by no means peculiar to AIDB children and their parents). A fourteen-year-old boy has threatened suicide several times, declaring his mother indifferent to him. The mother has driven to the school from Mobile, and for three-quarters of an hour we watch her, her son, a wise and empathic counselor, and the school's principal talk about what is happening to this family. The biological father has spurned Peter because of his deafness, yet even though a stepfather likes him and pays him favorable attention, he yearns for his "first daddy." The estrangement between mother and son is obvious—the aloofness each uses for self-protection, the hurt pride each displays.

All over the world youths and parents struggle with one another in similar ways for similar reasons. What distinguishes this confrontation is the obvious difficulty a mother and a son have in speaking to each other. The mother's signing is inadequate, and the youth is ready to use such a failure as an immediate indictment of her. Wiseman dwells on this scene not to show a special psychopathology, but to remind us of universals that transcend difficulties such as deafness—the failures of trust and love that mark the lives of so many of us.

In all four of Wiseman's documentaries of AIDB, teachers are heard at some length discussing the progress of various students, their small victories and persisting troubles. Often the talk becomes psychological, the dreary jargon one hears everywhere in this country today. Several times the viewer is transported from a concrete, arresting teaching situation to an abstract psychological discussion, with banal words such as "individuation" and "adjustment" filling, if not fouling, the air. So it goes, the bemused filmmaker seems to be telling us.

At such moments I kept wishing Anna Freud *had* visited AIDB before she died. She had little use for psychological pretentiousness and enormous respect for the daily fortitude and intelligence of the many teachers she knew in the course of her life. Often enough, I remember, she presented herself as the one who needed to learn— and she would have learned a lot had she gone to Alabama or, for that matter, seen Wiseman's films. She put in a considerable number of clinical hours observing and working with blind children, and in volume 5 of her *Writings* ("Research at the Hampstead Child-Therapy Clinic and Other Papers") she takes note several times of the stumbling blocks and quandaries that blindness and deafness (or bodily impairments of various kinds) can present to children. The young take in the world—including the image of a mother, a father, and, needless to say, themselves—through their eyes. The young also hear the words "yes" and "no" every day—the encouragement and the disapproval that create a conscience that works effectively (but not imperiously, crazily) in later life.

It is probably no accident that *Deaf* is a noisier, more truculent film than *Blind*. In the former, the teachers sometimes—no matter the camera's presence—seem sorely tested, even on the verge of an outburst. The deaf children are more combative, the blind more self-effacing. In psychoanalytic language, the deaf sometimes experience special hurdles in "super-ego formation"; the blind may be particularly tested by the vicissitudes of "narcissism." For years, however, Anna Freud urged on her psychoanalytic colleagues restraint in such formulations, common sense in their application to individuals or groups of people, and, most insistently, the research initiative she called "direct observation": keeping theoretical conjecture to a minimum until, as she once put it, "we have something to contemplate." Wiseman's films would have held her close attention, would have prompted her, I suspect, to want to look at the entire footage he secured in Talladega.

Even as the psychoanalyst must struggle with his or her subjectivity, a filmmaker such as Wiseman presents us with a mix of objective reportage and a particular artist's attitude. He is at pains to let us hear the school officials talk about budgets and political lobbying in the state capital, Montgomery, because he wants to make the point that much of the sensitivity and compassion we have witnessed is enabled by tough, shrewd, behind-the-scenes bargaining sessions. He asks us to listen to A. D. Gaston, the ninety-two-year-old black Birmingham entrepreneur, talking of "dream power," of *his* "handicapped" (segregated) earlier life as a grandson of slaves, born in turn-of-the-century poverty, because Gaston's speech is animated and entertaining, but also, one suspects, because yet another bigshot comes across as occasionally full of himself and full of hot air, and we had best remember that neither blindness nor deafness (Gaston's words are translated beautifully into sign language) need deny anyone an exposure to life's funny or absurd moments. Wiseman the filmmaker and editor is also Wiseman the visual poet, the social critic, the ironist—someone probing social reality, yes, but also arranging it, composing it, as artists or writers do. During the days when I watched these four powerful films, I kept reading reviews of them, and biographical accounts of the man who had to fight considerable odds to make them, to have them shown uncut. He is on record as having taken on the very people who can stand between his work and thousands of viewers, the Corporation for Public Broadcasting, where an endemic insularity often threatens and where, in Wiseman's words, "personal politics, the buddy system, jealousy, and pop ideology dominate the panel discussions."

One way Wiseman's critics get back at him is by calling his work "boring" or "repetitive" or "too demanding." I kept seeing such comments in the reviews, even from those who in general admire Wiseman's work. My wife, a schoolteacher, suggested that we show the films to some children the same age as many who appear in *Deaf* and *Blind*, ten to thirteen, and we did. They were utterly taken by what they saw. They scarcely moved. They remained silent. At moments they gasped in admiration or disbelief. (True, they were suburban children going to fine schools, and they were no strangers to serious assignments pushed by their elders.) We gave the films to one of our sons, who had been working with troubled ghetto children. He and they, too, sat still and were held spellbound throughout both *Blind* and *Deaf*. Afterward the boys and girls voiced a flurry of questions and offered a range of lively comments.

Exactly who is "bored" by these films? Perhaps some of us are offended because as experts or announcers we have been denied employment, refused permission to do what we otherwise do so commonly on television and elsewhere in our national life: make pronouncements, assert our authority, get seen and heard. Wiseman's are not the neatly packaged, carefully timed productions that feature smooth-speaking narrators and self-assured pundits. For years Wiseman has kept the experts at bay. His films feature only the inhabitants of the particular world he aims to regard closely. He has had no trouble finding "average" men, women, and children who have a lot to say about this life, about their fate.

Throughout his career Frederick Wiseman has dared explore directly the fullest range of human experience. In film after film he has rendered us as we are—the complexities, ambiguities, ironies, inconsistencies, contradictions that inform our life. He is akin, really, to some of our writers of short fiction, anxious to comprehend through a particular angle of vision our contingent lives: the way we are shaped by institutions, certainly, but the way we can stand up to them, take only so much from them, or find our own ways of breaking free of them. His careful, respectful, persistent regard for plain, ordinary people puts him in the company of writers such as Raymond Carver, Richard Ford, Bobbie Ann Mason, Toni Morrison, James Alan McPherson—storytellers, not social scientists. While sociologists increasingly play with banks of computers and spew an impenetrably mannered, opaque, highfalutin language and most anthropologists stay resolutely in the Third World, Wiseman and his camera attend the contours of our daily life, and in the end, as with fiction, help us better see and hear ourselves.

Robert Frank's America

To some extent we see the world we are looking for. We select for ourselves visually what our minds and hearts crave to notice. Such a remark can be a mere banality, yet it can also become charged with significance if realized in connection with a particular experience. I remember, for instance, walking with a child who was a pediatric patient of mine, a sick boy who would soon die. He kept observing vulnerability—birds chased away by people, squirrels scurrying up the trunks of trees in fear, an elderly lady trembling as she negotiated her way through a crowded street. I had been noticing the weather: it was a sunny, briskly comfortable day, the sky's blue unmarred by clouds of any kind, and spring's always touching, if sentimental arrival—daffodils holding their heads high, the earth fully exposed and soft after the snow had beat its last retreat, the bushes almost palpably ready to begin donning their green clothes. But the boy would have no part of me and my angle of vision, my particular perceptual field, the objects I chose to attend. When he saw me admiring those daffodils, he addressed me in this unforgettable way: "They'll die soon. They'll turn brown and wither away. Then no one will look at them anymore."

I was devastated, of course. I knew he was talking about himself; was telling me how sick he felt; was telling me of his awareness that he had all too little time left. Years later, when I'd gone into child psychiatry and watched children watching the world, heard children telling me what they saw (and what they couldn't bear to see), I would often remember that boy, one of my first child patients, actually, and an important teacher. When Anna Freud lectured to us, told us out of her vast experience as a child psychoanalyst how "differently each of us sees even the same scene, selecting from it what we want to emphasize out of our personal needs and nature," I thought, yet again, of that boy: he knew how such a process, at once cognitive and emotional, works—and told me so, ever so poignantly, after he'd realized how sad I'd become upon hearing his remarks about the daffodils. Like not a few patients, he wanted to heal, even as he needed to be healed; and so, once more, the doctor was helped by the person in need of help, with this remark: "Oh, don't feel *too* bad, doc, because they *are* pretty, right now, so we can enjoy them a little bit." Then he did allow himself to do exactly that, to look and look.

Robert Frank came here from Switzerland to look and look—brought with him his own particular sensibility, and soon enough offered us in *The Americans* an aspect of ourselves. He did not show us all there is to see, obviously, but a selected number of images meant to convey one more lyrical observer's examination of this wonderfully sprawling and changing subcontinent, its people so diverse, its social and cultural history so dramatic and compelling to contemplate and so thickly textured. Even as Frank's photographs offer—well, in a way, *him* as much as the "Americans" he chose to connect with, as a photographer and, later, as someone assembling a portfolio, a book, so we readers will have our individual responses to what is offered by Mr. Frank, who (to make matters even more complicated, as I fear is necessary) might well now choose different photographs from among the many he took, and might well choose to take others altogether, were he on some more contemporary self-assignment.

All of the above is a prelude to a wish, so to speak—my constant personal wish that Robert Frank could have known the William Carlos Williams of the 1930s and 1940s and early 1950s, who gave us in poems and short stories and novels and essays a series of remarkably vivid and searching portraits of ourselves—of our manners of speech, our habits and preferences, our ideals, our worries, our aspirations. I well remember seeing *his* eyes at work—as set, in their ways, as that sick child's were. I well remember, as mentioned, trudging with him up and down those New Jersey tenement-house stairs during his medical rounds, a plain doc, seeing plain people: the poor, the hard-pressed, the newly arrived in America, men and women and children who, often enough, never paid him. Not in cash, at least; they did give him rather a lot as that writing doctor knew—they gave him themselves, in all their diversity, exuberance, vitality, assertiveness, melancholy, bitterness, apathy, gave him the ambiguities and contradictions and inconsistencies that make us what we are, make us more than a match for the various categorical-minded theorists who want to declare their unequivocal findings. "Look—over there," he'd exclaim as we'd walk the streets of Paterson, an industrial city that has harbored so many different immigrants over the generations. I would look—often enough to be interrupted by another, similar situation: a poet at work, noticing and noticing, preparatory to the crafting of words and phrases, of images and metaphors and symbols, for him the evening's effort that followed all that daily doctoring.

What Williams saw was in certain respects what Frank saw: waiters and waitresses, people riding buses and trains and motorcycles, children in playgrounds carving out their various territories, real and imaginary, barber shops, billiard parlors, gas stations, tables and chairs and juke boxes and statues and cemeteries and cars everywhere—cars, the great ticket to American citizenship. "If I couldn't get me a car when I was grown, I'd ask the Lord to call me back," said a black Alabama sharecropper's young son to me in desperate hope, in fearful expectation, he who barely had enough food to get him by, but who saw the automobile as a virtual incarnation of God's judgment: either saved in America, or destined never to be of any use at all here, hence someone to be "recalled" (even as the rest of us know about automobiles that get recalled!).

I remember Williams with his own car, forgetting to shift, stalling, squeezing the brakes too hard, cursing the motor, the tire that had disappointed, fallen flat—roaring with excitement at the other cars passing by, their inhabitants roaring themselves, the horns, the lights flashing, the radios blaring, the voices working their way into the (mostly) modest streets. "Voices!" / he once virtually shouted (in *Paterson*), "multiple and inarticulate, voices / clattering loudly to the sun, to / the clouds. voices / assaulting the air gaily from all sides." A bit further on (picking up ironically on Alexander Hamilton's characterization) he would refer to "the 'great beast' come to sun himself," his Americans—and how hard he worked as a poet to capture their language, its nuances, its moments of strength, its weaker spells, its victories and defeats. Once I asked him, as others had before, why he didn't stop practicing medicine and work as a poet full-time. "Hell, I can't do that," he shot back, and he explained sternly, "These people feed me! Their tough, plenty tough struggle to stay afloat, to keep breathing, gives me life, keeps my head alive and humming." He, who would write *In The American Grain*, could never stop finding his fellow citizens enlivening, a challenge to the imagination.

And so with Frank's *The Americans*: a statement of the life and death that a particular bourgeois Swiss man, poised with a camera, happened to find as he crossed a particular continent at a particular time in his and its life. Frank was no muckraker, no Dorothea Lange or Lewis Hine, despite those who want to appropriate him politically, even including (maybe) himself. There is a great and raw dignity in his glimpses, his gazing, his inspections and arrangements of a few of the billions of fragments of what the abstract mind tries to summarize with a sound, a word: "reality." This is a mid-century watch of sorts, scenes obtained by a lens both misty and keen-eyed. The moving spirit is more the lyricist (albeit grim or downcast or sardonic or appalled or enraged) than the social analyst, the political activist, or the moralist. I may be wrong (is the issue with respect to photographic impressions really one of right or wrong?), but I sense affection and surprise and perplexity more than outrage and horror in a Robert Frank whose own sensuality, one comes to believe, is fired by that of lots of other people.

True, there is death, too, literally and symbolically, in these presentations (in the form of representations) of our life. Yet, a certain gauzy restraint obtains; the camera's holder is excited as well as saddened, just as in the Bible the angel of Death is never denied his dramatic, powerfully stirring possibilities as a continual presence in our lives. I think it would be a mistake for us to appropriate the bleak, cheerless, heavy-hearted side of Frank's footage in the service of a wholesale, embittered denunciation. Lord knows, America is not perfect; and there is a long tradition of the outsider arriving to criticize this country, with even one as usually shrewd and open-eyed as Dickens, alas, succumbing to bitterness, as in the notes, letters, and essays that he wrote while he worked his way across the nation. I believe it is the enviable power and the great mysteries of our giant nation that sometimes induce such an angry response—the sprawling energy and promise of the mighty geography, the apparently endless procession of "others" who have yearned out of their desperation and hope for these shores, and who, by God, have gotten here, have become part of what is here.

It was a storyteller's dream, Kerouac's words wedded to Frank's pictures—yet another stab into the American dark. The two of them gave all of us readers and viewers a bit of light, and we were grateful. To this day my students look at Frank's look at their country, its people, and remember places and things, and they read Williams's *Paterson*, and Whitman, and get sentimental—a danger; but they also become truly, cannily observant in a contemplative way, as they catch a sharper-than-usual glance at the crowded, hassled urban landscape. "There be plenty of sick ones, and death will come and take me soon," that Alabama child's mother once told my wife and me, "but I'm not ready to quit this place, yet, and who knows what a smiling God may have in store for us here." Us here, in America.

Photographers under Twenty-Five

Today's young photographers (say, under twenty-five) have grown up in a century that itself has witnessed the emergence from obscure infancy of an art, even a profession that is now thoroughly grown up, able to exert its particular hold on our aesthetic and moral imagination. The camera has become a mainstay of our ordinary life—both the camera that brings us snapshots and family albums and the camera that brings us the movies, not to mention the constant presence in our homes of television. In a sense, then, this has been a century of hugely expanded vision, maybe not in the introspective, ethically awake use of that word, but in the more literal meaning: we can see so very much, through telescopes that take us across unimaginable distances, across aeons of time, and through microscopes that get to the very heart of matter, and, again, through the constant parade of images that come our way at our beck and call—a TV button pushed, a movie ticket bought, the click of a picture-taking instrument that we have purchased at no enormous cost. Even our newspapers, magazines, and books, means to a different kind of visual experience, the sight and contemplation of words, have become more insistently illustrative, and, of course, the book as itself a pictorial rather than a textual event is nothing new.

All of us are sighted, as it were, in ways and to a degree that we may take for granted, may never fully realize. Indeed, as I look at the photographs taken by young photographers, and read the personal statements that sometimes go with them, I once again remember conversations I had with Erik Erikson, a distinguished psychoanalyst (hence someone trained to listen carefully, to attend the spoken language of those who lie prone, their eyes unable to see him) but also an artist whose promising career took a turn when he met Anna Freud in Vienna and, shortly thereafter, began a course of training in what he once called "looking within"—an activity he contrasted to that of his earlier life, when he "looked at the world outside [himself] and tried to represent it to others, in a personal way, of course." Erikson was actually much given to reflection upon that word *looking*—even decades after he'd stopped making sketches and woodcuts, in favor of making sense of what analysands told him or, through the study of lives such as those of Luther and Gandhi, the study of history itself, as it gets shaped by such individuals. I well recall how he started one long discussion we had, triggered by that word *looking*—remember him trying to remember his own youth, lived in the first decades of this century, as compared to the youths of those he treated psychoanalytically or encountered as a much-revered college professor in the later decades of the same century: "I think our eyes are worked harder now—but maybe we take them for granted more."

He paused, prepared to expand upon the irony he had just summoned, and then, in a long reminiscence, tried to explain his sense of an important generational distinction:

When I first became involved with psychoanalysis, I was in my twenties and I wasn't sure where I was going in life. I was an artist—people called me that: I did drawings and woodcuts. Then I got a job teaching—in a school whose children were the sons and daughters of people being psychoanalyzed by Freud and his colleagues. That's how I got into [psychoanalytic] training—Anna Freud felt I'd do well, working with children. She was then developing a whole new field: child psychoanalysis. I remember saying to her one day [in analysis with her] that 'I'm not for this,' words to that effect. She wanted to know why—of course!—and even now I can hear myself replying: 'You people are listeners, and I'm someone who learns in a different way.' She wanted me to go on, and I did; I told her that my eyes were the way I took in the world, more so than my ears. She didn't say anything more—the [analytic] hour winded down; but the next day we were back at the same subject, and she very nicely told me, at one point, that 'child analysis really needed visual people.' I didn't know what she meant, so she explained herself. She reminded me that young children take in the world through their eyes; language comes later. Then she gave me a bit of a lecture—she was a precise, clear-headed teacher. She said that in analysis we have to learn to *see*, as well as to hear; we have to 'take in' the person we're working with, through our eyes as well as our ears. We were getting into a lot of psychological symbolism, obviously; I'll spare you the details! But what I remember from that hour—well, I was given a kind of sanction: I'm someone who engages with the world through my eyes, and they will be as important in my work with patients as they are when I'm working on a canvas or with a pencil or pen and paper.

Back then, in our psychoanalytic conferences, everything was talk: the patient said this, and that, and we had this or that to say in response [as discussants of the case]. In contrast, I was always asking about *appearances*—and I hoped I wasn't being 'superficial'. As I look back at that time, and compare it with our time, I realize how different this world is. Now, our eyes are constantly being given something to do! Back then, many psychoanalysts talked of closing their eyes, while they listened, listened very intently. Now, we look and look and look—and our patients are telling us that they saw this, they saw that, at the movies and on TV and in the magazine advertisements. You have to have come from another world, maybe, to appreciate what this one is like—and yet, I'm not sure a lot of people really *notice* things, pay attention to them, even if they're able to see everything, it seems, just by looking at the [movie or television] screen. Anna Freud once said, 'People hear, but they don't necessarily listen,' and I would add that these days, people look, but they don't necessarily see.

The issue, of course, is attention—whether it be visual or aural: what it is that impresses itself upon us to the point where we pay heed, go beyond the blur of sight or sound, focus on an image or a remark in such a way that we are given reflective pause? Under such circumstances, a person is going through an experience, a moment in time that matters—something truly witnessed, something truly heard and kept in mind, as opposed to the rush of things that the existentialist philosophers (and psychologists) call "everyday-ness": the inattentiveness that characterizes a headlong or bored or distracted or self-absorbed drift or plunge through time, when we are "turned off," a description that applies to the relationship be-tween our sensory apparatus (eyes and ears) and our cognitive and ethical eyes. In contrast, a breakthrough moment has us, suddenly, alive to the world, and, of course, to ourselves: now we are awake to what is out there, and awake to ourselves as part of what makes up a particular scene, so that the self experiences both itself and what (who) is around it. Not that the choice is *only* ours; sometimes we are seized, so to speak, by the world, grabbed by its press of events, of stimuli, shaken into a wakefulness that brings us to full (emotional, sensual, moral) life—hence the phenomenological insis-tence that "the self is the way an individual structures experience." On occasion we cry, amidst boredom, for such "experience." At other times, we are all too preoccupied, hence relatively impervious to such "experience"; the world passes by us, locked as we are within a consciousness that is often more semi-consciousness.

Youth is for some, who live in the relative comfort of the bour-geois West, such a time of self-absorption: of a well-known willfulness that fuels a decided turn from the ordinary, the conven-tional, and a seeming indifference (if not hostility) to what others take seriously. Once, working psychiatrically with such a young per-son, I heard all of the foregoing given a sharply knowing, almost revelatory condensation: "I'll be in a daze, because that's where I want to be, I guess, and then suddenly, I'll see something, I'll really grab on to it, and then I'm not just me and my thoughts, I'm me letting the world come inside. I call it, getting hit by a sight."

I kept thinking of him, under twenty-five then, as I looked at the photographic "sights" that certain young men and women have cho-sen to display—their take on what is around them, their visual grasp of things, their capture, as it were, of a "hit" sent their way. Their particular sights become, for us, a collective or generational sighting. They memorialize, courtesy of the camera: streets and rooms and stores and fields and cars and public conveyances, a phone booth here, a bed there, and through it all, human beings in various shapes and sizes going through the motions of life, and thereby, one speculates, bringing to life (giving direction and purpose to) these youthful observers who, as Erikson reminded us, have it in their capacity to roam a particular world so that what they come to regard seriously, the rest of us are enabled to glimpse, then perhaps take in, and finally take seriously—a visual culture yet again comes at us, even in books, once the exclusive province of words that (as William Carlos Williams once put it) "you hear, while reading them."

I think of Williams, too, (and once more) as I look at those photographs, those "sights"—they transport me from one observed or imagined world to another. Williams was, like Erikson, an artist as well as a writer. He painted pictures, looked at them with enormous interest, and had close friends such as Marsden Hartley and Charles Sheeler, whose canvases attracted much attention from those who visited galleries and museums. He was a determined "localist," ever ready to spot the arresting, the ironic, the amusing, the melancholy, or the scary in the neighborhood where he lived, on the streets he traveled to do his medical work. In his stories and his verse (and especially in *Paterson*), he cast his eyes upon scenes he knew well, even as his ears had recorded for him the rhythms of a language-in-the-making, the vernacular expression of immigrant, working-class life. "I use my eyes and ears to find my wits," he once tersely put it. Similarly, these young men and women try to apprehend what is available, courtesy of luck and chance and circumstance: it is their fate to be *here*, to notice what is *there*. Out of such a world as Paterson, so ordinary and humble, comes nothing less than inspiration, Williams knew—and so it has gone for these young photographers, who have dared take to heart (again, the refrain) what he put forward as a challenge: "outside/outside myself/there is a world ...."

Such a world is always a mix of the objective and the subjective—the individual's sensibility coming to terms with an observable reality. Even as painters explored themselves, the range of their own feelings and attitudes, through the representations they gave to the external world (Expressionism), today's photographers know to look inward, upon occasion, by looking outward; know to let their minds play with, amplify, modify, and distort what their eyes have chosen to recognize, their hands (courtesy of technology) to record—a camera's click becomes, in no time, Cartier-Bresson's "decisive moment." To grow up, actually, is to be able to experience such an awareness: time selected and considered; time wrested from eternity, from its endless succession; time now become the occasion of an event that the eyes want to do more than behold—want to possess, then share with others, in the hope that one person's "moment" becomes that of another, even if from afar.

"We learn from one another," Dr. Williams once said impatiently, after hearing a medical student ask him about his patients and their "role" in his writing life, the time for which he had to steal, bits and pieces, from an extremely busy medical practice. Today's photographers tell us in their personal statements, and through their pictures, what they have learned from the people and the places that have figured in their lives. In backlots and buses, in bedrooms, the camera, in knowing, subtle hands, brings us up close to a late-twentieth-century American life in all its variety. We have here the universals of human experience: we all eat and sleep and form attachments, and, alas, we form grudges, feel distrust and worse. When I look at a photograph in which a woman sits on the side of a bed and a man stands with his back toward her, his face toward me, the viewer, I think of Edward Hopper's expeditions into such rooms:

love and its affirmations, its possible discontents, the strange and haunting intimacy that stirs minds mightily, the minds of the ones who are or have been making love, and the minds of the rest of us, who look and remember and wander and wonder in our thoughts. Hopper, like Williams (whom he much admired), took to the streets near his home, and what he didn't actually see (and, later, use in his work), he saw in a different sense: the imagination can create its own world of sight and sound, hence Hopper's wonderfully suggestive, evocative paintings, which "tell" of restaurants and movie houses and offices and living rooms or bedrooms, of porches and railroad stations, each the beginning of a story that the viewer is meant to extend and conclude. The viewer's personal stamp gets imposed upon what is, after all, pigment artfully arranged on a piece of cloth tacked up or framed for a painting.

Erikson was right—we today *see* so very much, courtesy of technology. But as a psychoanalyst (and as a person), Erikson knew that all of us, no matter where and when we live, and no matter how long we have been here and how long we have to go, must do as these people in these pictures do: get something to eat; travel to work or to our homes; have fun, play; connect with others; laugh, or look sad because we feel low; take in the world (its beauty, its ugliness) and give back to the world (our ways of being, acting). To be under twenty-five, then, and graced with the skill to take touching or powerful or arresting or unsettling pictures is, finally, to be a human being, put here with that camera of cameras, the mind's eye, and all it can envision, suppose, guess, dream, gather— and offer to others.

The Bible As Documentary

For a quarter of a century the novelist (and poet and playwright and essayist) Reynolds Price has drawn a writer's inspiration from the Hebrew and Christian Bible. *Palpable God* (1978) brings together Price's translations from both those sacred texts, including "The Good News According to Mark," the oldest, briefest, most pointed of the four gospels. In the same book Price also offers a powerfully suggestive essay on "the origins and life of narrative"—with a first paragraph that sounds a clarion call for any of us who, smitten by a documentary impulse, may choose to learn about the lives of others, then offer what has been discovered to a world more needy than we may have realized:

> A need to tell and hear stories is essential to the species *Homo Sapiens*—second in necessity apparently after nourishment and before love and shelter. Millions survive without love or home, almost none in silence; the opposite of silence leads quickly to narrative, and the sound of story is the dominant sound of our lives, from the small accounts of our days' events to the vast incommunicable constructs of psychopaths.

Now, in *Three Gospels*, Price extends his Biblical foray; puts forth a translation of the fourth gospel, that of John; gives us again his translation of Mark from years ago; and brings to each of those efforts substantial introductions that both shine with a luminous knowledge, a sound judgment acquired out of a devoted scholarship, and sparkle with an expository originality, savvy, verve. Moreover, Price takes a bold further step and dares to give us "an honest account of a memorable life," his own "modern apocryphal gospel," which gets its own explanatory preface. All of the above comes to us from a gifted storyteller who has become not a theologian or a Biblical "authority" but his own kind of scholar, fluent in Greek, versed in the particulars of an historical era, and quite determined that we keep in mind the heart of the matter with respect to the four gospels—that they offer what certain individuals close to a charismatic teacher and healer remembered about his brief, eventful, history-shaking life: the gospels as, in our terms, an oral or documentary history that got told, written, and then transmitted over the generations.

We are reminded constantly by this contemporary translator and narrator of "good news" (what "gospel" means) that we ourselves observe the world and convey our impressions to others (our children, grandchildren, students, and friends) and that such a deliverance of the seen, the heard, the remembered and the told is quite natural. "Such spans of time [the years between the death of Jesus and the writing of, say, Mark]—stretched across no more than two or three contiguous lives—are not necessarily fatal to an oral tradition that has urgent reasons for reviewing itself," Price observes, and he then presents this challenge to a certain segment of the academic world: "Yet, in recent years, as Christian scholars have grown more and more punitively self-limiting in the structures they set around their work—structures that amount to degrees of suspicion unfamiliar in sober historians of other fields—such unimpeachable-sounding traditions have been severely questioned and often rejected with striking degrees of misrepresentation." It is as if the subject matter of the gospel writers (whom Price calls "reporters," and whose narrative strategies he finds affecting and compelling because they make, as he puts it, "sound human and literary sense") requires an ironic, formidable skepticism: "If the gospels did not concern the life of someone with alleged divine origins, most students would have long since accepted the early testimony."

Not that Price means by such "acceptance" a conviction that is faith; rather, the issue has to do with the conventional relaying of events—history as it was shaped in the past (and is now as well) by those who want to recall, describe, and chronicle events. In Price's pointed comment: "a great teacher's pupils preserve his memory." To be sure, there are plenty of inconsistencies to be considered, plenty of mysteries and confusions that don't yield to the assertions and explanations of these four narrators; and Price speaks of "fresh documentary evidence" as a potential cloud that would diminish the authority of these stories. Yet, for him, the gospels are a documentary record that has, in fact, been scrutinized as thoroughly as any in our recorded history and still has a persuasive tug to it, one that has certainly stood the test of time. Of course, there were four gospel writers, and their different approaches to a story remind us of the central issue of all narrative, of documentary writing, of reporting, of historical exposition: who chooses to emphasize what, and for which reasons.

In his *Quest for The Historical Jesus*, Albert Schweitzer needed no overwrought psychological theory to help him realize the earthy obvious: that biographers, bent on the telling of lives, aiming at an evocation of what happened to whom (and when, and why) will inevitably be telling us about themselves—and so Price, referring to the "various lives" of Jesus written in the nineteenth century, speaks of "the Jesus wanted or needed by their individual authors." (He creates such a Jesus himself, as he is candidly at pains to inform us.) In the brief preface to his own "account" of the life of Jesus Price speaks of the "magnetic" consequences of a life that has so clearly shaped history and too, he acknowledges a writer's temptation: to draw upon four chronologies of a singular life in hopes of constructing "a harmony of all known gospel themes." Things were similar, of course, back then; the individuals who give us Jesus picked and chose their way through what was said, heard, recalled, and stressed in accordance not only with *what was*, but with who *they were* as individuals, and who their informants happened to be. Mark heavily relied upon Peter, and some believe that John was an eyewitness who decided late in life that he wanted to confide his memories, not to mention turn them into a soaring, commanding affirmation whose spell would hold others in its steady, demanding grip for thousands of years.

No question, Mark was the leanest of the gospel writers; his is a bare-bones, disciplined presentation that denies us much of Jesus' moral preaching, not to mention the unfolding of the resurrection story. When the three women who dearly love Jesus and surely miss him come to pay their early-Sunday-morning respects, they are told by a young man that "He was raised," and they are urged to go inform His disciples of that outcome, whereupon, in Price's version of Mark, "Going out they fled the tomb—they were shuddering and wild—and they told no one nothing for they were afraid."

To a modern sensibility, even one disposed toward religious faith, such a conclusion is easier to contemplate than that of John, who renders the risen, yet returned Christ directly. Here, Mark's women in terrified flight become John's women who, with others, conversed with the man-become-God. Price contrasts, further, Mark's "no-nonsense reportage," his "bat-out-of-hell commitment to vivid ac-. tion" with John's vivid, metaphoric narration—the "prose story-teller" as against the "lyric visionary poet." These two are far more attractive to Price than the moral educators (as he sees them) who gave us the other two gospels—even as Price himself is, in keeping with Dr. Schweitzer's rule of thumb, both a poet and a spinner of yarns, short and long.

These two gospels and Price's own story are wonderfully inviting, enchanting in their narration; they tug at the mind and heart both. Price is a careful Biblical scholar in all three gospels, yet he is un-afraid of contemporary idiom when it seems appropriate (though never "smart," a modern wise guy determined to flaunt jazzed-up talk, to be "with it"). This mix of the respectful, even the erudite and the relaxed, the informal, when fitting, doesn't grab the reader abruptly, and so it isn't easily shown in any particular citation; rather, it is a matter of cumulative tone, of subtle shading, of a language that in its sum offers an immensely enveloping presentation of characters, events, and commentary. A translator has wanted to write of

Jesus in a special way. Other twentieth-century novelists (François Mauriac, Shusaku Endo) have given us biographies of Jesus; and D. H. Lawrence drew on the life of Jesus in his novel *The Man Who Died*. But Price brings us an extraordinary kind of documentary writing: it calls upon those other documentary narratives, called the gospels, yet it is assembled and presented by one of our century's own—and only a few years short of the second millennium.

In keeping with today's documentary tradition, Price summons the visual for himself, even as he offers the narratives of two gospel writers, and his own narrative to boot, for the rest of us. In *A Whole New Life*, an account of his struggle with a spinal-cord tumor, he tells us of a "happening" (his visionary encounter with Jesus) with matter-of-fact candor, yet quietly, tactfully: this is what, unaccountably, crossed my mind, touched my heart, a sighting, a pictured encounter of sorts. Now Price, the contemporary novelist, puts himself in the shoes of an ancient documentarian. To do so, he stands up boldly to the academic world, describes certain "theological claims" as "foolish excess baggage," even as he struggles to make sense of a gospel writer in the way we try to figure out diaries, letters, recorded testimonies, or "oral histories": "Certainly John's unique details of the ensuing arrest [of Jesus] in the garden suggest either eyewitness or a canny novelistic fabrication."

At one point, referring to a particular narrative manner and capability, Reynolds Price speaks of "John's theophanic shockers"— the striking metaphors that characterize that fourth gospel. The phrase is emblematic of John's present-day translator, his learned buddy, as it were, who gives us an erudition that mixes casually with the colloquial, the unceremonious, just as the young Jesus took the religious scholars by surprise with his vast learning whereas the older Jesus became a carpenter, spent his time with humble peasants, fishermen, and became the moral and spiritual leader of what this "latter-day" translator and gospelist calls "a small and threatened, largely working-class movement" whose ultimate fate we know, yet rightly still ponder.

The Bible for Children: Documentary Variations

For those of us who do documentary work, the matter of "truth" is a constant challenge, even a provocation: we try to lay claim to the actual, to what *is* (the palpable, the audible, the visible), but we keep realizing (if we dare keep our minds open) the many-sided and contingent nature of what gets called "reality," never mind a creed worthy of worship. We know, as we attend people closely, observe over time their manner, and pay heed to the rhythms of their language, the turns and shifts in their expressed thoughts, that even the soundest of us has to contend with inconsistencies and contradictions of word, of conviction, of feeling, of intent. What holds for the observed surely holds for the observer; we who regard others juggle within ourselves a range of views and values, not all of them coherently.

Under such circumstances, it is not hard to imagine what can happen on any day of a documentarian's life: a decision, a judgment is made about a person, a place, or an incident and is thereupon rendered, and the result is a double filtration of sorts: a selection of what to document, preceded and enabled by a selection made within the selector—attitudes and points of view summoned or set aside in order to arrive at a particular verbal or visual presentation. Put differently, a rendering of the external requires choice, and to make those choices, a writer or a photographer or a filmmaker has to come to terms with himself or herself—with the interior world through which the world outside must pass before it gains access to the reading, viewing eyes of others, the audience addressed in books, galleries, movie houses. All of the above is surely a matter of common sense, yet must be repeatedly stressed: we pick and choose our way through the perceptions that come to us, even as we "perform" in various ways for our readers, our viewers. But before doing so, we also "perform" for those others whom we are "studying," yet who are also an audience of sorts for us, hence that additional "variable": documentarians vary in what they will elicit from any given person or locale.

These days, we know to get insistent and specific about such matters. Ruth Bottigheimer does just this in her book, *The Bible for Children: From the Age of Gutenberg to the Present*. She refers to considerations of "class, country, century, and confession" to account for the variations in the Biblical stories that have been offered children over time—her way of reminding us that even with respect to religious and spiritual authority in the Bible the subjectivity of the translator, the illustrator (both living in a given era and national or cultural setting) encounters the so-called objectivity of the received canon or text, itself the outcome of earlier such meetings between human beings desirous of coming to terms with the stories of other human beings as those stories have been variously transmitted over the generations.

Children are, of course, a mirror of ourselves. We see in their future a chance to affirm our own earthly gropings toward immortality; what they learn to believe and do extends our hold on the things of this world. No wonder, then, many of us place such store by what our children learn, what they believe, what they look at or read; and no wonder even the book of books, Holy Scripture, becomes yet another aspect of that attentive parental concern—a series of narratives that have to pass the muster of particular mothers and fathers who live at a particular time and in a particular world.

Although a book with the title *The Bible for Children* will deservedly attract the attention of religious educators or literary critics, who will learn a lot about the way stories from the Hebrew Bible, especially, have been shorn of their brutality, violence, and sexual candor in keeping with social and cultural shifts in attitude, those of us who work with patients, who teach, say, literature or history in schools and colleges, or who are social scientists trying to understand how and why this or that society has been evolving in one or another way, will find much to consider in what is really a story about the fate of stories: how a received tradition is not "set in stone" but rather becomes the teller's to alter, to bend in accordance with what he or she finds proper, right, necessary, and believable. Editors, it must be remembered, are also narrators; they have their own ways of becoming a shaping part of books, films, and collections of photographs, even of those presented to the public as documentary, and even of texts regarded as spiritually authoritative, sacred—"the word of God."

So it was, says Bottigheimer, that "in general God's anger was gradually edited out of children's Bibles all over Europe in the course of the eighteenth century." So it was that around that time "authors and editors stripped their children's Bibles of outrageous narratives of rape, murder, incest, and betrayal that had elicited God's wrath and retribution." So it was that nothing less than "God's character" became radically transformed. He who had once been an inscrutable, hugely demanding, sometimes moodily unpredictable, even vengeful power gradually turned into "an educator of humanity," a thoroughly reasonable and even-handed and judicious presence who hovered benignly over all of us, if we would only be prayerfully receptive, responsive, attuned to His good intentions for us. The God who had Abraham ready to sacrifice his son Isaac and who had young Søren Kierkegaard (he who was unwilling to take seriously those kindly, "enlightened" Bibles for children) quaking in his boots, became the God of—well, such a deity has given way, really, to our rationalist notions of how we ought to treat one another *here* (never mind that *there* called heaven or hell). In Ruth Bottigheimer's apt concluding phrase, those Bible stories for children of yore (and of this present age as well) "mingle sacred text with secular values."

Bottigheimer's book is really a chronicle of those values as they have emerged and then come to bear upon the poetry and prose and parables that make up the Holy Book as it has been tendered young ones during this now fading second millennium.

For the author of this most instructive exercise in Biblical scholarship, in a literary criticism sensitive to historical knowledge, not to mention the assumptions of today's social science, the Bible becomes "a human document," and even its chronology, never mind its content, becomes subject to the knowledge of, the rules that govern "documentary history." We are asked to keep in mind that today, as in the past, the secular bears down hard on the sacred, hence the imprint of modern psychology and sociology on many of our contemporary children's Bibles—a turning toward "human beings as a centrally important component of Bible composition" rather than, say, an emphasis on God's unknowable, arbitrary, mightily insistent, pervasive impact on our lives.

In one century the Western world moved from Pascal to Rousseau, and soon enough the latter's abiding interest in human beings, in who *we* are, what *we* think (rather than who the Lord is, what the Lord might have in mind for us), would give us a God who is as eager to take notice of us as we are to take ourselves ever so seriously. It is no big step from this contemporary, culturally sanctioned egoism to a theology that has God hungering for *us*, rather than vice versa, or at least a God whose "thou" (we mortals, rather than we sinners) is more or less on a parity with His "I." Put differently, theology, as with children's Bibles, responds to a forceful social history that occupies its own territory in our unconscious assumptions, which we don't so much spell out as assume—hence Karl Barth's or Martin Buber's or Teilhard de Chardin's God. Protestant, Jewish, and Catholic, those theologians carry Darwin and Freud and Marx in their bones as they contemplate the Other Who, these days, can't be free of us, our yearnings (sometimes directed outward toward the heavens), our conceptual imagination, with its hierarchies and explanatory notions, narratives.

As certain historians have proposed (Phillipe Ariès and others), the very notion of childhood is tied to the specific conditions of certain places and times; and so a children's Bible is a memorial to ourselves and our habits of thought, an artifact (a foresighted skeptic might say) that might one day be regarded with curiosity, perplexity, amusement, even as we regard archaeological discoveries with the wry condescension that comes with today's muscle and might as it glances at what has crumbled under the weight of the centuries. Who of us, in that regard, will dare leap into the end of the next millennium and try to imagine how our twentieth-century ideas about children, or the Bible, or even science will then fare? If every present is a prelude to a future that in some way negates the past, the documentary history of children's Bibles will warrant many future chapters (though of course such efforts will be controversial insofar as they distance both the writer and reader from an unskeptical commitment to compliant faith).

While reading *The Bible for Children*, I remembered some moments I had a few years ago when I did documentary work with children. I was interested in these children's religious beliefs, in their thoughts about God, the Bible, our purpose (if any) on this planet. These were Catholic, Protestant, Jewish, Islamic, and essentially agnostic children. Some of those youngsters, barely ten, were startling in their capacity and willingness to edge close to the moral and cultural (and documentary) perspective that informs not only Bottigheimer's book but our secular, materialist world. One girl, a professed Catholic, kept asking not me but a nun who was teaching a Sunday-school class, why the four gospel writers wrote their stories, and why, before them, the prophets of the Hebrew Bible had done likewise. At first, the nun was confident and quick in her answer—to let others know of God, His commandments, and His incarnation in Jesus. But the youngster was almost brusque in her impatience with such a response—it was all too obvious and predictable, she seemed to indicate with her face, and with this further question: "But how did they know they were right, in what they said?" A pause, then she went on: "A lot of people say things, when they see things—so, how do you know which person has said it right; and besides, you can change your story sometimes."

The nun nodded. She hesitated before she answered, then told her questioner and her class, "God chose among people, and they're the ones in the Bible [as authors]." The class was silent for a few seconds, while the girl who had set the above in motion sat at her desk fidgeting. She opened her mouth as if she were about to ask something more, but then she closed her mouth, and looked around the room as well as at the teacher, who awaited further inquiry on the part of these fifth- and sixth-grade American children, alive in the year 1989. Finally, the silence was broken by a boy sitting across the room. He seemed to be apologizing before he even posed his question. "I don't mean to say something wrong, but"—he stopped to gather his strength, and then came another "but," followed by silence. The children were now more alert, more watchful than before. The teacher waited, then reconsidered: she could either move on, or she could signal her encouragement of this line of discussion, of questioning. She did the latter, smiled at the boy, asked him to share his thoughts with the rest of us. He still hesitated—but then he took the plunge: "Sister, I'm sorry, but I was wondering how you know if God told those people to tell us something, or if they just did, because they wanted to."

The nun was soon enough letting us all know that the issue was faith, rather than proof—that, in her words, "you know because you believe." The children, in response, relaxed considerably—except for the boy who had just sent that question our way, and the girl who had paved the way for his potential slide toward skepticism. Their brows were slightly furrowed; their faces resisted the ready smile of acceptance, of spiritual consent. In a second, we were onto other matters, while I kept wondering what those two children may have thought later on, in one or another private moment with themselves, even as I remembered other children who had also gotten caught up in what I suppose could be called a bothersome detail of the documentary method: what constitutes divinely sanctioned inspiration or declaration—as against private opinion that has no broader standing in a community or a nation at a given place and time?

Later, going home, I thought of quite another setting wherein I had heard questions put to a teacher, who kept fielding them as best he could: the anthropologist Oscar Lewis trying to explain why he selected this rather than that person to get to know, and why he selected these words or these stories rather than others as he assembled his portraits, biographies, or "oral histories," and as he made his various assertions with respect to what is, what was, and what should be, all propounded over the course of time. At one point, a little vexed with the unrelenting "methodological" scrutiny of his respectful but quizzical academic fans, he smiled and told us, "Maybe, sometimes, I hear a voice that says, *this* is the way to go, *here*, not there"—after which a relieved silence descended upon us, a moment of secular silence, actually, that seemed to affirm the validity of inspiration as a proper rationale for a writer. We wouldn't have dared, of course, to wonder where such inspiration comes from or how it actually gets communicated, transmitted, as that boy had been wondering—and so the mystery was still there, accepted as such, courtesy of our kind of faith, of belief: not in God, but in a writer's, a researcher's, a documentarian's subjectivity as it takes hold of objectivity, the muse our nearest approximation of God.

The Documentary Impulse

As every parent knows, by the second year of life children are learning words and exploring the world earnestly, persistently. They talk up a storm, and they poke, pry, and peek—anything to see more, touch more, or feel in command of yet another aspect of the world around them. Soon enough, at three or so, they are giving accounts of what they have seen, heard, and discovered, the stories and more stories that boys and girls tell their parents and others—descriptions of what has been heard, observed, overheard. Theirs is an appetite for the concrete, the specific—a wish to fathom people, places, things in all their particularity. This eagerness to catch hold of, to catch sight of, to survey and inspect, to learn and then convey to others what the eyes and ears have taken in, this restless insistence upon taking measure of things, figuring them out, and eventually doing so with words, so that others may become fellow witnesses—therein lies the documentary impulse in its first and sturdy expression: I want to know, then tell.

Soon enough, of course, young children are at school, where they continue to take stock of what is available to them, within the classroom and in a neighborhood. In so doing, they take in knowledge and learn to speak of it—learn to render narratively the learned, the beholden. Many of these children draw and paint what they have come to regard, another way of recording what has been acquired. These same children are frequently ready to speak of their dreams—to announce a nighttime visit, a journey, an experience, a matter of words and pictures, of images and encounters, all remembered and when told given a second life. Indeed, I remember a child informing a third-grade class I taught that she liked to "find out all there is about something," and would then sometimes have a dream about it that evening, her way of sealing a discovery: "When I have a dream about a place it sticks in my mind, and I keep thinking of it."

What children very much want to do—find out what is happening around them, and relate what they have learned to themselves and to others—the rest of us also have an interest in doing: this is the documentary impulse as an expression of our creaturely interest in exploration, narration. Of course, each of us will have a particular manner of conveying what we have come to know; documentary expression allows the writer, photographer, or filmmaker the appropriate leeway. The point is not submission to a standard mode of presentation, or an escalation of language and of thinking—the idiosyncratic abandoned in favor of the abstract, the general. The point is loyalty to "the thing itself"—and to the task of sharing what has been witnessed with others. Here, as noted earlier, nonfiction embraces fiction: the (imagined, observed) ruminations on our concrete reality that make up fiction have their parallel in the variations on concrete reality that make up documentary expression.

Moreover, the documentarian is, after all, a writer, a storyteller, and as Nadine Gordimer reminds us unforgettably in "Letter from His Father" (her notion of a letter Kafka's father might have wanted to send to his son), writers use those around them to achieve their ends: anything and everything is potentially on call for the storyteller. The documentary narrative, then, will be as cleverly engaging as the particular writer (or photographer or filmmaker) can manage to be— even as Nadine Gordimer has Kafka's father scratching his head in amazement (and indignation) at what his son has done with a family's reality in order to convey certain (fictional) truths. And so with documentary expression: through selection, emphasis, and the magic of narrative art, the reader or viewer gets convincingly close to a scene, a subject matter, and sees the documentary as one of many possible takes, not *the* story, but *a* story.

The documentary impulse, then, is to seek to know in such a way that the telling really works, connects others to an observed situation. It is the impulse to reconnoiter, to scout successfully, and report back, to send signals (and more) about what has been spotted or surveyed. "I went and saw my granny's house," a third-grader once told our class, "and here I am to tell you all about it, all that happened to us when we went there." A reflective, knowing pause, followed by this ambitious proposal: "I hope by the time I'm through, you'll all be granny's guests, like we were!" Soon enough, the student was on her narrational way—and as she regaled us with memories, moments, anecdotes, incidents, pulled us out of ourselves, away from where we were, filled our minds with a report from elsewhere, I realized I was in the presence, there, at that moment, of a documentary impulse become realized: the exploration, the representation for interested others.

But why do such work in our adult lives—why avail ourselves of the documentary impulse? No question, as indicated, we do so out of a natural curiosity, even as the reader or viewer joins us for a similar reason. Yet, many documentarians have seen wrongs in the world, have wanted to change it. Even as there is a call to service in many of us, our way of connecting with others, of trying to be of help to them (and thereby, of course, helping ourselves), there is a need for us to stop and think about what we are doing as we work at that service: as we tutor children, talk with the elderly, build homes for those in need of solid shelter, offer ourselves as nurses and doctors to those ailing but without medical care. The experience of service can soon enough prompt a need for reflection—and so it is that documentary work can itself become a kind of service: the narrative work done among those vulnerable "others" can enable us to stop and reflect upon who "they" are, and what "we" are trying to accomplish. The call to documentary work is an aspect of the call of stories, of our wish to learn about one another through observation of one another; that way, we can consider how we are getting on with one another, serving each other, with documentary work as the reflective side of such service—those stories and pictures a chance for us to wonder how we are doing as we try to affirm ourselves by reaching toward others, helping to make a difference in a neighborhood, a nation.

Epilogue

"Documentary Studies"

A Course on Documentary Work

Anyone who desires to teach a course or courses under the rubric of "Documentary Studies" will have more than enough books, collections of photographs (slides), and films to consider. I have already mentioned some of these in the foregoing pages. Indeed, as my colleagues at Duke University's Center for Documentary Studies have learned, a wide range of course offerings readily appears in response to the interests of the students and faculty both, once institutional permission has been granted. What follows, then, is one person's way of thinking about a particular subject matter, his way of sorting out its elements and drawing upon what has been written, photographed, and filmed. In the preceding pages I have discussed documentary work that I find important and illuminating; I use such work as mainstays of my teaching. I also call upon or make reference to other efforts, and here they are. Needless to say, not all the books mentioned are now in print (though they can be found in at least some libraries), and a teacher will have to track down certain slides and films from various collections, archives, "resource centers," and, again, libraries.

To begin with, there are books: those that offer words, those that offer pictures, and those that offer a mix of the two. There are also, books that offer fact, ones that offer fiction, and those that blur the distinctions. There is a history of documentary work, as well—going back, as I've indicated, to the Bible itself, and certainly including such classics as Daniel Defoe's *Journal of the Plague Year*. There are also films, including films that readily connect to still photographs or to particular writings. All in all, I think of an ideal introductory course as one that can call upon history, upon different categories of documentary work, and upon other work (journalism, the social sciences, fiction) that connects with the documentary tradition. One can also use a particular subject as a means of organizing a course— race, for instance, or war, or class, or economic dislocation (poverty), or regional life, or the environment. Time, too, can become an organizing principle, not only the years as chronology, but a certain year as a means of doing comparative reflection: 1936, say, as the year Agee and Evans went to Alabama, Orwell went to Lancashire and Yorkshire, William Carlos Williams labored hard and long over his *Life along the Passaic* stories, and the University of North Carolina was in high gear with its sociological inquiries into "cotton culture."

All of the above—ways of seeing, as it were, the various kinds of documentary impulses as they have been implemented, expressed, and handed to others for contemplation—will become each teacher's opportunity to summon in his or her own way, and each student's chance to receive and consider a somewhat idiosyncratic "field of study" (with its studies done in the "field") that properly resists somewhat the classificatory schemes that exert their powerful hold on so many other academic realms and fiefdoms.

I now go ahead, then, with some thoughts about what I would try to teach, and how I would organize that teaching, were I to have a year or more with students. I would start with the Bible, and with Reynolds Price's wonderfully helpful essays, discussed earlier, and his rendering, across the span of almost two millennia, of another's (the apostle John's) documentary narrative. I would then leap to Defoe's *Journal of the Plague Year*; its mix of fact and fiction, its narrative authority and cogency, and its evocative and suggestive power make it an important landmark in documentary work. In the early eighteenth century this novelist and essayist summoned fictional devices (the construction of scenes, character portrayal, and attention to detail, all worked into an energetic story) and, utilizing a range of historical sources, was able to carry his readers back a half a century, to create and re-create a particular moment, to render a time, a place, to give voice to what was felt by individuals.

The next century, the nineteenth, offers a wide range of possibilities. More and more writers attended closely various kinds of "life," and they developed and expanded strategies for conveying the various truths and lessons learned in the course of pursuing such an interest. In America, Thoreau addressed the Concord and New England worlds around him—the naturalist as careful observer, chronicler. In England, George Eliot's early writing, *Scenes of Clerical Life*, the debut of a great novelist, offers portraits of individuals, character sketches. Eliot asked her friend George Henry Lewes to tell a publisher in this way about her proposed writing: "It will consist of tales and sketches illustrative of the actual life of our country clergy about a quarter of a century ago." In *Scenes* Eliot has yet to work the men and women in her head (perhaps first glimpsed in her daily life) thoroughly into stories. That is, she has yet to develop sustained (and sustaining, or convincing) plots. We are given "moments," incidents meant to tell us about a person—who is a certain "type," or, in the author's sense of things, who is representative of what exists, what would be found by social inspection.

Eventually, of course, Eliot would give us *Middlemarch*, a finely plotted, carefully intent examination of an English village as it goes through social and political change. In a sense, the village Middlemarch is the novel's central character; its complex life is ours to contemplate. Eliot does not deny us extended authorial comment, the direct intervention of the narrator in the service of psychological, social, and moral reflection. She is looking back one generation to England's "age of reform," her own kind of historian at work— even as Tolstoy, in *War and Peace*, did likewise so that his readers could be carried back a generation to the French invasion of Russia that reached the outskirts of Moscow. In *War and Peace* Tolstoy not only creates his own (fictional) characters, but he calls upon those from history itself: Russia's generals, Napoleon and his aides. Indeed, as the title suggests, *War and Peace* offers military history, carefully evoked, even as it portrays a nation's upper bourgeoisie confronted with a major threat to its existence. Moreover, in an appendix, Tolstoy furthers the possibilities of the novel by offering an extended essay of historical reflection—thoughts on what (and who) causes events to take place, and why. This enormous fictional world draws directly upon factuality, offers moral and philosophical reflection in the form of an extended essay, and is yet another opportunity for us to contemplate the various ways in which made-up stories can be bearers of social observation, cultural comment, historical description and analysis, personal reflection, speculation.

Later in the nineteenth century, another Russian storyteller (and playwright), Chekhov, contributed more explicitly to the documentary tradition—indeed, embodied several aspects of it in an effort as important and instructive as it is (relatively) unknown. Already coughing up blood (a foreshadowing of the tuberculosis that would take his life at forty-four) at the height of his success as a playwright and writer of short fiction, Chekhov decided to go to the penal colony in Sakhalin Island, off the Siberian Coast, an enormous undertaking in 1890 (the journey from Moscow by train and boat took eighty-two days). Before he left he read everything he could get his hands on—articles and books about the island, about the condition of Russia's prisons. He amassed a long bibliography and took voluminous notes: he was the methodical medical scientist, preparing for a field trip. Once on the island, he contacted a wide range of people and interviewed hundreds of prisoners and those who guarded them, fed them, and supervised the workings of the penal colony. He devised a questionnaire, handed it out, and then interviewed those who had answered the questions. He kept notes, tried to remember what he'd seen and heard, and also wrote discursively about his impressions. He recorded in a journal stories he'd been told, incidents he'd witnessed, anecdotes he'd come to hear. For three months he was a constantly energetic fieldworker, on the job day and night.

When Chekhov returned to Moscow he started writing a full description of this distant world he'd come to know well—but there were interruptions. He wrote fiction. He worked as a doctor in response to an outbreak of cholera. He himself fell ill. But in 1895, he finished his documentary report, *The Island: A Journey to Sakhalin*—a mix of statistics, summaries of scholarly reading, direct observation, anecdotes and stories, and a scrupulously attentive description of a particular world, its physical terrain, its climate, its range of humanity. The book had no significant consequences for Sakhalin's prisoners, their keepers, or, indeed, the doctor and writer who had ventured so far to get to know them. Soon enough, the book, a model of a social documentation with occasional flourishes of literary excellence, of storytelling savvy worthy of its author, would disappear; and it is now sadly unknown by many who try to do the kind of broad research, and the kind of literate, humane, responsive writing to such research, that Chekhov attempted.

Perhaps no other writer of fiction has come as close as Chekhov to accomplishing a documentary project that called upon both a scientist's research and a short-story writer's command of narrative writing—a sense of what matters, an eye for the telling and the dramatic detail, and a moral sensibility that informed the effort but was kept under careful scrutiny, lest a doctor's decency, his righteousness, and his soulful responsiveness to others turn into a screech of self-righteousness. Yet, contemporaries of Chekhov (or immediate predecessors) whom we primarily know for their fiction were also quite interested in taking note of the nineteenth-century world around them and offering what they discovered, and surmised, to others. Stephen Crane, who, like Chekhov, also died young of tuberculosis (he was only twenty-nine) explored the Bowery slums of New York carefully and energetically before he wrote *Maggie, A Girl of the Streets*, and even as he wrote fiction and poetry, he worked at reportage; and of course Mark Twain, who was born thirty-five years before Crane and died ten years after him, was an American master of descriptive writing that depended, ultimately, on his own experiences, on the sights and sounds he took in, treasured, and, in time, worked into narratives handed to others: autobiography summoned for fictional purposes by someone uncannily able to observe himself with the distance of the observer.

Theodore Dreiser was another powerful writer who drew lavishly upon his own experiences for fiction; he was also a journalist who for years learned how to take stock of particular moments, scenes, events, and do them sharp, knowing justice. His social fiction— unlike that of, say, Balzac, in *La Comédie Humaine*, and Zola, who drew primarily upon their reservoirs of imagination—followed his long career as a much-admired newspaperman and magazine writer who for years lived and worked in Chicago, St. Louis, Pittsburgh, and New York City, where he pursued stories to write (nonfiction) rather than the writing of stories (fiction). Meanwhile, others (who would not write novels) wrote their accounts of America's ordinary people, the humble, the impoverished, and the lowly: Jacob Riis's *How The Other Half Lives* (1897) and *Children of the Tenements* (1903), Charles Loring Brace's *The Dangerous Classes of New York* (1880), Lewis Hine's crusading use of the camera as an early-twentieth-century instrument of social investigation, to which he added writing, as in *Tasks for the Tenements* (see Judith Mora Gutman's wonderfully accessible yet erudite *Lewis Hine and The American Social Conscience* [1967]).

In England, an important documentary tradition, verbal and visual, gave interested readers and viewers Henry Mayhew's *London Labor and The London Poor* (1851 and 1860), an extraordinary study of a great city's tradespeople (see *The Unknown Mayhew*, by Eileen Yeo and E. F. Thompson, published in 1971, for a full account of Mayhew's work as a social investigator—his fictionalized portraits and his firsthand, factual reports); Mayhew's writing was illustrated with woodcuts that were inspired by Richard Beard's daguerreotypes. In 1877 the writer Adolphe Smith collaborated with the photographer John Thompson to offer *Street Life in London*—Mayhew's capital city a generation later, now quite visibly present courtesy of the camera, even as essays tell us of "the seller of shellfish" or "the street locksmith" or "street doctors," whose "pills, potions, and quack nostrums" had a ready clientele in a population as vulnerable physically as it was at constant risk socially and economically. Those narrative accounts include direct remarks from "informants" as well as a fluent writer's chronicle of what is to be witnessed, overheard. A similar tradition can be found for another capital city, Paris, as Louis Chevalier makes clear in *Laboring Classes and Dangerous Classes in Paris During the First Half of the Nineteenth Century* (1973). Victor Hugo's *Les Misérables* had its counterparts in a series of social surveys and studies of wayward or indigent families.

Once the twentieth century arrived, of course, documentary work (and its near and distant kin, various kinds of social-science research) began to flourish as photography came into its own as an instrument of both aesthetic contemplation and social portrayal; and soon enough, of course, the movie camera would arrive. This century's events, in a sense, have been presented to us not only by historians but by various documentary projects that, taken together, give us access to the struggles of people the world over for a halfway decent life, for self-respect and the comprehending assent of others.

Any course, needless to say, on that documentary history, and its antecedents in earlier centuries, will respond to the wishes, the capabilities and experiences, the ideas and ideals of the one who organizes and teaches it. In the classroom, as in documentary fieldwork, the crucial issue is the way a teacher's subjectivity comes to terms with an objectivity that is out there and that has now been defined, surveyed, and rendered by an investigator in his or her particular way. For me, a course on documentary work would begin with a contextual insistence on the past, and not only the written past of the books already mentioned—of Dickens as a traveler in America (his "American Notes"), Henry James as an exile returned to America (or as an enamored visitor in Italy), or de Tocqueville as a witness to American democracy—but the visual past: Rembrandt's humble people of Amsterdam, his portraits of the elderly, of Jews and blacks, of his neighbors and their life; Daumier's poor folk and Van Gogh's miners and Münch's factory workers and Kollowitz's "humiliated and scorned," and, nearer to our time and our nation, the so-called Ash-Can Artists, George Bellows and John Sloan and George Luks and William Glackens and Everett Shinn and Robert Henri (who urged them all on, even as he inspired Edward Hopper's social realism). In that regard, I would also put Edward Lucie-Smith's *American Realism* (1994) before my students, and Marianne Doezema's *George Bellows and Urban America* (1992).

With respect to documentary film, I'd call upon Robert Flaherty's *Nanook of the North* (1922) and Pare Lorentz's *The Plow That Broke the Plains* (1936) and *The River* (1937). Indeed, I would encourage an acquaintance with the history of the documentary film—with books such as Erik Barnow's *Documentary: A History of the Non-Fiction Film* (1974), Lewis Jacobs's *The Documentary Tradition* (1971), and Robert Snyder's *Pare Lorentz and The Documentary Film* (1968), not to mention Pare Lorentz's small but arresting book *The River* (1938), with its words and photographs. These books have their own bibliographies, and they describe a host of films that can require a seminar (or two or three) of exclusive attention to this one aspect of documentary work. But for those who want to read and look at photographs and films in a more inclusive manner, there are wonderful opportunities—a showing of, say, Lorentz's *The River*, with readings from Mark Twain, and then, comparatively, a move from the Mississippi River to the Rio Grande, as in Paul Horgan's mighty, two-volume *Great River* (1954).

The mainstay of a course on documentary photography would surely offer students a long look at Depression-era America: the pictures of Lange and Shahn and Evans and Rothstein and Wolcott and Lee and Vachon, some of them now absorbed into an American iconography—social pain on the plains, in the Delta of Mississippi, on the streets of our small towns. As Williams said, "the thing itself" ought to be there for a class—slide after slide from the FSA collection, and especially from the less familiar archives of that collection, as in *Let Us Now Praise Famous Women: Women Photographers for the U.S. Government, 1935–1944* (1987). All along, of course, the work of those photographers has been connected to words, as in the work of Agee and Evans discussed at such length in this book, but also in other ways: *Land of the Free* (1938), Archibald MacLeish's poetry and the works of FSA photographers; Herman Clarence Nixon's *Forty Acres and Steel Mules* (1938), an essayist's evocation of the rural South of the 1930s; *Hometown*, Sherwood Anderson's important and lyrical tribute to an America he dearly loved, written in 1940 (toward the end of his life) and connected to FSA photographs by David Anderson (1968); and *The American Writer and The Great Depression* (1966), wherein the novelist Harvey Swados offers "writers of diverse origins and temperaments" who tried to come to terms with the disastrous consequences of the 1930s economic collapse—in their fiction and essays, their plays and magazine articles, and yet again, the America of the FSA photographic tradition.

That tradition has itself been documented: by William Stott in *Documentary Expression and Thirties America* (1973); by F. Jack Hurley, in *Portrait of a Decade: Roy Stryker and the Development of Documentary Photography in the Thirties* (1972 and 1977); as part of a broader cultural development, by Maren Stange in *Symbols of Ideal Life: Social Documentary Photography in America, 1890–1950*. Not that the FSA photographers were the only ones to try to come to terms with that era's misery. One of the best-known collaborative documentary efforts of the time was *You Have Seen Their Faces*, by Erskine Caldwell and Margaret Bourke-White (1937); James Agee's scorn notwithstanding (in *Let Us Now Praise Famous Men*), that book touched many thousands of readers, and still does, as does Erskine Caldwell's *Tobacco Road*, with its presentation of early-1930s rural Georgia. (A 1974 edition of it displayed some of Bourke-White's photographs.) Another well-known writer of the 1930s, John Steinbeck, gave us, unforgettably, *The Grapes of Wrath*, but also, in the documentary tradition, *The Forgotten Village* (1940)—words and pictures of northern, rural Mexico. A last book to mention in connection with 1930s documentary work: *A Long Road Home: In the Footsteps of the WPA Writers*, Geoffrey O'Hara's fine effort to remind us how much of this country was observed and described by writers and photographers enabled by federal grants to look and listen, to attend a nation in distress and respond with the clarity of straightforward prose or a lens directed honestly, sensitively, searchingly.

By the 1950s, America had survived the Great Depression, entered and won a war against totalitarianism, and begun the last half of the twentieth century, whose waning years we now inhabit. Photographers such as Robert Frank (*The Americans*) and Henri Cartier-Bresson (*The Decisive Moment*) became well-known documentarians, ever alert to our funny and sad times, often catching us by surprise or with an ideological intent; they were artists of the apparent and the accidental as the revelatory, the unyielding. Down south, Danny Lyon gave us our civil-rights struggle (see his *Memories of the Southern Civil Rights Movement* [1992], and his research into Texas prisons, *Conversations with The Dead* [1971]), and in the Midwest, Wright Morris sang and snapped away to create his memorable *God's Country and My People* (1968). A recent book that devotes considerable attention to Wright Morris, and to other writers who have in one or another way connected themselves to photography, is Jane Koff's *Literature and Photography* (1995)—a fine anthology indeed.

The problem, actually, for anyone who teaches documentary photography as something to be contemplated (rather than practiced) is selection—amidst a rising tide of books, which to point in the direction of students? I suggest the following in my classes: George Tice's *Paterson*, with which we read William Carlos Williams's *Paterson*; Lee Freidlander's *The Jazz People of New Orleans* (1992), with which we listen to Billie Holiday, Charlie Parker, Louis Armstrong, and read Whitney Balliett's writings on jazz and a companion effort, Peter Guralnick's *Searching for Robert Johnson* (1989); *Russell Lee's FSA Photographs of Chamisal and Penasco, New Mexico* (1985), which I link to *River of Traps*, by William de Buys and Alex Harris (1990); *Carry Me Home*, Debbie Fleming Caffery's careful look at Louisiana's sugarcane country, its scenes, its people (1990), and, not least, Eudora Welty's small gem *One Time, One Place* (1971), which goes well with another small gem, *A Way of Seeing*, by James Agee and Helen Levitt (1965).

To move from a preponderance of pictures to documentary writers more or less on their own, there are, again, certain classics: Oscar Lewis's *Children of Sanchez* (1961), and *La Vida* (1966); Studs Terkel's *Division Street* (1967) and *Working* (1972); Theodore Rosengarten's *All God's Dangers* (1974); Bruce Chatwin's *Songlines* (1987) and *In Patagonia* (1977); Joseph Mitchell's brilliantly plain, unaffected descriptive writing for *The New Yorker*, most recently collected in *Up in the Old Hotel* (1993); and also from *The New Yorker*, Alec Wilkinson's *Big Sugar* (1989) and *A Violent Act* (1993); Theo Richmond's *Konin: A Quest* (1995), a reconstruction, really, of a long lost Polish village by an Englishman whose Jewish ancestors once lived there—a most compelling, affecting "return," through the personal memories of various people interviewed; Ruthie Bolton's *Gal* (1994), a documentary masterpiece written pseudonymously, with the shaping encouragement of the novelist Josephine Humphreys—a "true life" by a humble black woman of Charleston, South Carolina; Veryln Klinkenborg's *The Last Fine Time* (1990); and, finally, John Berger's *A Seventh Man: Migrant Workers in Europe*, with photographs by Jean Mohr (1975).

Historians, sociologists, and anthropologists can and sometimes do write up their work in such a way that it connects quite tellingly, vividly with the documentary tradition—offers its kind of explorative writing, its kind of direct observation of people and neighborhoods. Within history, there is, of course, the entire "field" or "sub-specialty" of "oral history." An excellent introduction to that kind of work (with a full bibliography of various kinds of oral histories) is James Hoopes's *Oral History* (1979). In anthropology, I think of *Visual Anthropology: Photography as a Research Method*, by John and Malcolm Collier (1987), an important book for those who use the camera to observe others; also, Carol Stack's *All Our Kin* (1974), and

Call to Home (1996) and William Foote Whyte's *Streetcorner Society* (1943), an account of a working-class Italian community, as well as Elliot Liebow's *Tally's Corner* (1967), a report of life among poor black people in a ghetto neighborhood. In sociology, I think of *Middletown*, by Robert S. Lynd and Helen Merrell Lynd (1929) and David Halle's *America's Working Man* (1984), a remarkable study of our contemporary "laboring" people, with powerfully suggestive interviews that bring the reader close to the people whose collective lives make up the "subject" of analysis.

Charles Van Onselen is a South African social historian, anthropologist, and sociologist—a writer who transcends the categories of social science and illuminates particular lives with the attentiveness and precision of a novelist. His *The Seed is Mine* gives us "The Life of Kas Maine, a South African Sharecropper, 1894–1985" (1996)—a major biographical study, and, by extension, an examination of a particular world. His earlier works, *New Babylon* and *New Ninevah* (1982), tell so very much about the making of modern, industrial South Africa in graceful, even entrancing prose.

Then, of course, there are novels that are linked to history, to events, such as Charles Chesnutt's *The Marrow of Tradition* (1901), meant to describe accurately, vividly the Wilmington, North Carolina, race riot of 1898; or Robert Tressell's *The Ragged Trousered Philanthropists* (1914), a novel about a group of workingmen, intended to be "a socialist documentary based on real people and real events." But in any novel, flashes of documentary writing can appear—Frank Conroy's chronicle of musicology in *Body and Soul* (1991), or Richard Ford's careful description of a rest station on the New Jersey Turnpike in *Independence Day* (1995), the novelist absorbing into a story a body of knowledge, or an aspect of today's highway reality.

Another list: books that have their own narrative identity, as it were, and that are surely of interest to those who teach and study (and do) documentary writing. See Jeanne Schinto's *Huddle Fever*

(1995), a marvelous account of "Living in the Immigrant City" of Lawrence, Massachusetts, a novelist's story of her day-to-day life there; Kathleen Norris's *Dakota*, the first of her two books, each of which she calls a "spiritual geography" (1993), akin in their own pastoral and lyrical way to Wright Morris's work; *But Beautiful: A Book About Jazz* (1996), Geoff Dyer's skillfully, soulfully arranged stories about certain jazz musicians—Lester Young, Charles Mingus, Thelonius Monk, Ben Webster, Bud Powell. Here fiction and non-fiction meet; here the critic and the short-story writer become one in the bravely idiosyncratic writer who summons all that is known (interviews, essays, films, journalism) in order to approach certain lives, to get under the skin of certain performers, and, overall, to bring them together, give each of them the suggestive life of words so that all of them will sing in our memory. *But Beautiful* is an arrangement, a series of improvisations, with some solo takes on some strange souls and a cross-country trip with Duke Ellington with stopovers at the houses of (the lives of) various kindred spirits of his. Speaking of such a journey—I imagine teaching *But Beautiful* with Peter Guralnick's *Lost Highway* (1979), another expedition (if not pilgrimage) in which an encounter with country music is the destination. Indeed, one can imagine traveling further on this road and taking up with Zora Neale Hurston, her *Dust Tracks on a Road* (1942)—again, the musical soul is linked through folklore to the stomping of a piano, the saxophone player's desperate, heart-stopping exhalations. The above books on music constitute a course within a course.

We have similar material on "coal miners"—two words that might easily prompt generalizations, categorizations, research studies (all valuable: socioeconomic "data," the nature and etiology of pneumoconiosis, or "black lung" disease), but words that can also prompt others to walk another street. John Yount, takes us to Switch County, Kentucky in his novel *Hardcastle* (1980); Meade Arble brings us to Pennsylvania with his *The Long Tunnel: A Coal Miner's Journal* (1976), a work of autobiography, of personal observation and reflection; Clancy Sigal asks us to come to Yorkshire's mining territory and meet his novel's characters in what is surely a documentary novel based on an author's extended experience, *A Weekend in Dinlock* (1961); and, on similar terrain, we have Orwell's *Road to Wigan Pier*, mentioned so often earlier in these pages, and *Pitful of Memories* (1995), a series of interviews with miners of Chesterfield, England, conducted by that city's teenagers; and, back across the Atlantic, *Harlan Miners Speak* (1970), the testimony of miners in the Kentucky Coal Fields, recorded in 1931, along with the remarks of such visiting observers and would-be compatriots as Theodore Dreiser, Sherwood Anderson, and John Dos Passos—whose novel *U.S.A.* is another breakthrough attempt to use documentary observation in a fictional setting. Finally, I'd ask students to spend time with *On the Mines* (1973), which offers David Goldblatt's photographs and an essay by Nadine Gordimer—here one learns of South Africa's miners in all their jeopardy—and Doris Ullman's Appalachian photographs, in all their hypnotic, otherworldly power.

Even as novelists can draw on history, can use documentary techniques (call upon diaries, letters, interviews, newspaper reports), as E. L. Doctorow does so effectively, so brilliantly in *Ragtime* (1975), historians can write a vividly descriptive narrative that is documentary in manner and substance: Richard Bartlett's *The New Country: A Social History of The American Frontier, 1776–1840* (1974); E. J. Hobsbawm's *Labouring Men* (1964); *The Poor in the Middle Ages*, by Michel Mollat (1986); and Kevin Starr's *Americans and The California Dream* (1973).

In documentary work, imagination encounters and tries to come to terms with reality; and the way in which that is done, the outcome achieved, is as various as the individuals involved in the effort, the struggle. I think of Alfred Kazin using autobiography (*Walker in the*

City [1951]), Carlo Levi mixing a diary, a series of sketches, socio-logical reflection, political analysis, and storytelling for the wonder-fully special and edifying and even inspiring mix that makes up *Christ Stopped at Eboli* (1947). I think of Danilo Dolci, also in Italy, struggling as a social activist, but also trying to do a survey of what he sees (and wants to change) in *Waste* (1964). I think of writers who have worked at different times and in different ways, yet who can be brought together as kin, who all attended a particular place: *San Francisco Stories* (1990), wherein Trollope and Dylan Thomas and Mark Twain and Jack London and Kay Boyle and many others are assembled to show us (tell us of) a famed (and, in their hands, a fabled) city.

I think, finally, of poets, those who in our time have taken William Carlos Williams at his (sharply summoning) word, mentioned earlier: "no ideas but in things," a national anthem for all who do documentary work—the telling (through words, through pictures) of the particular. Martin Espada does Dr. Williams proud in *City of Coughing and Dead Radiators* (1993), and so does Jane Kenyon in *Otherwise* (1996); these are two poets hovering over two landscapes, an urban scene and a rural one, and giving us the heartfelt tenderness that informs an attention to what is, what happens—documentary work as a kind of love that becomes expressed in those words, those pictures, a kind of love that is handed over, thereby, to others.

Index

Index

Index